ISSUES in CULTURAL and MEDIA STUDIES

Series editor: Stuart Allan

Published titles

News Culture
Stuart Allan

Television, Globalization and Cultural Identities
Chris Barker

Modernity and Postmodern Culture
Jim McGuigan

Sport, Culture and the Media
David Rowe

MODERNITY and POSTMODERN CULTURE

Jim McGuigan

OPEN UNIVERSITY PRESS
Buckingham · Philadelphia

Open University Press
Celtic Court
22 Ballmoor
Buckingham
MK18 1XW

email: enquiries@openup.co.uk
world wide web: http//www.openup.co.uk

and
325 Chestnut Street
Philadelphia, PA 19106, USA

First Published 1999

A catalogue record of this book is available from the British Library

ISBN 0 335 19915 1 (pbk)   0 335 19916 X (hbk)

Library of Congress Cataloging-in-Publication Data
A catalog record for this book is available from the Library of Congress

Typeset by Type Study, Scarborough
Printed in Great Britain by Biddles Limited, Guildford and Kings Lynn

This one's for Madge

These our actors,
As I foretold you, were all spirits, and
Are melted into air, into thin air:
And, like the baseless fabric of this vision,
The cloud-capp'd towers, the gorgeous palaces,
The solemn temples, the great globe itself,
Yea, all which it inherits, shall dissolve,
And, like this insubstantial pageant faded,
Leave not a rack behind.

Prospero in *The Tempest*, William Shakespeare

CONTENTS

SERIES EDITOR'S FOREWORD

The use of the term 'postmodernism' is no longer restricted to weighty theoretical discussions in elite circles. Indeed, its appearance in mass media discussions concerning topics as diverse as architecture, drama, fashion, literature, music or film has become almost a daily occurrence. That said, however, the actual significance of the various claims being made about 'postmodern culture' continues to be the subject of much controversy.

Jim McGuigan's *Modernity and Postmodern Culture* explores the complex interplay between the modern and the postmodern in a manner which critically extends previous debates in radically new ways. His approach builds on a range of rich insights derived from close readings of the work of several influential theorists, including Baudrillard, Beck, Castells, Giddens, Habermas, Haraway, Jameson and Lyotard. At the same time, however, this is not an engagement with theory for theory's sake alone. Rather, McGuigan draws on these interventions with an eye to investigating specific instances of social and cultural change in a number of exigent contexts. A guiding imperative of this line of enquiry, stretching as it does to encompass issues such as theme parks, screen culture, information technology or environmental risk, is to render problematic the accepted tenets of much postmodernist thought. In sharp opposition to those voices calling for the abandonment of the Enlightenment tradition of critique, then, McGuigan is seeking to help establish a conceptual basis to sustain further elaborations of the forms and practices of critical reason.

The Issues in Cultural and Media Studies series aims to facilitate a diverse range of critical investigations into pressing questions considered to be central to current thinking and research. In light of the remarkable speed at which the conceptual agendas of cultural and media studies are changing, the authors are committed to contributing to what is an ongoing process of re-evaluation and critique. Each of the books is intended to provide a lively, innovative and comprehensive introduction to a specific topical issue from a fresh perspective. The reader is offered a thorough grounding in the most salient debates indicative of the book's subject, as well as important insights into how new modes of enquiry may be established for future explorations. Taken as a whole, then, the series is designed to cover the core components of cultural and media studies courses in an imaginatively distinctive and engaging manner.

Stuart Allan

ACKNOWLEDGEMENTS

When it was first suggested to me that I might like to write a book about postmodernism, my initial response was sceptical. I felt that there were already far too many books on postmodernism (and still do). However, I was tempted by the suggestion. Perhaps I would find something useful to say, specifically, as it has turned out, about the relations between post-modern culture and reflexive modernity. I was encouraged at the beginning to proceed by Zygmunt Bauman, Roger Bromley and Derek Longhurst, to each of whom I owe my gratitude. Without such encouragement I most certainly would not have written this book. I also very much appreciate the sensitive editorial advice that I have received from Stuart Allan. And, yet again, I thank Lesley, Christopher and Jenny for putting up with me during the madness of writing a book.

INTRODUCTION

We live in interestingly uncertain times. Nothing seems to stay the same for very long. The unexpected constantly happens. No belief or system is unassailable, except that is for **capitalism**. The ideological hegemony of market forces and the endless search for profit and capital accumulation now rule the world almost unchallenged. Some might reasonably object that this is not a novel condition. It has been the state of the world for hundreds of years, since capitalism emerged as a set of economic arrangements, a means of doing business, technologically dynamic, socially and culturally revolutionary. Capitalism was taking shape in the later part of the eighteenth century. The industrial revolution in Britain resulted eventually in a complex division of labour and capacity to mass produce. The political revolutions in America and France enunciated the values of capitalist civilization, especially modern rights of citizenship. Capitalism spread from its original base in Europe, through trade and in alliance with political, cultural and economic imperialism. Wherever it went, capitalism came into conflict with traditional ways of life. It heralded a modernization which took many different forms. And, out of the very culture of capitalism itself there emerged its alter-image, the modern counterculture of socialism, which in the communist states of the twentieth century apparently represented the possibility of another kind of civilization (Bauman 1992). By the end of the twentieth century, however, 'the enemy' had been defeated. Communism no longer offered a viable alternative to capitalism and, in the capitalist states themselves, social democracy became less socialistic. In a sense, the story of **modernity** had been completed. The traces of 'traditional', pre-capitalist society were ever diminishing traces and the dream of a socialized means of production and collectivist mode of being was but a dream. Yet, at the very same moment that modernity, in the form of capitalist civilization, broadly speaking, commanded the stage, it was announced that the scene had suddenly changed. Modernity was being superseded: by what exactly was not quite clear so it was called *post*modernity.

The postmodern's advent did not, of course, mean the end of capitalism. Instead, it was said to be a shift in knowledge and culture. If there was a transition occurring from one civilizational form to another, from modernity to postmodernity, the transformation was wrought by knowledge and culture, different ways of knowing, representing and identifying, rather than the more conventionally material factors of economics and the use of nature. The postmodern declaration is, then, first and foremost, to do with ideas and subjectivity, how we think and signify: it is not primarily a claim concerning 'material reality'. The declaration is supported by the assumption that there is no 'objectively' discernible material reality; in any case, not one situated beyond thought and signification. **Postmodernism** can thus be seen, at the extreme, as a philosophical idealism and a cultural reductionism, an inversion of, say, economic reductionism. For this reason, among others, postmodernism is widely contested by those who wish to argue, for instance, that there is a complex interaction between economy and culture and that sociality is reducible to neither bread and butter nor fun and games. The postmodern imaginary, in its philosophical and sociological claims, has been challenged on a number of grounds by critics such as Alex Callinicos (1989), Christopher Norris (1990), John O'Neill (1995) and Terry Eagleton (1996). Although I agree with a great many of the criticisms made by these authors, I do not disagree with postmodernism in quite the same way. My position is closer to that of Krishan Kumar (1995) who, while sceptical of postmodern claims, argues there is some truth in them and that they are important signs of the time.

In this book I make a basic distinction between postmodern*ism* and postmodern*ity*. For me, postmodern*ism* refers to philosophical ideas, mainly derived from poststructuralist theory, and cultural formations, especially associated with global popular culture. Postmodern*ity*, in contrast, refers to societal or civilizational claims; and, quite specifically the argument that we are living through the transition from a modern to a postmodern period in history. Because I believe modern civilization is best understood largely as *capitalist* civilization and, since capitalism has not been superseded, then, I disagree with the idea of a postmodern society. Moreover, I think it is an extraordinary act of hubris to call one's own period in history 'postmodern'. Yet, I do take certain aspects of philosophical postmodernism and broader claims concerning the *postmodernization of culture* very seriously. That is why this book is entitled *Modernity and Postmodern Culture*. Also on terminology, my use of the term 'civilization' in referring specifically to capitalist modernity, it should be noted, is meant to draw attention to capitalism's status as an advanced stage of social development, not just an economic system, and a stage of social development, indeed, that is now widely held to be insurpassable.

My general aim is to explore the complex interplay between the modern and the postmodern, which I believe is preferable to constructing too stark an opposition between modernist and postmodernist perspectives on culture and society. The heated rivalry and clamorous disputation that once characterized discussion of the modern and the postmodern have died down somewhat in recent years. For many unreconstructed modernists, I suspect, this is because they never thought postmodernism was more than a passing fad. On the other hand, I suspect that postmodernists are similarly complacent in believing they won the day. Their case remains unproven.

Radical claims about an epochal shift from modernity to postmodernity, in particular, are less convincing than Anthony Giddens's (1990) *accentuated modernity* thesis, by which he means the **globalization** of modernity's transformative dynamics. In an earlier phase of modernity, traditional ways of life had persisted and, in some parts of the world, predominated. What is most unsettling about the latest phase of modernity, as it spreads around the world and revolutionizes every aspect of existence, then, is an acceleration in the longer term trend of 'de-traditionalization' (Heelas *et al.* 1996). From this perspective, the confusions, anxieties, resistances and fresh possibilities associated vaguely with postmodernity are explained more satisfactorily in relation to the globalization of modernity.

The argument of this book departs, however, in two major respects from Giddens's original analysis in *The Consequences of Modernity*: first, with regard to his conception of modernity; and second, with regard to his conception of postmodern culture. Giddens's model of modernity is multidimensional, including four equally weighted and autonomous institutional dimensions: capitalism, **industrialism, surveillance** and military power. For him, *capitalism* is an exploitative system of commodity production and circulation. *Industrialism* is distinguishable from capitalism in so far as it refers expressly to the transformation of nature and use of inanimate sources of power. Influenced by Michel Foucault (1977 [1975]), Giddens defines *surveillance* as 'the supervision of subject populations in the political sphere' which is 'characteristically . . . indirect and based upon the control of information' (Giddens 1990: 57). *Military power* is a feature of traditional society but, peculiarly in modern conditions, the means of violence are monopolized legitimately by the state and the conduct of war is industrialized through the deployment of increasingly sophisticated weapon systems.

Although it is necessary to consider such institutional dimensions in terms of their relative autonomy from one another, so as to appreciate their specific properties, Giddens tends to play down the primacy and undervalue the coordinating role of capitalism. Industrialism, surveillance and modern military power have existed at least notionally without capitalism, as in the old Soviet Union, but they arose historically and have developed most fully within the civilizational frame of capitalism. Furthermore, it can be argued, that communist states, their particular forms and deformities, were conditioned by coexistence with capitalism, which included borrowing from as well as subordination and resistance to capitalist civilization. In the world today, the environmental damage caused by industrialism, the intrusiveness of electronic surveillance and the military capacity for mutual extermination are inexplicable without reference to the interests and dynamics of globalizing capitalism.

Giddens rejects postmodernity on both philosophical and sociological grounds: he believes that rational knowledge of the social world is possible and that this can be derived from analysis of the institutional parameters of modernity in a 'late', 'high' or 'radicalized' phase. He confines 'the postmodern' to culture but in a very narrow sense, which gives rise to my second point of disagreement with Giddens's general account. For Giddens, postmodernism is restricted to the contemporary avant-garde: 'Post-modernism, if it means anything, is best kept to refer to styles or movements within literature, painting, the plastic arts, and architecture. It concerns aspects of *aesthetic reflection* upon the nature of modernity' (1990: 45). Such a view is inadequate, though it is given support by promotion of the 'postmodern' avant-garde (such as by Zurbrugg 1993). The problem with Giddens's narrow conception of postmodernism is that it is insufficiently distinguished from **modernism** in the sense of diverse experimental movements in the arts that flourished in the earlier twentieth century, before 'postmodernism' came onto the scene. Modern art was never defined in terms of a particular style or aesthetic theory yet what the various movements had in common was indeed '*aesthetic reflection* upon the nature of modernity'.

To clarify the point, a brief digression on modern art is in order. John Berger (1972 [1969]) identified 'the moment of Cubism' from 1907 to the beginning of the First World War in 1914 as crucial, particularly because he wanted to challenge the equation of modernism, more typical of postwar Dadaism, Surrealism and Expressionism, with the 'acceptance of unreason, . . . social desperation, . . . extreme subjectivity and . . . forced dependence upon existential experience' (Berger 1972: 159). Rather, if Cubism is taken as exemplary, rationalism, hope, dialectics, scientific detachment, at a time of rapid change and possibility, are more in evidence. This was the moment of high imperialism and, in opposition, an international socialist movement that was not yet discredited by events; the moment of modern physics, physiology and sociology; the moment of electricity, radio and cinema, the mass-circulation press, synthetic materials, motorcars and aeroplanes. It was the moment when Cubism broke with Renaissance space, replacing art as a *mirror* with art as a *diagram*, 'the diagram being a visible, symbolic representation of invisible processes, forces, structures', in effect, the liberation of the sign from static vision. The 'aim was to arrive at a far more complex image of reality than had ever been attempted in painting before' (Berger 1972: 150, 153). Objects were abstracted, such as cubes, cones and cylinders, seen and represented from different angles laid over one another and on a surface in which the flux of time could be represented spatially. Although de-familiarizing and philosophically profound, Berger observes, 'All modern design, architecture and town planning, seems inconceivable without the initial example of cubism' (1972: 134). Compare this strange yet immensely consequential avant-garde with, say, Todd Gitlin's (1989: 350) summary of the recombinant culture of postmodernism – 'Anything can be juxtaposed with anything else' – which recalls Cubism but at a different time in space, when the juxtaposition of signs upon signs in an endless present has become very familiar and commonplace everywhere. Instead of a totalization of different points of view, however, everything is seen in fragments.

If the 'post' in 'postmodernism' merely referred to the latest manifestations of modern art as an elite practice, a laboratory of representation, it would be a good deal less significant culturally than is suggested by the argument of this book, which follows Fredric Jameson's (1984) insight that postmodernism is 'the cultural logic of late capitalism'. Postmodern culture, from this position, is best understood as culture in general, including contemporary mass-popular culture, media texts and everyday experiences, conceived on the model of a force field or structure of feeling. That is a much more satisfactory means of understanding what is going on culturally now than a limited and elitist conception of postmodernism which is indistinguishable from the memory and residual trace of avant-garde modernism. Various checklists of postmodern culture are given in the literature, such as Dominic Strinati's (1992: 2–3) five defining characteristics:

1 the breakdown of the distinction between culture and society
2 an emphasis on style at the expense of substance and content
3 the breakdown of the distinction between high culture (art) and popular culture
4 confusions over time and space
5 the decline of the 'meta-narratives'.

These various aspects of postmodern culture are discussed in this book, though not in that order.

We begin with Jean-François Lyotard's declaration concerning the decline of grand- or **metanarrative**, which is aimed more than anything else at the boldest modern story of all, Marxism, a project that sought with mixed results, to say the very least, to change the course of the world for the better. For Lyotard, the postmodern is an **epistemological** condition, a condition, that is, which is to do with how knowledge is legitimized. However, this is not how postmodernism is most popularly apprehended, which is in the built environment and in entertainment forms. Accordingly, Chapter 1 proceeds to consider postmodern architecture and the **hyperreality** of Disney as an instance of popular postmodernism. Chapter 2 returns to the modern, specifically the **Enlightenment** tradition of thought dating originally from the eighteenth century and looks at how it has been challenged. Particular emphasis is placed upon how poststructuralist theory questions modern rationality and reason. My argument here is that intellectual **modernity** is unduly reified and, to an extent, misrepresented in the attack upon it and that, in fact, it has always been a contradictory project. The contradictions are still being worked out. Chapter 3 discusses the postmodern scrambling of images with reference to the work of the most controversial postmodern thinker, Jean Baudrillard, and then considers Jameson's rather more critical arguments concerning the relations between postmodern culture, global capitalism and the technological changes brought about by electronics and computing. Chapter 4 examines questions of **identity**, its fracturing and hybridization, the relations between western culture and the rest of the world, and Giddens's arguments about the reflexively modern self (partly in anticipation of discussion of reflexive modernity in Chapter 6). In Chapter 5, Manuel Castells's theorizing and analysis of '**network society**' is examined. The publication of Castells's three-volume *The Information Age* in the dying years of the twentieth century is, in my view, one of the most important achievements of social and cultural analysis that that century has bequeathed the next. It is hugely illuminating of debates concerning modernity and postmodern culture. The final chapter, on reflexive modernity, suggests, as does the chapter on Castells, that there are more satisfactory ways of understanding social and cultural change than can be derived exclusively from postmodernist thought. Ulrich Beck's reflexively modern thesis on '**risk society**', though different from Castells's network paradigm, makes sense of some of the most salient features of contemporary culture and society, particularly to do with struggles over 'the environment', social movement politics and the role of science.

This book, then, is concerned with social and cultural change in the present, the contours and meanings of our own time and, coincidentally, at the turn of the millennium. The study of the present lacks certain advantages of studying the past, not least of which is a sense of perspective on more or less completed processes. The processes under consideration here are incomplete and their treatment, in a short book that aims to be accessible, is necessarily selective and partial. To study the present is an inherently risky business in which one is bound to make mistakes which become only too evident when they are eventually seen with the benefit of hindsight. The intellectual risks are worth taking, however, since some critical understanding of one's own time is a vital resource for surviving it, let alone changing it.

1 | DECLARING THE POSTMODERN

Introduction

Accounts of 'the postmodern' often begin with a search for its first usage. So, for instance, Arnold Toynbee's worries after the Second World War about what he saw as a transition from modern bourgeois to a fully democratic 'post-modern' civilization or casual use of the term around the same time in the title of an article on architecture may be cited. You can even find reference to its use in the nineteenth century, or so I am told. This search for an original meaning is not only trivializing and probably futile but also seriously misleading. It distracts from an understanding of why, at a certain point, 'postmodern' discourse became significant, which was during the 1970s. It coincided with a crisis in capitalist civilization which brought about a transformative resolution that is still immensely consequential, as David Harvey (1989) has argued. Towards the end of that decade, we find the declaration of a postmodern condition of knowledge, the first declaration to be considered in this chapter. Also, in the 1970s, architects began talking earnestly about postmodernism, and with good reason, as they sought ways to make up for the manifest deficiencies of much modern architecture. Cultural commentators also began to notice something strange going on in entertainment forms, particularly the emergence of the hyperreal, which unsettled the relations between representation and reality. This unsettling was not new for avant-garde and modern art. What was comparatively new was that it should be happening so markedly in mass-popular culture. This, no doubt, emanated from the counterculture of the 1960s. And, in fact, there are many other instances of the emergence of postmodernism in, say, literature and fine art.

It seems to me, however, that the declarations made concerning philosophy, architecture and entertainment are the most significant and exemplify much of what is at stake when considering modernity and postmodern culture. They also illustrate something of what Andreas Huyssen (1992) has called 'the specifically American character of postmodernism'.

Legitimizing knowledge

In the postmodern curriculum it is obligatory to refer, early on, to Lyotard's text of 1979, *The Postmodern Condition* (henceforth *The Pomo Con* for short). Meeting such an obligation, however, rarely involves paying too much attention to the official status and strategic role of this text. Once Lyotard's big idea is grasped, that overarching stories of progress, particularly Marxism, are no longer credible, then the entertainingly 'postmodern' features of recent cultural change can usually be broached more or less straightaway. A few of the possible selections and combinations available in this respect are, for instance, the displacement of 'reality' by media imagery, the concatenation of messages that taken together have the complex effect of a discontinuous collage of signifiers, the depthlessness and ephemerality of **signs**, the pose of cool detachment, the fragmentation of social relationships and the hollowing out of identity, that is to say, not characteristically the themes with which Lyotard himself was mainly concerned. Normally it is mentioned, in passing, that *The Pomo Con* was commissioned by and submitted to the Quebec Government's *Conseil des Universités* and the significance of Lyotard's subtitle is noted, 'A Report on Knowledge'. This 'report' of some 25,000 words is accompanied, as an appendix, by Lyotard's later essay of around 5000 words, 'Answering the Question: What is Postmodernism?', in the English translation (1984) from the original French. In that essay, Lyotard discusses postmodern culture in the aesthetic sense. Until the publication of *The Pomo Con*, Lyotard was best known, but not so well known, for his unorthodox Marxism tempered by Freudianism and his interest in avant-garde art. For a student of the humanities and soft social sciences, to read the appended essay is a familiar enough experience of participating in a language game concerning art and politics. To actually read *The Pomo Con*, however, is a rather different experience.

What on earth were the governmental officials of higher education and research in Quebec thinking about when they hired this vaguely lefty French philosopher and arty type to tell them about the state of science and the tasks of university research and education towards the end of the twentieth century? The ways of the Gallic mind are indeed strange to the more pedestrian English mentality. In effect, the purpose of such a text is that of a discussion paper to facilitate strategic decision making. Although unusually so, Lyotard's *Pomo Con* is indeed a policy document. His remarks on science, technology and education make it recognizably so. On science and technology, Lyotard observes that the most significant developments in the second half of the twentieth century were to do with communication. Linguistics and its general applicability to various branches of knowledge, cybernetics and its relation to computing and management, digitalization, information transfer, storage and retrieval, genetic coding and its implications for biological engineering and medicine, these are the cutting edges of latterday science and technology. The computer is at the heart of the postindustrial body politic, with enormous capacity for symbolic manipulation and accelerating the technological transformation of work and, where possible, the replacement of labour by machines. Economic process is increasingly driven by information and its commodification, a fact which presents the university with great challenges and possibilities. The university's function is to produce competent people to do the necessary and it is not so much in competition with business research and development as in partnership.

How does the university student fit in? Nearing the end of his report on knowledge, Lyotard discusses the traditional role of university education in reproducing the elite professions, the 'professional intelligentsia', doctoring and lawyering, ruling the nation and so forth. This will not end and in the most prestigious institutions, the *grandes écoles*, the ivy league colleges, the Oxfords and Cambridges, a liberal education where there is space for 'useless' knowledge, from the point of view of manifestly practical application, will persist. Research funding, public and private, however, is overwhelmingly devoted to hard science and technological development across the universities and in specialist institutes, around which a 'technical intelligentsia' is produced. There is a third and residual category of student, the utility of whose education is in some doubt: 'the remainder of the young people present in the universities are for the most part unemployed who are not counted as job seekers in the statistics, though they outnumber the openings in their disciplines, arts and human sciences' (Lyotard 1984 [1979]: 49). These are the relatively cheap subjects that have grown with the expansion, the massification, of higher education. They are frequently called into question along with several other questions that are asked about the purposes of the 'postmodern university' (Smith and Webster 1997). Lyotard's observation is cynical yet when one considers that, in Britain for instance, something like 50 per cent of graduate employment is unrelated to the subject of a first degree in a direct way, the function of mass higher education, especially in the humanities and social sciences, is difficult to justify on exclusively vocational grounds. Lyotard does not seek to justify it at all.

Sociology has been and now the newer interdisciplinary subjects, most notably cultural and media studies, are frequently cited as purveyors of useless knowledge for those outside the charmed circles of the reproduction of the social elite and the serious business of technocracy. There are all sorts of things that can be said in defence of such education: acquisition of advanced literacy and communicative competences, learning how to learn with the advantages it brings in a 'flexible' labour market, sheer pleasure in knowledge, the cultivation of critical intelligence and the capacity to bear witness against injustice, can all be cited as in some sense 'functional' and 'useful'. The fact of the matter is, however, that these are not the most widely spread features of mass higher education. In the USA, as Alan Ryan (1996: 12) notes, 'two-thirds of all students are in programmes in "business studies"; and many of these are closer to remedial reading and writing courses than a Harvard MBA'. Whether Ryan is right or not about the actual quality of business studies, it is quite likely that many students on such programmes are firming up their basic literacy and numeracy skills while receiving a pre-vocational education in what, before the advent of mass higher education and comparative de-industrialization in 'the most highly developed societies' (Lyotard's phrase), they would hitherto have learnt on the job. Evidently there is also a certain production of what might be called a 'lumpen intelligentsia'. Yet, few remain marginalized indefinitely. Most appear to benefit at least in terms of a correlation, if not necessarily causation, from going to university and occupational income, including those reading sociology and cultural and media studies.

For Lyotard, it must be stressed, the postmodern condition is fundamentally an *epistemological* condition. It is to do with the production and legitimation of knowledge. Whatever we may wish to say, for instance, about society and culture is, of necessity, mediated by our tacit assumptions and conceptions regarding how and what we may know. In the modern 'western' world, science came to be seen as the touchstone of knowledge, the cardinal means of knowing, displacing traditional knowledges that were in the past legitimized by the authority of religion. Science is only one way of knowing, however, and it has not been solely responsible for its own legitimation. Other ways of knowing, according to Lyotard, generally take the form of narrative. For example, the great world religions tell stories about the world and our places within it. Modern scientific knowledge has typically contested the authority of religion, giving rise to bitter disputes that have festered on or been resolved with more or less satisfactory truces. Lyotard sees science and narrative as simply incommensurate ways of knowing. They are different 'language games', in the sense given to the term by Ludwig Wittgenstein (1958 [1953]), meaningful discourses that are established in use. Narrative discourse seems truthful when it is plausible to its addressee, when it is apprehended as intuitively or commonsensically correct. In comparison, scientific discourse has tended to be unintelligible to non-specialists and many of its breakthroughs have seemed implausible at first, as counterintuitive, as offensive to common sense. Scientists, in any case, are expert at establishing their own jargon and rules of validation which are not dependent upon mundane and commonsensical understanding.

Yet, modern science, irrespective of the pretensions of scientists themselves, was not actually its own source of *social* legitimation. It has depended upon narrative for that: big stories, metanarratives, stories about stories, that make sense of the role of science. Lyotard identifies two major narratives that have legitimized modern science: narratives of *emancipation* and of *speculation*. The second of these comes closest to scientists holding the exclusive right and power to legimize their own work: 'science for science's sake'. This pure, speculative idea of science, although congenial to many scientists, was never the dominant one and its lack of justification according to social utility has made it extremely vulnerable. In one way or another, in contrast, narratives of emancipation have stressed the social usefulness and purpose of science and modern knowledge generally. Emerging with the European Renaissance of neo-classical thought and culture (fourteenth, fifteenth and sixteenth centuries), through the ages of Reason (seventeenth century), Enlightenment (eighteenth century), Progress (nineteenth century) and Analysis (twentieth century) – in the conventional periodization of the history of ideas – big stories have been told about the growth of (scientific) knowledge and its contribution to human improvement. One latterday version of the metanarrative was Marxism, which styled itself as the science of history with a big story to tell about progression through the **modes of production** – feudal, capitalist, socialist, communist – and the ultimate emancipation of the working class and hence the whole of humanity. Quite apart from any function it may have performed, particularly in the Soviet Union, as the legitimizing narrative of science, Marxism was already losing its power to convince even socialist critics of capitalism of its political story by 1979 when *The Pomo Con* was published; a loss of credibility that was dramatically confirmed, in the eyes of many, ten years later with the fall of the Berlin Wall. Although supposed to be of much broader significance, Lyotard's (1984: xxiv) definition of '*postmodern* as incredulity toward metanarratives' clearly has the Marxist version of Enlightenment uppermost in mind.

There is, then, according to Lyotard, a crisis of narrative legitimation of science and uncertainty about the prospects for human emancipation in the postmodern world. Under these conditions, how does science legitimize itself? Scientific legitimation is achieved now according to the criterion of *performativity*, that is, 'the optimization of the global relationship between input and output' (Lyotard 1984: 11). The computer terminology of 'input' and 'output' is not incidental to this observation. Power over knowledge production takes on the character of cybernetic cost-accounting where what goes in must be measurably and demonstrably justified by what comes out. Lyotard (1984: 4–5) talks of 'the mercantilization of knowledge' in 'the post-industrial society' where there is a 'hegemony of computers'. This takes us into 'the real world' of investment in research and development: 'It was more the desire for wealth than the desire for knowledge that initially forced upon technology the imperative of performance improvement and product realization' (1984: 45). Knowledge, according to the criterion of performativity, is thus reduced to instrumental value. That is a fact, according to Lyotard, and he is not at all sentimental about the ways in which knowledge has been thought to be otherwise. He is particularly scathing of the modernist defence of critical knowledge and consensual truth (see Habermas 1988 [1967]).

Lyotard, however, does not entirely dispense with critique: he just sees it as being rather limited and localized in the postmodern world. This is partly evident in his notion of *paralogy*:

> Paralogy must be distinguished from innovation: the latter is under the command of the system, or at least used by it to improve its efficiency; the former is a move (the importance of which is not recognized until later) played in the pragmatics of knowledge ... The stronger the 'move', the more likely it is to be denied the minimum consensus, precisely because it changes the rules of the game upon which the consensus has been based.
>
> (Lyotard 1984: 61)

Although Lyotard distinguishes 'paralogy' from 'innovation', none the less, it is an idea very close to that of 'discovery' in the arts as well as in the sciences, and is typified by its obscure originality, a move in the game which eventually changes the rules of the game but is not seen as such immediately and may be met with fierce resistance. Lyotard's own declaration of the postmodern condition with regard to the fragmentation and performativity of knowledges may itself be viewed as a paralogy, a move that merely created a local disturbance at first in the humanities and social sciences, the larger implications of which are perhaps still not fully appreciated.

While Lyotard believes that a rational consensus on what counts as knowledge and which contributes to a universal emancipation of humanity is implausible and, indeed, undesirable, he does believe, nevertheless, that *justice* is a value worth defending and advancing. He relates this directly to the use of computers right at the end of *The Pomo Con*. For him, and anticipating many subsequent debates, the computer may be seen as the means of perfecting control in the market system or, alternatively and simultaneously, a means of popular empowerment through access to information and, therefore, participation in the knowledge game.

When one reads the appended essay, 'Answering the Question: What is Postmodernism?', it is evident that Lyotard is not entirely happy with an unqualified embrace of the postmodern. For example, he writes, 'I have read that under the name of postmodernism, architects are getting rid of the Bauhaus project, throwing out the baby of experimentation with the bathwater of functionalism' (1984: 71). Further on he displays something of the modernist intellectual's weary exasperation at what has popularly become understood as 'postmodern culture': 'Eclecticism is the degree zero of contemporary general culture: one listens to reggae, watches a western, eats McDonald's for lunch and local cuisine for dinner, wears Paris perfume in Tokyo and "retro" clothes in Hong Kong; knowledge is a matter for TV games' (1984: 76). It also becomes evident that Lyotard's own conception of 'postmodern culture' is not like this at all but, instead, somewhat closer to the modernist impulses of avant-garde art. He states this view paradoxically or, should we say, paralogically: 'A work can become modern only if it is first postmodern. Postmodernism thus understood is not modernism at its end but in the nascent state, and this state is constant'. Moreover, 'The postmodern would be that which, in the modern, puts forward the unpresentable in presentation itself; that which denies the solace of good form' (1984: 79, 81). Scientific knowledge, then, may have become postmodern but not art, according to Lyotard's appendix to *The Pomo Con*. The modernist project of endless experimentation, creating new ways of seeing, presenting the unpresentable, has not lost the force it gathered at the turn of the nineteenth and twentieth centuries. Yet, this does not seem to capture the texture of 'general culture' at the turn of the twentieth and twenty-first centuries: postmodern *popular* culture and, for instance, its concretization in architecture and the built environment routinely encountered by people every day.

Learning from Las Vegas

As a small child in London around 1960, I lived in the groundfloor flat of a Victorian house with an outside toilet and no bathroom. On my way to the park, I would pass new blocks of high-rise flats soaring above my head and

I desperately wished to live in one of them but never did. These houses in the sky represented the future in the present, the promise of a brave new world. A decade later, however, across the Atlantic, they began blowing up much the same kind of apartment blocks as those of my childish modernism. Famously and much quotedly, the architect and architectural critic Charles Jencks gave a precise place and date to the death of modern architecture:

> Modern Architecture died in St Louis, Missouri on July 15, 1972 at 3.32 p.m. (or thereabouts) when the famous Pruitt-Igoe scheme, or rather several of its slab blocks, were given the final *coup de grace* by dynamite. Previously it had been vandalised, mutilated and defaced by its black inhabitants, and although millions of dollars were pumped back, trying to keep it alive (fixing the broken elevators, repairing smashed windows, repainting), it was finally put out of its misery. Boom, boom, boom.
>
> (Jencks 1984 [1977]: 9)

Conforming to Le Corbusier's rationalist prescriptions for modern urban living, Pruitt-Igoe had won an award from the American Institute of Architects for its design in 1951, yet like many similar schemes it proved to be, in effect, uninhabitable. It took people away from the street and piled them in little boxes on top of one another, leaving vast windswept spaces of lawn and pathway between the blocks, spaces that prohibited rather than facilitated ready concourse. Modern public housing did not make people better, nor did it solve problems of inequality and alienation: in fact, it exacerbated them.

What was the alternative? One example, again taken from Jencks, is that of the Byker Wall estate in Newcastle, north eastern England. In 1976, flats and houses were built on the inside of derelict factory walls, thus 'incorporating old buildings into the pattern which is meant to shield the community from traffic' (Jencks 1984: 85). The arrangement of the homes is irregular. Some have balconies, some do not. There are inside stairways and outside stairways. Most of the housing on the estate is at ground level. Importantly, as an illustration of how to avoid the unintended consequences of modern architecture, the architect of the Byker estate, Ralph Erskine, set up his office on the building site and consulted with people who were to be rehoused there about where they would like to be located and with whom as neighbours. One can view this as a later modern **reflexivity** with feedback loops and learning processes or, alternatively, as a fundamental break into something completely different, into a postmodern mode. Jencks himself, although an advocate of Post-Modern (he always uses upper-case and the hyphen) architecture, would not see this as a stark judgemental choice that has to be made.

The crucial aspect of Jencks's definition of postmodernism is *'double-coding: the combination of Modern techniques with something else (usually traditional building) in order for architecture to communicate with the public and a concerned minority, usually other architects'* (Jencks 1986: 14). **Double-coding**, in this definition, refers to a simultaneous textual appeal to popular taste, that of 'the public', and expert taste, that of cultural elites such as the architectural profession. At the semiotic level, this is a more important feature of the definition than decorative concealment of the enduring methods of modern architecture. Also, the doubling effect is usually understood as much more complex than is conveyed by Jencks's most elementary definition of postmodern architecture. The postmodern text is not necessarily confined to just two meanings but, through various stylistic hybrids, it may suggest a multiplication of meanings resulting from an opening out to differences of interpretation. The basic contrast between the ideal types of modern and postmodern architecture, then, is that of unity and plurality, suggesting unliveable order, on the one hand, and habitable disorderliness, on the other hand. Postmodernism is characterized by picking and mixing, in principle, constructing a built environment and, more generally, a semiotic landscape that resists fixity of meaning. This may take a diversity of forms and, although it is frequently associated with nostalgia by raiding older styles, as Jencks notes, it does not typically dispense with techniques that are modern.

Robert Hughes (1991 [1980]) has pointed out that, quite apart from the much derided **utopianism** and functionalism, modern architecture is founded in the use of three materials: steel, concrete and glass. The steel-framed building of Louis Sullivan's Chicago office blocks at the end of the nineteenth century provided the infrastructure for large-scale modern architecture so that brick, when used now, serves as cladding rather than as building block, which is normally the case in the postmodernist revival of brick. The second material, concrete, developed in Germany in the early years of the twentieth century, made it possible to put up huge structures quickly and at comparative inexpense. Concrete suffers the passage of time very badly: it does not weather well and cracks. It is the material more than any other which now represents modern architecture as disastrous error. Much less controversial is the third material, glass, the most utopian of the three materials. Stained glass was a great decorative feature of pre-modern architecture, particularly in the glory of the medieval cathedral, which did not, however, exploit the properties and propensities of glass itself ('lightness, transparency, structural daring': Hughes 1991: 175) to anything like the same extent as some of the most impressive constructions of modern architecture. Take, for instance, Ludwig Mies van der Rohe's Seagram Building (1956–8) in New York, aided by Philip Johnson who much later produced the postmodern confection of the AT&T Building. This citadel of corporate America, the Seagram Building, is by no means a modern system-built block. Mies used expensive bronze rather than steel and his specifications were of such a high standard that he managed to leave an enduring monument to what Hughes describes as 'an architecture of ineloquence and absolute renunciation' (1991: 184).

It was a long journey from the Bauhaus, of which Mies van der Rohe had become head in 1930, to the Seagram Building. The Bauhaus, an art and design school dedicated to experimental modern design, was founded by Walter Gropius in Weimar, Germany, in 1919 and moved to Dessau in 1925. Students and teachers at the Bauhaus believed they were 'starting from zero', that all past traditions of pointless decoration must be swept aside: form must follow function. It was a hothouse of ideas and experimentation, epitomizing the ideal of advanced learning and research. Politically, yet rather diffusely, the Bauhaus was associated with the Left and inevitably came a cropper in Hitler's Germany of the 1930s, although by then its revolutionary character had been much diluted. Mies himself was quite prepared to produce designs for the Nazis before decamping to the USA towards the end of the 1930s. Gropius also wound up in America.

The conservative American critic Tom Wolfe has complained bitterly about the consequence of that exodus of European modernists to the USA in his *From Bauhaus to Our House*: 'the reigning architectural style in this, the very Babylon of Capitalism, became worker housing, as developed by a handful of architects, inside the compounds, amid the rubble of Europe in the early 1920s' (1983: 68). Wolfe himself much prefers, in contrast, the luxury hotels of John Portman, built in the 1970s and 1980s, acme of extravagant *post*modernism, 'with their thirty storey atriums and hanging gardens and crystal elevators' (Wolfe 1983: 94). That view, however, might best be understood as a preference for the rich and immoderate over the poor and modestly practicable. 'Postmodern' hotels like Portman's can be seen, contrary to Wolfe's judgement, as a continuance rather than a break with what the American architects Henry-Russell Hitchcock and Philip Johnson (1966 [1932]) named 'the international style' and extolled fervently as long ago as 1932, before the European exodus from Nazism. The international *post*modern style, which no doubt has its local variations as did the international modern style, updates and often actually refurbishes the kinds of hotels, airport lounges and office blocks that appear wherever serious business is being conducted around the world. These buildings may now be witty and ambiguous instead of solemn and univocal but the interests they serve are evident and their homogeneity of style, indeed, in spite of regional nuances, is often quite striking.

With regard to architecture, the shift from the modern to the postmodern is not just about the finer points of architectural style but about the construction of the built environment as a whole. For example, at the height of modern architecture new buildings were erected with little attention to context, unconcerned about how they looked and functioned in relation to older buildings in the vicinity. Up to a point, that was understandable since Corbusierian schemes for the total reconstruction of the built environment were rarely implemented, except in very extreme cases like Brasilia where an entirely new capital city was built. Unlike Haussmann (see Berman 1983), Le Corbusier was never to be given the blank slate of a central Paris razed to the ground. Modern buildings, in effect, often tended to violate the places in which they were built, blocking out views of great old buildings and generally trampling on the remnants of the past. A vital feature of postmodern architecture, then, is the alternative attention to context, fitting into place and acknowledging the traces of history, a certain kind of holism, in fact.

Nan Ellin has usefully summarized the broad lines of the shift from modern to postmodern urbanism:

1 In reaction to modernism's clean break with the past and regarding of the future as a model → Historicism; historical quotation; an architecture of memory and monuments; the search for urbanity (in its pre-industrial incarnation).

2 In reaction to decontextualism, internationalism, models, neutrality, razing and flattening of sites, the International Style → Contextualism; importance of site/place; regionalism, vernacular design; pluralism; a search for 'character', urban identity, unique features, visual references, creation of landmarks, genius loci, and urban legibility; populism.

3 In reaction to totalising rationality, functionalism, Taylorism, the machine metaphor (mode of production as model for the city and for architectural practice), 'Less is more', 'form follows function', technological 'honesty', separation of functions (the city divided into its constituent parts) → Use of symbolism (with that being its only function), ornament, superfluous elements, wit, whimsy; the metaphors of collage, bricolage, assemblage, text, or simply older cities (Vidler's 'third typology'); emphasis on human scale (the human figure re-enters the design); 'more is more'; 'Form follows fiasco'; no zoning or 'mixed-use' zoning.

4 In reaction to the political agenda of the Modern Movement, the utopian belief that a new architecture will engender a new and more egalitarian society along with the desire to bring this about (assuming environmental determinism), the belief in salvation through design, the belief in a perfectible world, the search for truth and

purity, faith in linear progress, faith in science and reason, faith in technocratic solutions, a certainty and hubris among architects and planners → Apoliticism, humility, a lack of faith and a search for something to believe in; anti-utopianism; belief perhaps in 'vest pocket utopias' or 'heterotopias'.

(Ellin 1996: 91–2)

Ellin's lists and contrasts indicate a global shift, the replacement of one set of assumptions by another on a wide scale, though the latter set of assumptions are said to be more diverse or, at least, generative of greater diversity. Still, it is interesting to note that the postmodern movement, similarly to its predecessor, has been enunciated in bold manifestos, as we have already seen, in passing, with Jencks's *The Language of Post-Modern Architecture*, originally published in 1977 and not so much setting out a new agenda as cataloguing what was going on. Even this text was not simply the record of error and its correction. Jencks had already picked up from Robert Venturi (1977 [1966]) the emphasis on complexity and, in his later work, Jencks has become emphatic about complexity. Drawing upon scientific theories of complexity, Jencks (1997 [1995]) makes out a polemic for translating the non-linear and wave patterns of nature, on ecological grounds, into architecture, furniture, decoration and public art. Venturi's own original arguments for complexity drew not so much on science and nature, however, as on history and culture.

In the introduction to Venturi's classic work, *Complexity and Contradiction in Architecture*, originally published in 1966, Vincent Scully compared the book with Le Corbusier's *Vers une architecture* of 1923 and suggested that it was likely to be seen, albeit superficially, as an inversion of the Swiss architect's modernist assumptions. It is significant that many of Venturi's examples of complexity and contradiction were actually drawn from Le Corbusier's own architectural works, such as the Villa Savoye. Venturi was not, then, quite the iconoclast that he was made out to be. Moreover, Venturi made it clear that he drew much of his inspiration from the historical styles of Mannerism, Baroque and Rococo, though this may well amount to a postmodernist move if postmodernism is understood in one of its meanings as a return to the pre-modern. Much more controversial were the lessons Venturi wished to learn from Pop Art and Las Vegas.

Right at the outset, Venturi stated his position succinctly:

I am for richness of meaning rather than clarity of meaning; for the implicit function as well as the explicit function. I prefer 'both-and' to 'either-or', black and white, and sometimes gray, to black or white. A valid architecture invokes many levels of meaning and combinations of

focus: its space and its elements become readable and workable in
several ways at once.

(Venturi 1977 [1966]: 16)

The critical departure is clear enough, the mistaken purity and singular
meaning of modern architecture, exemplified by Mies van der Rohe's 'less is
more', the principal target of Venturi's postmodernist manifesto. Venturi
stopped well short, however, of a deconstructionist position. He declared
himself a holist who was looking for a more complex whole than that of
'Orthodox Modernism'. Complexity derives from exploiting contradictions
between different materials, angles and shapes, sources of contradictoriness
that recall Eisensteinian montage. Venturi, moreover, insisted that the
ambiguity which necessarily results from a complex architecture does not
necessarily mean incoherence. Venturi's first book also registered the impact
of structural linguistics and its key insight that signification is not just
secondary to the world of material objects but constitutive of it in the realm
of meaning. Against the modernist dismissal of ornamental rhetoric, Venturi
celebrated symbolization and the ironic play of signifiers. In the 1960s, this
was not to be found in the utopian projects of high modernism but, rather,
in complex old buildings that had survived obliteration of the past. It was
also to be found in the new semiotic landscape of commercial and entertainment culture which Pop Art focused upon:

> Some of the vivid lessons of Pop Art, involving contradictions of scale
> and context, should have awakened architects from prim dreams of
> pure order, which, unfortunately, are imposed in the easy Gestalt uni-
> ties of the urban renewal projects of establishment Modern architecture
> and yet, fortunately are really impossible to achieve at any great scope.
> And it is perhaps from the everyday landscape, vulgar and disdained,
> that we can draw the complex and contradictory order that is valid and
> vital for our architecture as an urbanistic whole.

(Venturi 1977 [1966]: 104)

Venturi's own architectural work of the 1960s, aimed at exemplifying complexity and contradiction, such as the Guild House apartment block for
elderly people in Philadelphia, was less than impressive. Subsequent research
on Las Vegas with Denise Scott Brown and a class of Yale students, however,
further confirmed his capacity to overturn conventional wisdoms in the profession of architecture. In the summer of 1968, when radical students were
revolting and American blacks were protesting against injustice, Venturi and
his colleagues took off for Las Vegas to stay gratis at the Stardust. What they
learned there was originally published in 1972 as *Learning from Las Vegas*
(Venturi *et al.* 1977 [1972]), an early statement of postmodern populism

(McGuigan 1992) and described by Jameson (1994: 141) as 'one of the classic texts of contemporary theory'.

The apparently random sprawl of settlements along highways, the billboards and neon lights hailing the motorist, the promise of quick and easy fun and sustenance, these features of the American landscape all came to a head in the Nevada gambling town of Las Vegas, the very sign of tacky glitz. Venturi and his colleagues deliberately suspended judgement of 'Las Vegas values' in order to examine how it worked as an urban environment. Their intent was not, however, dispassionate objectivism: 'Learning from the existing landscape is a way of being revolutionary for an architect' (Venturi *et al.* 1977 [1972]: 3). For a start, the buildings, casinos, motels and gas stations are all turned towards the highway, towards the auto culture of the USA, Route 66 and all that. Ground-level parking at the front, then, is a distinctive feature and one to be appreciated in Venturi's estimation. The buildings are 'decorated sheds' adorned by symbols of consumption, with 'rhetorical front and conventional behind' (ibid.: 90). They are contrasted favourably with the 'ducks', in Venturi argot, of high modernism; buildings that are themselves symbols, like Mies van der Rohe's stuff. And, of course, the contrast (the contradiction?) between the inside and the outside of casinos is a wonder to behold: 'artificially lit, air-conditioned interiors complement the glare and heat of the agorophobic auto-scaled desert' (ibid.: 49). Late-night gamblers, thus, need not be alarmed by the rising sun. Wolfe had already noted it; Venturi and his colleagues further acclaimed it: the bizarre mix of styles of the casino-hotels, such as 'Miami Moroccan' and 'Yamasaki Bernini cum Roman Orgiastic' (ibid.: 80). None of this represents disorder but, instead, the logic of a 'pleasure zone':

> For the architect or urban designer, comparisons of Las Vegas with others of the world's 'pleasure zones' . . . – with Marienbad, the Alhambra, Xanadu, and Disneyland, for instance, suggest that essential to the imagery of pleasure-zone architecture are lightness, the quality of being an oasis in a perhaps hostile context, heightened symbolism, and the ability to engulf the visitor in a new role: for three days one may imagine oneself a centurion at Caesars Palace, a ranger at the Frontier, or a jetsetter at the Riviera rather than a salesperson from Des Moines, Iowa, or an architect from Haddonfield, New Jersey.
>
> (Venturi *et al.* 1977 [1972]: 53)

The city of signs with its architecture of communication, studied by Venturi and Scott Brown in the 1960s, had developed exponentially by the time they revisited it for a BBC television programme nearly thirty years later (*Virtually Las Vegas*, The Late Show, BBC 2, 16 January 1995). By then, Las Vegas was receiving nearly 30 million visitors a year and was the fastest growing city in the USA, driven by its entertainment economy and its increasing attractiveness as a retirement resort for the well-heeled elderly. Venturi and Scott Brown had wanted to study the Las Vegas Strip from the perspective of an architecture adapted to the automobile back in the 1960s. Now, Las Vegas has become much more pedestrianized in order to cope better with the numbers and to facilitate the virtual realities it constructs as extensively, if not more so, than Disney. Scott Brown bemoaned a loss of 'purity', particularly the decline of the art of neon lighting with its bulbous shapes in the dark, having been replaced in many cases by square and rectangular screens of moving images and words. Venturi himself, however, appreciated the 'aesthetic tension' between the 'pure signography' of Treasure Island and the Forum at Caesars Palace, on the one hand, and what he called the 'reality', on the other hand, of an older Americana inscribed in the signs on the shops along the Strip, like Kodak.

In spite of the potential catastrophe that might result from sucking the Colorado River dry or from Las Vegas's sinking water table, Larry Wolfe, chairman of MGM Grand Hotel, could state insouciantly, 'We'll run out of roads, we'll run out of water, we'll run out of clean air, long before we run out of the demand for [*sic*] customers' (*Virtually Las Vegas*). Scott Brown and Venturi were not asked to comment, persumably because their interest in Las Vegas was always exclusively aesthetic. On the question of the aesthetic, both Jon Jerde, the architect of Treasure Island, and Charles Jencks, who was also interviewed, were agreed that Las Vegas had become Disneyfied and may even have gone beyond Disney in the entertainment stakes.

Disneyfying

In postmodernist writing, what Michael Real once called the 'Disney Universe' (Wasko 1996) is often held up as the epitome of hyperreality, a space where representation itself has become more real than the reality it ostensibly depicts. Jean Baudrillard is frequently cited to this effect. However, Baudrillard's initial observations on Disney (1983 [1981]; reprinted in a better translation in Baudrillard 1994a [1981]) were an echo of Umberto Eco's much more substantial discussion in his essay of 1975, 'Travels in Hyperreality' (reprinted in Eco 1987). Although Baudrillard's (1988 [1986]) later remarks on Disneyfied America were read by some Americans, according to Norman Denzin (1991: 142), 'as an indictment of the American character by a European snob', it is Eco who much more richly deserves that touchy accolade.

Eco positioned himself near the beginning of his essay: 'Cultivated Europeans and Europeanized Americans think of the United States as the home of the glass-and-steel skyscraper and of abstract expressionism. But the United States is also the home of Superman' (Eco 1987: 4). He had already remarked, 'Holography could only prosper in America, a country obsessed by realism, where if a reconstruction is to be credible, it must be absolutely iconic, a perfect likeness, a "real" copy of the reality being presented' (Eco 1987: 4). It is this combination, the fantasy of a flying man and the look of reality, which encapsulates Eco's original take on hyperreality. He also noted a then comparatively new mania for replication in American museums, reconstructed oval offices and the like. The curatorial cult of the authentic artefact was no longer a restriction, which is so even in 'serious' presentations of the past such as the pilgrim settlement at Plymouth. And, when it comes to 'entertainment', anything goes. Eco observes: 'Disneyland is more hyperreal than the wax museum, precisely because the latter still tries to make us believe that what we are seeing reproduces reality absolutely, whereas Disneyland makes it clear that within its magic enclosure it is a fantasy that is absolutely reproduced' (Eco 1987: 43).

This 'faith in fakes', so strikingly manifest for Eco in the audio-animatronics of the Caribbean Pirates and the ghostly holography of the Haunted House, was interpreted by him as 'iconic reassurance'. It spoke of something else, distraction from a pervasive uneasiness that is felt in the richest country in the world. National identity generally, not only in the USA, is at least partly constructed by reassuring icons, something with which to identify, for instance, in the conservative British attachment to a once 'glorious' past represented by royalty, castles and grand country houses. It is understandable, then, that in the capitalist nation which has been most insistently committed to constant transformation and the endless turnover of consuming pleasures, with a shaky sense of history and perhaps a fragile sense of reality, the reassurance of something felt as real is so eagerly sought. Whether this is quite what Eco meant or not, it is reasonable, none the less, to suggest that his interpretation of hyperreality was leavened by a gesture towards an explanatory hypothesis concerning a persistent 'real world'. For him, one can assume, there was still a difference between hyperreality and reality, that the explanation might be to do with relating the two levels or modes to one another. Not so, Baudrillard.

In 'The Precession of Simulacra', originally published in 1981, Baudrillard stated his view provocatively:

Disneyland exists in order to hide that it is the 'real' country, all of 'real' America that is Disneyland (a bit like prisons are there to hide that it is the social in its entirety, in its banal omnipresence, that is carceral). Disneyland is presented as imaginary in order to make us believe that the real is real, whereas all of Los Angeles and the America that surrounds it are no longer real, but belong to the hyperreal order and to the order of simulation.

(Baudrillard 1994a: 12)

Briefly, Baudrillard repeated his point in *America*: 'it is Disneyland that is authentic here. The cinema and TV are America's reality' (1988: 104). Such a declaration needs, of course, to be considered in terms of Baudrillard's general thesis on the rise of a culture of the simulacrum in which representation has lost whatever referential function it might once have performed, a thesis to which I shall return later in this book. This apart, Baudrillard is not necessarily making a particularly startling claim, no more startling, in fact, than Benedict Anderson's (1991 [1983]) measured argument that all nations are 'imagined communities'. How could they be otherwise? Nations are made up of large numbers of people, sometimes very large numbers of people, who never meet one another but are supposed to share something in common. That the imagined community of the USA is constructed by its entertainment industry is undoubtedly a novel historical departure but hardly surprising when one considers just how economically important is the business of pleasure for the USA.

It is interesting that, in 'The Precession of Simulacra', Baudrillard simply repeats the myth of the cryogenic preservation of the late Walt Disney, apparently without irony, while noting a correspondence with the frozen Disney Universe:

By an extraordinary coincidence (but this derives without a doubt from the enchantment inherent in this universe), this frozen, childlike world is found to have been conceived and realized by a man who is himself now cryogenized: Walt Disney, who awaits his resurrection through an increase of 180 degrees centigrade.

(Baudrillard 1994a: 12)

Walt Disney was indeed fascinated by the idea of being frozen prior to death until a miracle cure could be applied to his reawakened body. In his case, the *Sleeping Beauty* scenario would have involved lung transplantation and elimination of advanced lymphatic cancer in a raddled 65-year-old body. The evidence is, however, that he died. As Marc Eliot observes:

Contrary to rumours that persist to this day, Walt Disney wasn't frozen. Sick jokes about it percolated through the studio for weeks after his death. One animator recalled a running gag at the time that freezing was Walt's attempt to make himself a warmer human being. In fact his body was cremated.

(Eliot 1994: 267)

Although Janet Wasko goes too far in dismissing postmodern debates concerning the significance of Disney that are associated with the name of Baudrillard as 'mumbo jumbo', a certain analytical realism is required; and not only about the fate of Walt Disney's body. She is right to suggest that:

> The continued extension and popularity of the Disney Empire seems especially ripe for the integration of political economic analysis with insights drawn from cultural analysis and audience studies or, in other words, analysis emphasizing the economic as well as the ideological, production as well as consumption.
>
> (Wasko 1996: 349)

There is a famous thesis on the culture and political economy of postmodernism, Jameson's (1991) postmodernism as 'the cultural logic of late capitalism', which is examined in Chapter 3 of this book. Sharon Zukin has challenged what she considers to be Jameson's argument specifically regarding postmodern architecture. For her, Disney World in Florida is not, as Jameson is said to have it, 'a symbol of capitalism' but, instead, 'the capital of symbolism' (Zukin 1991: 232). Zukin's position, however, can be interpreted as a refinement of the broadly Jamesonian perspective rather than, strictly speaking, a contrary one. She is concerned to stress the significatory power and controlled behaviour of Disney's most extravagant landscape, the 29,000 acres of reclaimed swamps near Orlando, where Walt had imagined building an Experimental Prototype Community of Tomorrow (EPCOT) and which has since become not an ideal place of permanent residence but the most extensive theme park and theme hotel complex in the world, an exemplary holiday destination, one of Zukin's (1992) 'postmodern landscapes'. Unquestionably, the construction of this 'stage-set landscape' could not simply be read off from and reduced to some general logic of capital accumulation. Even Zukin, then, who in her own work does not neglect the economic, unlike many commentators on the postmodern scene, is anxious about economic determinism. The trouble is that in contemporary cultural analysis there is a tendency for virtually any recourse to the economic to be accused of such reductionism. Yet, I would argue, along with Wasko, we cannot make sense of Disney unless we see it as both a fantasy universe and a business.

Business first: the Disney Company is now one of the major media conglomerates in the world, vying for pole position in terms of size. In 1995, the

25-year-old prohibition on combining programme making with command over television networking in the USA was abolished, whereupon Disney bought ABC/Capital Cities. There was an exquisite historical irony in this take-over since the ABC network had showcased Disneyland with a regular television programme in the 1950s. It was heralded by a promotional preview, *The Disneyland Story*, the year before the park actually opened in 1955. Thus, the deal with ABC enabled Disney to lay down two principal foundations for future success: theme parks and television. Also, with the *Davy Crockett* show, as well as the standard cartoon fare, television boosted the Disney merchandising of ancillary products that had started back in the 1930s. There was a falling out between Disney and ABC in 1960 when Disney thought he was being ripped off and the network decided to cancel both *Walt Disney Presents* and *Mickey Mouse Club*. Disney then moved to NBC to make *Walt Disney's Wonderful World of Color* in 1961. The ABC shows had been in black and white (Eliot 1994).

As Douglas Gomery (1994) has argued, the historical development of the Disney Company is not a smooth story of success upon success. Even the 'initial Golden Age' from 1922 to 1946, when Walt Disney established his niche market in animation and pioneered the feature length cartoon to much and deserved acclaim with classics like *Snow White* and *Pinocchio*, was not without its ups and downs. The bitter strike of animators at the Burbank Studio in 1941 and Disney's authoritarian response, indicative of his extreme right-wing politics, coincided with a crisis of profitability due to the comparative commercial failure of *Pinocchio* and *Fantasia*. The 1950s recovery carried the company past Disney's death in 1966 until the delayed succession crisis of the 1970s, which was eventually resolved by the appointments of Michael Eisner and Frank Wells in 1984. Between them they brought about one of the most spectacular business success stories of the 1980s. For instance, the management guru Tom Peters (1994a) has said that Eisner's 'wacky brilliance . . . was the right potion for launching bedraggled Disney on a sparky new trajectory' (1994a: 281). The appointment of Jeffrey Katzenberg to run subsidiaries Touchstone Pictures and Hollywood Pictures and to launch the Disney Channel, resulting in such commercial winners as *Three Men and a Baby* and *Pretty Woman* and the second most widely distributed cable channel in the world, was also critical to the success story. However, diversification was not, in Gomery's opinion, the most important strategy. He identifies two other strategies that were decisive in his judgement: 'Strategy one: if a corporation is languishing, sell some of the assets. Eisner and Wells did this in spades by packaging and proffering the "classics" of Disney animation in the home video market.' And, 'Strategy two: do more of what you are already making money with. So Eisner and

Wells expanded Disneyland in California and Walt Disney World in Florida'
(Gomery 1994: 81).

Alan Bryman (1995) has suggested that Gomery's account is too narrow
and he also questions the commonly held view that Eisner is a 'serial vision-
ary' in the Walt Disney mould. Eisner's general strategy was to generate business on a number of different fronts at once, including the revival of
animation and product merchandising through the Disney shops. In effect,
advantage was taken of the synergistic opportunities that conglomeration
gives and which is further accentuated by the vertical integration resulting
from the ABC/Capital Cities merger. Edward Herman and Robert McChesney outline the marketing advantages:

> When Disney, for example, produces a film, it can also guarantee the
> film's showing on pay cable television and commercial network tele-
> vision, and it can produce and sell soundtracks based on the film, it can
> create spin-off television series, it can produce related amusement park
> rides, CD-Roms, books, comics, and merchandise to be sold in Disney
> retail stores. Moreover, Disney can promote the film and related
> material incessantly across all its media properties.
>
> (Herman and McChesney 1997: 54)

This is not by any means an isolated case. The day after Disney bought into
network television in 1995, Westinghouse acquired CBS, which was fol-
lowed within months by the Time-Warner/Turner Communications merger.
The trends are towards massive agglomeration and concentration of ownership and power in the field of information, communications and entertainment. These mega-media corporations are in a commanding position in
national and global markets. And, still, the US-based firms dominate.

Bryman (1995) has addressed the question of whether Disney is modern
or postmodern, both in terms of business operation and cultural form. He
considers the applicability of George Ritzer's (1993) 'McDonaldization'
thesis to Disney theme parks. Ritzer stresses how goals of calculability, control, efficiency and predictability have become intensified in modern
organizations. Control and efficiency are clearly evident in the training of
employees, the corporate culture of clean-cut appearance and enthusiastic
service to customers, and how customers themselves are moved in and
around the parks from attraction to attraction. Services are delivered
efficiently and they are of a predictable and by all accounts customer-
satisfying quality. The theme park experience is quite different, though,
according to Bryman, from the crude calculability of a fast food restaurant
in which quality tends to be equated with quantity. However, if visiting, say,
Disney World is seen within the actual context of a vacation, as Ritzer

(1998) does, then consumers quite evidently do calculate the cost-benefit of the package. In developing his McDonaldization thesis, Ritzer now concedes the value of a Baudrillardian perspective on the consumption of signs, post-modern reflexivity and so forth. This may undermine his own argument about rationalization and standardization. Alternatively, from the point of view of production, it is clear that the parks exemplify modern rational organization on the grand scale. Hierarchy and rigid division of labour in the Disney Company would suggest a modern rather than a putatively post-modern *modus operandi* with its crazy ways for crazy days (Peters 1994b). The craziness is all in the entertainment, not in the organization.

On the postmodernism of Disney's entertainment culture, Bryman sug-gests the evidence is somewhat inconclusive. Venturi, Eco and Baudrillard certainly saw something like postmodernism in the Disney Universe. There is plenty of pastiche and plenty of de-differentiation between fantasy and reality, postmodern features that are said to appeal to the 'post-tourist'. Yet, in the end, there is a grand narrative that links all the particular stories together. As Bryman observes, specifically with reference to Disney World and the corporate sponsorship of pavilions at EPCOT by AT&T, Exxon, General Motors and others, 'The extolling of the corporation, of con-sumerism, of technological progress, and of individualism has much to do with the propagation of ideals that are in Disney's self-interest and that of the companies with which it is associated' (Bryman 1995: 189). Further-more, 'in getting across the larger political-economic themes associated with capitalism, corporations, consumerism and so on, Disney's technical wiz-ardry and capacity to present *the* view has to be acknowledged' (ibid.: 190).

The approach taken by Bryman is described by him as 'an implicit politi-cal economy' (1995: 189). Such an approach does not claim that analysis of political and economic determinations eliminates the need for careful interpretation of representation and meaning. What it does suggest, how-ever, is that without such analysis, interpretation is insufficient. Susan Davis (1996), in her discussion of the theme park phenomenon, adopts a similar perspective. She wants 'to shed a different, political economic light on the modern pleasure dome' but she also insists, 'I am not abandoning the con-cern for understanding theme park landscapes as representation' (Davis 1996: 339, 400). While providing pleasure for millions by appealing to the child in all of us, the theme park has been at the heart of a very profitable development in media conglomeration and monopolization. Disney is not alone in this respect. Other media conglomerates, such as Universal Studios, have theme parks and benefit from vertical integration and synergistic exploitation of product in the information age (see Wasko 1994). In addition to inventing the modern theme park experience, however, Disney has a particularly strong brand image which was established long ago by Walt and his deified character, Mickey Mouse, and that is instantly recognizable across the globe. Tokyo Disneyland quickly proved to be a huge success and, after a troubled start, Disneyland Europe soon picked up business. The cultural-economic-political complex, of which Disney is a prime example, is spreading rapidly around the world, capturing the attention of middle-class consumers wherever great wealth is being created. It tells a story, indeed a grand narrative, about the triumph of capitalism and the joys of sovereign consumption, and, in this sense, may be seen as modern.

Conclusion

In this chapter I have examined three declarations of the postmodern, in philosophy, in architecture, and in entertainment. Each makes a strong case for a major cultural transition that is taking place, though the crisis of modernism and its supersession by something completely different is perhaps most sharply delineated with regard to the built environment, resulting from the evident failure of much modern architecture and planning. This is of greatest consequence for people in their daily routines where they live and work. Commercial leisure spaces, on the other hand, are where the postmodern imaginary is given its most glittering expression. The themed environments of Disney and Las Vegas, discussed here, are popular harbingers of cultural postmodernism, originating in the USA and becoming globalized. Intellectual apprehension of the postmodern imaginary, however, tends to focus upon the intersection between French theory and American culture, the former illustrated in this chapter by the ideas of Baudrillard and Lyotard. This seems to view the widespread cultural phenomena that are labelled 'postmodern' as, at least partly, the effect of poststructuralist thought. While we undoubtedly need concepts and analytical frameworks to make sense of anything, such a view is called into question by the argument of this book that something like postmodern culture happens and is best understood in relation to material conditions of existence that are substantially transformed by the development of capitalism.

Lyotard's original thesis, none the less, has profound implications, although he himself baulks at the supersession of cultural modernism. The profundity of his claim is to do with the very conditions of knowledge, the ostensible collapse of grand narratives of legitimation, exemplified politically by Marxism but with much broader ramifications. In Jurgen Habermas's (1987a [1985]) term, however, Lyotard is guilty of a 'performative contradiction' with his declaration of the postmodern condition. On announcing the collapse of grand narrative, Lyotard tells us a grand narrative about postmodernity. Yet, this narrative is not even held firmly by its own proponents. Baudrillard denies that he is a postmodernist, as do many other thinkers thus labelled. Jencks has sometimes stressed the continuity rather than the break between modern and postmodern architecture. As for Lyotard, whether he contradicts himself or not, there is an obvious lacuna in his position: the failure to register the persistently grand narrative of capitalism, which is writing new chapters and, as some critics have suggested, is told in a popular form by businesses like Disney.

MODERNITY – A CONTRADICTORY PROJECT

Introduction

The declaration of a postmodern condition signifies a momentous change of mind. It entails, in effect, the rejection of intellectual modernity, how the modern world has been theorized and rationalized, towards something else. To appreciate what is at stake in substantiating or countering the postmodern claim, it is necessary to be clear about the basic contours of *intellectual modernity*, which may be thought of as a 'mind set', a 'cultural dominant', an 'episteme', in Foucauldian terminology, or perhaps, in Raymond Williams's term, a 'structure of feeling'. In this respect, intellectual modernity is partially distinguishable from *historical modernity*, something that has demonstrably happened and is still happening. Roughly speaking, this can be equated with capitalist civilization; and, while certain ideas, such as individual freedom and equality before the law, may have been historically functional to the formation of capitalism, they are not reducible to it nor are they always found with it. To suggest, however, that the era of historical modernity has passed is much less credible than the claim that the categories of modern thought have become unconvincing in certain quarters of western culture.

On receiving the Adorno Prize in Frankfurt in 1980, Jurgen Habermas (1985 [1981]) declared modernity to be 'an incomplete project'. He was not talking about the potential of capitalist civilization to further extend its reach, to eliminate communism and the final vestiges of traditional society. Rather, Habermas was responding to a movement in ideas and cultural expression that had announced the exhaustion of intellectual modernity. In his view, there were 'old conservatives' making out such a case who were by conviction, in any event, hostile to modernism as an aesthetic and cultural movement. What was comparatively novel, however, was the emergence of a school of 'young conservatives', in Habermas's provocative depiction, such as Michel Foucault and Jacques Derrida, scions of French modernism and gurus of **poststructuralism**, who were undermining modernity philosophically:

> The 'young conservatives' recapitulate the basic experience of aesthetic modernity. They claim as their own the revelations of a decentred subjectivity, emancipated from the imperatives of work and usefulness, and with this experience they step outside the modern world. On the basis of modernistic attitudes they justify an irreconcilable antimodernism. They remove into the sphere of the far-away and the archaic the spontaneous powers of imagination, self-experience and emotion. To instrumental reason they juxtapose in Manichean fashion a principle only accessible through evocation, be it the will to power or sovereignty, Being or the Dionysiac force of the poetical.
>
> (Habermas 1985: 14)

Thus, Habermas deliberately but implicitly indicated the philosophical source of an assault on modern reason, without actually naming him, the aestheticism of Friedrich Nietzsche. The extreme counterpoint to Marxism in nineteenth-century German thought, Nietzschean irrationalism was the acknowledged inspiration, in the second half of the twentieth century, for Derrida's critique of 'logocentrism' and Foucault's of 'Man' (see Callinicos 1989; Sarup 1993 [1988]). Nietzsche had reacted against the optimistic claims of modern science, reason and democracy; and, in so doing, his ideas have appealed to both conservatives and some radicals.

To challenge the possibilities of rational discourse, human understanding and emancipation was indeed an attack on the promise of intellectual modernity, though in line with a certain kind of aestheticizing modernism which privileges the poetic over the prosaic. That the actual administration of modern society, moreover, has had 'terroristic' features, sometimes coupling together instances of bureaucratic instrumentalism with state violence, as in the East German communist regime, further encouraged anti-modern sentiment. This was not in itself sufficient reason, however, for rejecting modernity wholesale, according to Habermas (1985: 12) 'instead of giving up modernity and its project as a lost cause, we should learn from the mistakes of those extravagant programs which have tried to negate modernity'. So, for Habermas, the errors of modernity could be corrected through critique and the practical control of instrumental reason by communicative rationality.

Habermas's hopes for renewing the modern project in this way are treated typically with incredulity by those tutored in poststructuralism's irrationalist story, its suspicion of the totalitarianism implicit in any rational project of renewal. Yet that point of view conveniently neglects the contradictoriness of modernity, its uneven combination of liberating and disciplinary forces. Lyotard (1984 [1979]) himself, after all, had used the cliché of baby and bathwater in defending the Bauhaus legacy against anti-modernism. Whether or not the modern project can ever be 'completed', nevertheless, it is vital to appreciate that modernity has been a contradictory rather than a wholly negative project. Most poststructuralists would probably agree since they still live practically in a world of modern assumptions and routine expectations – for instance, when travelling by air – whatever their disgruntlement. It is useful, in this context, to reflect upon Habermas's observation that 'in the entire Western world a climate has developed that furthers capitalist modernization processes as well as trends critical of cultural modernism' (1985: 13).

Enlightenment reasoning

Intellectual modernity tends to be characterized by the legacy of the eighteenth-century Enlightenment in Europe, especially in France. Modern consciousness was not simply dreamt up in the eighteenth century nor was it exclusively the product of the free-thinking French *philosophes*. An important precursor to the Enlightenment was Renaissance humanism and the recovery of classical thought in the city states of Italy from the fifteenth and sixteenth centuries. The invention of 'Man', which, as Foucault (1970 [1966]) has shown, became the object of the nascent human sciences during the Enlightenment, was inaugurated by the Renaissance, graphically so in the rules of perspective. If the Renaissance placed 'Man' at the centre of the Universe, then he did not remain there incontestably for long. The centrality of 'Man', so threatening to Papal orthodoxy, was qualified by the Copernican revolution in astronomy. Modern science, in effect, called both theology and subject-centredness into question. The Church had insisted that the Sun went round the Earth and the flatness of the Earth was a commonsensical matter of ordinary perception.

In his *Philosophical Letters* from England, published in 1732, Voltaire took pleasure in mocking the conventional wisdom of his French compatriots:

In Christian Europe people gently aver that the English are fools and madmen: fools because they give their children smallpox to keep them from having it: madmen because they lightheartedly communicate to

these children a disease that is certain and frightful, with a view to pre-
venting an evil that may never befall them.

(Voltaire 1961 [1732]: 41)

Voltaire admired British empiricism and his scientific hero was Isaac
Newton, whom he compared favourably to his own countryman, the
rationalist René Descartes. Descartes had reasoned deductively from first
principles whereas 'natural philosophers' in Britain tested out their propositions experimentally and thus came up with a more satisfactory account of
gravity. In continental Europe the construction of rational systems of
thought had taken precedence over empirical science. Voltaire was sceptical
of such system-building and he satirized it ruthlessly in the character of Dr
Pangloss in his picaresque novella, *Candide*, written in 1758. Pangloss, a
caricature of Leibniz, one of the inventors of calculus, is the voice of philosophical wisdom in the household of Baron Thunder-ten-tronck, the baron's
kept mind. He is introduced through the eyes of the novella's eponymous
hero, the innocent young man, Candide:

> Pangloss taught metaphysico-theologo-cosmolo-nigology. He proved
> incontestably that there is no effect without a cause, and that in the best
> of all possible worlds, his lordship's country seat was the most beauti-
> ful of mansions and her ladyship the best of all possible ladyships.
>
> (Voltaire 1947 [1758]: 20)

Voltaire's satirical wit in this characterization illustrates a little understood
aspect of Enlightenment thought, its sceptical attitude towards excessive
rationalism. It was, arguably, not so much Reason writ large that typified
Enlightenment reasoning but, rather, the critical cast of mind, as Peter Gay
stresses in the first volume of his monumental study of the Enlightenment:

> The philosophes' glorification of criticism and their qualified repudi-
> ation of metaphysics make it obvious that the Enlightenment was not an
> Age of Reason but a Revolt against Rationalism. This revolt took two
> closely related forms: it rejected the assertion that reason is the sole, or
> even the dominant spring of action; and it denied that all mysteries in the
> world can be penetrated by inquiry. The claim for the omnicompetence
> of criticism was in no way a claim for the omnipotence of reason. It was
> a political demand for the right to question everything, rather than the
> assertion that all could be known and mastered by rationality.
>
> (Gay 1977a [1966]: 141)

Gay makes his point so emphatically in order to counter the standard
critique of the Enlightenment's pretensions, which is now so frequently

repeated in poststructuralist and postmodernist writing. Yet, it must be said, the *philosophes* did have pretensions that are easily pilloried today, such as the project of an encyclopaedia that would cover all knowledge. As Jean D'Alembert declared, in 1751, in his *Preliminary Discourse to the Encylopedia of Diderot*:

> The work whose first volume we are presenting today has two aims. As an *Encyclopedia*, it is to set forth as well as possible the order and connection of the parts of human knowledge. As a *Reasoned Dictionary of the Sciences, Arts and Trades*, it is to contain the general principles that form the basis of each science and each art, liberal and mechanical, and the most essential facts that make up the body and substance of each.
>
> (D'Alembert 1963 [1751]: 4)

The very idea of encapsulating 'the principles' and 'the most essential facts' of all the arts and sciences in an encyclopaedia indicates the vaunted ambition of the Enlightenment at its height. From a present vantage point, the sheer impossibility of realizing such an ambition seems obvious, although the Internet is sometimes extolled in a similar manner. The *Encyclopedie* was immensely successful in its time. It was required reading or, at least, a necessary possession for the educated classes of Europe in the second half of the eighteenth century. Over half its circulation was outside France. The text was revered by the American revolutionaries who overthrew British colonial rule. French was then the 'universal' language of European civilization. There was also, for example, a close and mutually informing relationship between the French *philosophes* and such figures of the Scottish Enlightenment as David Hume and Adam Smith.

Gay has argued that the Enlightenment 'republic of letters' functioned like a 'family' but, as in all families, there were squabbles and occasionally fundamental disagreements. Jean-Jacques Rousseau famously fell out with all his Enlightenment colleagues and this was at least partly to do with his proto-Romantic emphasis on Nature over Culture. Even the Enlightenment attitude to progress, which is so casually decried by postmodern thought, was no simple matter. Unlike the nineteenth century's embrace of Progress with a capital P, the Enlightenment view was less a systematic theory of history, as in Hegelianism, than an optimistic policy programme, according to Gay (1977b [1969]). Enlightenment thinkers dared to imagine a better world and made practical proposals for its accomplishment, not always realistically, of course, as in the Marquis de Condorcet's case for 'the perfectibility of man', written courageously in hiding from the blood-thirsty Jacobins in the 1790s:

> Such is the object of the work I have undertaken; the results of which will be to show, from reasoning and from facts, that no bounds have

been fixed to the improvement of the human faculties; that the perfectibility of man is absolutely indefinite; that the progress of this perfectibility, henceforth above the control of every power that would
impede it, has no other limit than the duration of the globe upon which
nature has placed us. The course of this progress may doubtless be more
or less rapid, but it can never be retrograde; at least while the earth
retains its situation in the system of the universe, and the laws of this
system shall neither effect upon the globe a general overthrow, nor
introduce such changes as would no longer permit the human race to
preserve and exercise therein the same faculties, and find the same
resources.

(extract in Kramnick 1995: 388)

The implication here is strangely prophetic, that the only necessary limits to
human improvement, ultimately, are ecological. It is not difficult to believe,
at this juncture in time, that the greatest peril of modernity is the damage it
does to the environment. Condorcet was not gazing into a crystal ball to
quite that extent but his cognizance of unpredictable ecological limits displayed remarkable foresight.

In my teaching I have occasionally asked students to decide whether they
agree or disagree with the following list of ten domain assumptions of the
Enlightenment, drawn up by Peter Hamilton:

[A]ll the *philosophes* would have agreed on the following list:
1 *Reason* – the *philosophes* stressed the primacy of *reason* and rationality as ways of organizing knowledge, tempered by experience and
  experiment. In this they took over the 'rationalist' concept of reason
  as the process of rational thought, based upon clear innate ideas
  independent of experience, which can be demonstrated by any
  thinking person, and which had been set out by Descartes and
  Pascal in the seventeenth century. However, the *philosophes* allied
  their version of rationalism with *empiricism.*
2 *Empiricism* – the idea that all thought and knowledge about the
  natural and social world is based upon empirical facts, things that
  all human beings can apprehend through their sense organs.
3 *Science* – the notion that scientific knowledge, based upon the
  experimental method as developed in the scientific revolution of the
  seventeenth century, was the key to expanding *all* human knowledge.
4 *Universalism* – the concept that reason and science could be applied
  to any and every situation, and that their principles were the same
  in every situation. Science in particular produces general laws
  which govern the entire universe, without exception.

5 *Progress* – the idea that the natural and social condition of human beings could be improved, by the application of science and reason, and would result in an ever-increasing level of happiness and well-being.

6 *Individualism* – the concept that the individual is the starting point for all knowledge and action, and that individual reason cannot be subjected to a higher authority. Society is thus the sum or product of the thought and action of a large number of individuals.

7 *Toleration* – the notion that all human beings are essentially the same, despite their religious or moral convictions, and that the beliefs of other races or civilizations are not inherently inferior to those of European Christianity.

8 *Freedom* – an opposition to feudal and traditional constraints on beliefs, trade, communication, social interaction, sexuality, and ownership of property (although ... the extension of freedom to women and the lower classes was problematic for the *philosophes*).

9 *Uniformity of human nature* – the belief that the principal characteristics of human nature were always and everywhere the same.

10 *Secularism* – an ethic most frequently seen in the form of virulent anti-clericalism. The *philosophes'* opposition to traditional religious authority stressed the need for secular knowledge free of religious orthodoxies.

(Hamilton 1992: 21–2)

The most common response to this 'modernity test' is that it is impossible. While it may be easy enough to agree with one part of an Enlightenment proposition, another part of it may be found disagreeable. This is the most important result of the test since it is, in my opinion, symptomatic of a deeply felt ambivalence towards intellectual modernity, a sense of undecidability that would tend to confirm the postmodernist view (see Bauman 1991). I insist, for the sake of the game, that my students must decide one way or the other on each of the propositions. Very few respondents return large scores for either agreement or disagreement. Most respondents, in my experience, tend to agree with about half the propositions but not necessarily the same half. This further suggests a general experience of hovering between the modern and the postmodern.

Ambivalence over Enlightenment reasoning is not just to do with the rise of postmodernism. Modernity, in this form, was always a contradictory project. The contradictoriness can usefully be considered in two ways: first, with regard to the tension between universalistic claims and particularistic practices; second, with regard to the tension between critical reason and instrumental reason. In concluding this section I shall elaborate upon the first of these tensions and return to the second in the next section.

History belied intellectual modernity. One of the three slogan words of the French Revolution, the violent eruption of Enlightenment reasoning in politics, was *egalité*. The *philosophes* themselves were ambivalent about equality. They were bourgeois with an interest in opposing feudal and monarchical power, though in many cases compromised by such power, but less materially engaged with universal emancipation. Take, for instance, the position of women. Women had a curious relationship to the Enlightenment *milieu*. Free-thinking women organized *salons soirées* where the great male thinkers of the day met, talked and had affairs with the women. Libertine conduct was one thing, and an outrage to conservative society, but the women were not seen as equal to the men intellectually. However, it was in the context of the revolutionary fervour to realize Enlightenment ideals towards the end of the eighteenth century that one of the great tracts of early feminism was written, Mary Wollstonecraft's *Vindication of the Rights of Women*, published in 1792. As Sheila Rowbotham (1974: 41) has observed, 'Mary Wollstonecraft applied the ideas of revolutionary men to the situation of women'. The Enlightenment thus provided a rudimentary language for women's liberation.

Socialism is another child of the Enlightenment. As Karl Marx was forever demonstrating, the capitalist system and its finest ideals were riven with contradiction. A fair day's wage for a fair day's work was revealed as a sham when the capitalist culled such great profits from creaming off surplus value. This material reality made a mockery of the egalitarianism so easily espoused by progressive thinkers but so absent from the actual workings of modern society. Political emancipation had to be enunciated in universal terms. Otherwise free and open public debate and democratic rhetoric were the merest of ideologies. Socialists of one kind or another found a language of emancipation in the gap between universalizing claims and particular practices. The *philosophes* were not themselves socialist but their ideals became integral to socialism. Similarly, Enlightenment revolutionaries like Thomas Jefferson owned slaves yet the Enlightenment was, in theory, opposed to slavery. The contradictions were manifold. Much of the dynamism for progressive change would come from exposing such contradictions ideologically and in political struggles to realize the possibilities enunciated by Enlightenment thought.

Values were universalistic but the social and political practices legitimized by the Enlightenment were not. As well as being masculinist and bourgeois, the Enlightenment was Eurocentric. The relation between what Stuart Hall (1992) calls 'the West and the Rest', historically, calls into question the pretensions of enlightened universalism. The formation of modernity coincided with European exploration and conquest, from Portuguese voyages to the African coast and Columbus's voyages to 'the New World' in the fifteenth century to high imperialism in the late nineteenth century and decolonization in the twentieth century, leaving legacies of dependency, impoverishment and international tension. It would be mistaken to assume, however, that the European and western view of the Rest has been only oppressive. Other cultures were not, in fact, necessarily considered inferior in Enlightenment thought. There has also been an enormous fascination with the 'exotic' in, for instance, Occidental Orientalism (Said 1985 [1978]). Hall has said it is more satisfactory to understand western discourse on the Rest relativistically rather than simply as oppressive ideology. He identifies four features of western discourse on the Rest:

1 idealization
2 the projection of fantasies of desire and degradation
3 the failure to recognize and respect difference
4 the tendency to impose Euopean categories and norms, to see difference through the modes of perception and representation of the West.

(Hall 1992: 308)

Liberation movements and reconstructions of identity have sought to throw off the structures and consequences of European imperialism and, in spite of the suppression of difference, they have drawn on progressive aspects of Enlightenment to do so, as exemplified by figures such as the South African President, Nelson Mandela. Mandela is in direct line of descent from Toussaint L'Ouverture, leader of the black slave revolt in San Domingo during the 1790s, whose story has been told so brilliantly by the West Indian Marxist, C.L.R. James in *The Black Jacobins* (1980 [1938]). Toussaint sought to apply Enlightenment principles of equality and reasonable governance in the struggle for what eventually became Haitian independence but he was betrayed by his French masters who were already reining back the revolutionary consequences of Enlightenment. Napoleon had Toussaint captured, taken to France and thrown into a freezing prison cell to die without trial.

Countering reason

In trying to make sense of what the Enlightenment was about and its relevance now, Immanual Kant's short essay of 1784, 'What is Enlightenment?' is the focus of considerable disputation. The bare bones of Kant's argument would appear, on the surface, quite straightforward and of enduring reasonableness. Kant says, 'Enlightenment is man's release from his self-incurred tutelage' and ' "Have courage to use your own reason!" – that is the motto of Enlightenment' (Kramnick 1995: 1). This seems to apply to all reasonable beings, though Enlightenment thinkers were always somewhat unclear about exactly who was included in that category and who was excluded. Certainly included were those aspiring to the status of a philosopher like Kant himself: 'By the public use of one's reason I understand the use which a person makes of it as a scholar before the reading public' (Kramnick 1995: 3). The assumed dichotomy of public and private could well be taken to suggest that women are excluded and there is further textual evidence to support such a reading. In addition, Kant hedges his bets throughout the essay by pointing out that freedom does not absolve the enlightened man from paying taxes or from exercising his professional duties as, for instance, a priest or civil servant. So, 'the propensity and vocation to free thinking' (Kramnick 1995: 7) was not without limits even in the public sphere.

From a feminist perspective, over two hundred years later, Kant comes across as a man of his time. The question then becomes of whether the implicit suppressions in Kant's discourse are to do with an insufficiently universal diffusion of 'enlightenment' or are integral to this foundational creed of modernity. Jane Flax's (1992) reading of Kant's essay favours the latter interpretation and suggests that, from a feminist perspective, the whole Enlightenment project is suspect from beginning to end. She says, 'Kant's essay is structured through and pervaded by gendered dichotomies' (Flax 1992: 233). These include child/adult and family/autonomy so that at a certain point the mother's and indeed the wife's care and nurturance become restrictive for the man of enlightenment in his public role. The positive terms of autonomy, independence and public expression are in binary opposition to what are, in this reading, the negatively linked terms of tutelage, guardianship and domesticity. Flax's technique here is an elementary deconstruction *à la* Derrida (see Norris 1987), opening up and dissolving the negatives in a set of binary oppositions, which in this case are shown to suppress the feminine.

Flax argues unreservedly, 'Modernization in Kant's story depends upon and reinforces a series of splits and renunciations. The world is split into two private spheres: the world of work and the family and two public spheres: the world of scholarship/knowledge and the state' (Flax 1992: 238). In the public realm two modes of rationality operate, the critical reason of the intellectual and the instrumental reason of the bureaucrat, while all that is irrational is confined to the private realms of the family and everyday working life.

Rationality is bought at the cost of the public/private split and by down-grading the emotionally feminine. Flax acknowledges two feminist responses to such reasoning. The first would deny that it is intrinsically gendered and therefore necessarily inimical to women's emancipation. The second takes the alternative view 'that the exclusion of women from most of modern culture is not contingent' (Flax 1992: 245), which is the view held by Flax herself. Moreover, such feminism is at odds with liberalism and democratic socialism since they are dependent upon the Enlightenment story: 'I am sceptical that feminist visions of gender justice or political life can be accommodated within any liberal or democratic-socialist state' (ibid.). For her, public discourse can never be any more rational than private discourse. As Flax recognizes, the position thus enunciated is not essential to feminism – some feminists think otherwise – so, where does it come from? The source is poststructuralism in one or any number of its combinations. This strand of thought has the great value of stressing the irrational in life and, as specifically in Flax's argument, draws attention to the interrelations between emotion and cognition, between feeling and reason. In this sense, it casts a compellingly critical light on the limitations of Enlightenment thought and the contradictoriness of modernity. The danger, however, is of a descent into an irrationalism that cannot ultimately distinguish a liberal or social-democratic state, on the one hand, from a totalitarian communist of fascist state, on the other hand.

Another reading of Kant's essay on Enlightenment was given by Michel Foucault in a lecture just two years before his death in 1984. This is ostensibly much less critical of Kant's position than the feminist reading and does not comment upon its gendered categories. In fact, Foucault's (1986 [1984]) lecture on 'What is Enlightenment?' is widely interpreted as signalling a partial *rapprochement* with the Enlightenment quest for 'truth'. From *Madness and Civilization*, originally published in 1961, through to the mature works, including his greatest book *Discipline and Punish* of 1975 and the first volume of *The History of Sexuality* in 1976, Foucault had ceaselessly unpicked the ruses of modern reason. He sought to demonstrate in later writings, under the explicit influence of Nietzsche, how regimes of truth are produced in networks of power and that all knowledge is irredeemably perspectival and particularistic. 'Truth', from this position, is an effect of power which has no adjudicatory function. Careful consideration of what Foucault actually says about Kant's essay indicates that he had not changed his mind greatly if at all, as Norris (1993) has pointed out and as Habermas (1994) clearly realized.

In his lecture, Foucault was at pains to stress that for Kant, and for himself, modernity is an attitude rather than an historical period: it is the critical attitude towards the present. In this respect, Foucault's counter-reasoning is in the tradition of Kantian critique but in very different historical circumstances and after totalizing thought and the delusions of liberal reform and revolutionary practice have been debunked:

> I do not know whether we will ever reach mature adulthood. Many things in our experience convince us that the historical event of the Enlightenment did not make us mature adults, and we have not reached that stage yet. However, it seems to me that a meaning can be attributed to that critical interrogation on the present and on ourselves which Kant formulated by reflecting on the Enlightenment. It seems to me that Kant's reflection is even a way of philosophizing that has not been without its importance or effectiveness during the last two centuries. The critical ontology of ourselves has to be considered not, certainly, as a theory, a doctrine, nor even as a permanent body of knowledge that is accumulating; it has to be conceived as an attitude, an ethos, a philosophical life in which critique of what we are is at one and the same time the historical analysis of the limits that are imposed on us and an experiment with the possibility of going beyond them.
>
> (Foucault 1986: 49–50)

A crucial move in Foucault's lecture on Kant is the recourse to Charles Baudelaire's essay on 'The Painter of Modern Life', written at the end of the 1850s. For Foucault, Baudelaire was a modernist in that he sought to 'break with tradition'. Baudelaire praised the art of the otherwise little-remembered Constantin Guy, which sought to capture fleeting moments of everyday life in Paris, 'capital of the nineteenth century' (Benjamin 1973a [1969]). The Baudelairean version of modernity is an essentially aesthetic one: it is about art and personal sensibility, not about the conditions of knowledge. According to Baudelaire (1972: 403), 'Modernity is the transient, the fleeting, the contingent'. In this essay, Baudelaire famously invented the figure of the *flâneur*, poetic observer, strolling through the public spaces of Paris (Tester 1994). One of the favourite activities of a *flâneur* was watching women, high and low. In his writing and apparently in his personal life, Baudelaire displayed, according to Janet Wolff (1990: 43), '[t]he classic misogynist duality, of woman as idealized-but-vapid/real-and-sensual-but-detested'.

In English, *flâneur* has been translated as 'dandy', though the French word itself is used in recent English-language writing since it retains more of the connotation of a strolling observer and less that of an idle peacock. Yet, it is quite clear in Baudelaire's text that the latter connotation is part of the character described. He is a snappy dresser; a work of art himself. The *flâneur*/dandy, furthermore, 'is *blasé*, or affects to be, as a matter of policy and class attitude' (Baudelaire 1972: 399). Further on he is referred to as the 'wealthy man' and '[i]f I speak of love in the context of dandyism, the reason is that love is the natural occupation of men of leisure' (1972: 419). 'But alas!', protests Baudelaire (1972: 422), 'the rising tide of democracy, which spreads everywhere and reduces everything to the same level, is daily carry-ing away these champions of human pride'. Baudelaire's ideal modern man, then, appears in such passages as a kind of degenerate aristocrat who is ren-dered romantically appealing by his aesthetic sensibility:

> Sophisticated minds will understand me when I say that he possesses that difficult art of being sincere without being ridiculous. I would will-ingly confer on him the title of philosopher, to which he has a right for more than one reason; but his excessive love of visible, tangible things, in their most plastic form, inspires him with a certain dislike of those things that go to make up the intangible kingdom of the metaphysician.
> (Baudelaire 1972: 399)

Albeit an old bohemian type, a picture begins to form here, in one of the classic inaugural texts of aesthetic modernism, of something like the post-modern theorist. Probably more Baudrillard than Foucault but with a cer-tain family resemblance.

Foucault invoked Baudelaire as the aesthetic counterpoint to Kantian criti-cal reason but his main inspiration was actually Friedrich Nietzsche rather than Charles Baudelaire. Nietzsche is a complex and difficult figure who was once considered the philosopher of Nazism, due to the machinations of his sister after his death in 1900, though now he is, perhaps, more typically seen as the philosopher of individual estrangement from the oppressive rational-ism of modernity (see Kaufmann 1968 [1950]). Nietzsche favoured Dionysian expressivity over Apollonian order, myth over truth, atheism over Christianity, and the superior insights of 'the Superman' over the 'herd' men-tality of egalitarian democracy. He can be seen broadly as a kind of link man between the Romantic reaction to industrialization and massification in the nineteenth century and the rise of intellectual postmodernity in the twentieth century, mediated by Heideggerian and poststructuralist philosophy. Alex Callinicos has usefully identified and summarized the principal Nietzschean themes that inform contemporary theory:

1 The individual subject, far from being the self-certain foundation of modernity, is a fiction, a historically contingent construct beneath whose apparent unity throbs a welter of conflicting unconscious drives;

2 The plural narrative of the self is merely one instance of the inherently multiple and heterogeneous character of reality itself: run-ning through the whole of nature, including the human world, is what Nietzsche called the 'will to power', the disposition of different

power-centres to engage in a perpetual struggle for domination whose outcomes alter both the relationships fundamentally constitutive of reality and the identities of the parties to those relationships;

3 The will to power is operative within human history: political and military struggles, social and economic transformations, moral and aesthetic revolutions – all are comprehensible only in the context of the unending conflicts from which successive forms of domination arise;

4 Nor is thought itself exempt from this struggle: modern scientific rationality is a particularly successful variant of the will to power, its urge to dominate nature originating in Plato's claim that thought can uncover the inner structure of an antecedently existing, and indeed unchanging reality; the only attitude appropriate to the seething heterogeneity of the actual world is perspectivism, which recognizes every thought as an interpretation, valid only within a conceptual framework the grounds for whose acceptance lie not in any supposed correspondence with reality, but in the purpose, construable ultimately in terms of the will to power, which it serves.

(Callinicos 1989: 64–5)

Nietzsche is cast as the evil genius behind the 'neo-conservatism' of 'neo-structuralism' that Habermas criticizes in *The Philosophical Discourse of Modernity* (1987a [1985]). Significantly, however, Habermas also locates this counter-discourse to intellectual modernity in relation to the rationalization of modern society that Max Weber explored. Under modern conditions, the application of rational procedures to the conduct of organized social life brings about administrative efficiency and the further disenchantment of traditional belief and practice. As Weber insisted, 'The decisive reason for the advance of bureaucratic organization has always been its purely technical superiority over any other forms of organization' (Gerth and Mills 1970 [1948]). The modern bureaucracy takes on the characteristics of a machine, operating impersonally to execute administrative tasks. It is a means for achieving ends on a day-to-day basis that are ultimately decided elsewhere. Yet, the very 'formal rationality' of modern bureaucracies, driven by economic and political imperatives, is routinely in tension with various kinds of 'substantive rationality' concerning meaning and purpose in everyday life (Weber 1964 [1947]). It is not surprising, then, that both nostalgic and anarchistic sensibilities should have found such a ready target in their revolts against modernity: the bureaucratic, machine-like civilization of market capitalism and state capitalism.

Yet, as Habermas (1987a: 336) remarks, 'The radical critique of reason exacts a high price for taking leave of modernity'. In effect, the poststructuralists, like Habermas's own mentors, Adorno and Horkheimer (1979 [1944]), assume that critical reason has been eclipsed by instrumental reason and, in consequence, they relinquish the project of modernity. Habermas himself believes that it is possible to reconstitute critical reason in the terms of a theory of communicative action whereby mutual understanding is sought through rational debate concerning criticizable validity claims. The alternative position, especially in the neo-conservatism of Foucault, is to assume that only power makes sense. Quite apart from the idealism of Habermas's position, there is a problem to do with abstraction. He is at his strongest, however, in arguing that communicative action is not so much a philosophical programme as a common feature of the life-world, that we do it anyway. On the other hand, the retreat from reason is also provided with greater justification by concrete historical instance rather than by abstract philosophizing. Poststructuralists, and particularly the avowedly right-wing *nouveaux philosophes* who succeeded them on the Parisian intellectual scene, were not slow in pointing to the manifest horrors of actual modernity. Their favourite example against French Leftism was the Gulag. Of equal significance was the Holocaust.

Zygmunt Bauman's award-winning study, *Modernity and the Holocaust* (1989), could well be taken as historical confirmation of the deepest poststructuralist/postmodernist suspicions of modernity *tout court*. Bauman (1989: 1) contests the view not only that the Holocaust was just 'something that happened to the Jews' but also that it represented an irrational disruption of modern civilization. Rather, it was something that happened in modern civilization and is explicable as a distinctly modern cultural and technical phenomenon. It became possible under conditions where the state monopolizes the means of violence and administers society through the impersonal processes of efficient bureaucracy, the very conditions that Weber had identified as characteristic of modern social rationality. Commenting upon what was learnt from the trial of Nazi war criminal Adolf Eichmann in Jerusalem in 1960, Bauman (1989: 19) observes: 'It is common knowledge now that the initial attempts to interpret the Holocaust as an outrage committed by born criminals, sadists, madmen, social miscreants or otherwise morally defective individuals failed to find any confirmation in the facts of the case'. In Hannah Arendt's haunting assessment, Eichmann's evil was banal. When he managed extermination, Eichmann was simply doing his job. The difficult thing to explain, however, is how the enormous organizational task of carrying out genocide daily could overcome 'animal pity'. It was achieved through bureaucratic detachment. Moreover, according to Bauman, the Germans were not even especially anti-Semitic until they were made so as a matter of practical policy: *'the perpetration of the Holocaust required the neutralization of ordinary German attitudes toward the Jews, not their mobilization'* (Bauman 1989: 185).

Crucial to the formation of the Final Solution, which evolved through the Second World War, was the modern project of creating a perfect society, what Bauman (1989) calls *'an artificial social order'*, one which in this case necessitated the elimination of European Jewry. Bauman is right to trace such an ideal, in general, back to the Enlightenment but it would be quite wrong to suggest – and I do not believe Bauman actually does – that the Enlightenment's project of perfectibility led directly to the gas chambers. Much more consequential was the separation of formal and substantive rationality, as Bauman (1989: 206) says, 'In a system where rationality and ethics point in opposite directions'. The most striking feature of bureaucratic rationality is the reduction of all problem solving to that of instrumental reason, how to do something rather than why to do it. The critical reason of enlightened thinking, on the other hand, refuses this separation between purpose and execution. It could, of course, be argued that in the Holocaust the Nazi purpose of eliminating Jews from 'the thousand-year Reich' was served by executing them. This had to be achieved, though, as Bauman argues, by innoculating the ordinary German perpetrators of genocide against common human feeling through the dehumanizing and distancing mechanisms of instrumental reason and the routines of bureaucratic rationality. That was what made the Holocaust possible.

Renewing the project

The late twentieth century debate on Enlightenment reasoning and the fate of intellectual modernity is often treated as a debate between Jurgen Habermas and Jean-François Lyotard. This may be partly attributed to Richard Rorty's (1985) essay, 'Habermas and Lyotard on postmodernity', where he unravels the contrasting ideas of the two theorists and resolves the differences between them in the terms of American Pragmatism by arguing that grand or metanarratives should be abandoned (Lyotard) while the practical reform of institutions should be sought in a more or less rational manner (Habermas). The fact of the matter is, however, that Habermas and Lyotard, in their major texts on the question of modernity, thought past one another rather than conducting discussion in the formal structure and context of a 'debate' with argument and counter-argument. No doubt *The Postmodern Condition* did have Habermas in sight as representing a *passé* theoretical modernism but this is not argued through. Habermas himself has paid scant attention to Lyotard. He is not even cited in 'Modernity – an incomplete project' and there is only one fleeting mention of Lyotard in each of *The Philosophical Discourse of Modernity* (Habermas 1987a [1985]) and *Postmetaphysical Thinking* (Habermas 1992a [1988]). In the collection of interviews with Habermas (1992b), *Autonomy and Solidarity*, edited by Peter Dews, there are several mentions of Lyotard but they are all in the editor's introduction. It would seem, then, that Habermas does not take Lyotard very seriously. He did take Michel Foucault seriously, though, and his Nietzschean alternative to the Kantian-Hegelian-Marxian tradition of which Habermas is the leading latterday exponent in social theory. The planned debate between Foucault and Habermas in the USA, however, never took place due to Foucault's untimely death in 1984 (see Kelly 1994).

To stress 'debate' in this way, as Gregor McLennan (1992) observes, does tend to rig consideration of what is at stake in the frame of Enlightenment reasoning where argument and counter-argument are valued, though this clearly has its origins in the dialogues of ancient philosophy and is integral to Habermas's theory of communicative action whereby he seeks to renew the project of modernity. From a Habermasian perspective, the tension is to do with the rational possibilities of mutual understanding and the obstructions mounted to such understanding by distorted communication and nihilism. For Habermas, the nihilistic tendencies of poststructuralism reiterate the counter-Enlightenment which accompanied the Enlightenment itself. The battle between reason and philosophical unreason is not, by any means, a new one. However, even the most dyed-in-the-wool philosophical modernist would not deny the force of many poststructuralist/postmodernist arguments and positions with regard to knowledge of the social. McLennan summarizes the issues involved:

> The post-modernist challenge to the Enlightenment model of social knowledge involves either rejecting entirely, or at least seriously questioning, the following typical Enlightenment tenets:
> - The view that our knowledge of society, like society itself, is *holistic*, *cumulative*, and broadly *progressive* in character.
> - That we can attain *rational knowledge* of society.
> - That such knowledge is *universal* and thus *objective*.
> - That sociological knowledge is both *different* from, and *superior* to, 'distorted' forms of thought, such as ideology, religion, common sense, superstition and prejudice.
> - That social scientific knowledge, once validated and acted upon, can lead to mental liberation and social betterment amongst humanity generally.
>
> (McLennan 1992: 330)

Although the arguments are many and diverse, McLennan helpfully suggests that there are really three broad positions in play. The first, in Habermas's words, involves 'taking leave of modernity', in effect, rejecting the Enlightenment legacy and giving up on modern reason. The second, and diametrically opposed position, more or less that of Habermas, regards the first position as dangerously irrationalist and so, instead, defends the Enlightenment legacy. The third position would accept that poststructuralism/postmodernism has indeed exposed some deficiencies of the Enlightenment but has no really constructive proposals for what should replace it. There is a problem, however, in setting out the problem in this way: it suggests possible moves in a privileged philosophical game that is abstracted from history.

Personally, I take the view that the project of *intellectual* modernity is revisable and, in theory, renewable. It was never a single, reified object in any case: there were always alternative positions and internal contradictions and struggle. There is nothing inherently at odds between the aims of the alternative and oppositional movements that have demonstrably made the world better – such as feminism and resistance to various forms of colonization – and the progressive aspirations of Enlightenment on the side of critical reason. Instrumental reason has not been without its uses either. One could cite, for instance, in this respect, extended longevity. Yet, we also know that instrumental reason in the form of an endless drive for economic growth has wrought terrible damage on a natural environment that sustains life. Radical environmentalism, however, stands firmly within an Enlightenment tradition of wishing to make the world better, of correcting error through criticism and struggle. Inevitably, this involves a holistic perspective, a sense of interconnectedness. In practice, however, struggle tends to be localized: 'think global, act local', in the old slogan of green politics. Foucauldian attention to particular struggles is attuned to such practice while simultaneously rejecting holistic understanding on the grounds that it is always totalitarian. In consequence, a Foucauldian politics lacks normative grounding and is in danger, under certain conditions, of becoming just another variant of instrumental reasoning where purpose is subordinated to administrative convenience (McGuigan 1996).

The Enlightenment promise of a better world, its speculations on what that might be like, opened up questions concerning what is desirable socially and how it should be sought. One of the most characteristic features of a postmodern mentality, in contrast, is to dismiss the possibility of human betterment as a delusion that has already been demonstrated by the dreadful record of past delusions. It is exactly the kind of conundrum set up by these contrary views that is dramatized in Steven Lukes's (1995) splendidly didactic novel, *The Curious Enlightenment of Professor Caritat* (*caritat* is the French word for charity). Nicholas Caritat, a professor of Enlightenment philosophy in Militaria, is arrested and imprisoned by the dictatorship for giving hope in his work to 'Optimistic elements', the underground guerrilla movement of the Hand. He is helped to escape in the disguise of his *Doppelgänger*, the all-purpose ideologist Dr Orville Globulus, by a former militant student of Caritat's, Julian, who is engaged in the Trotskyist practice of 'Entryism' as an army officer of the oppressive regime. Julian gives Caritat the mission 'to find grounds for Optimism'. As Julian says, 'We know what we are against, but what are we for? . . . What is left? We need to know what we can hope for' (Lukes 1995: 22). Under the alias of Dr Pangloss, Caritat is sent off to visit other societies, to search out 'the best possible' and report back to Julian and the oppositional forces of Militaria. In turn, Caritat visits Utilitaria, Communitaria, Proletaria (in a dream) and Libertaria.

The Curious Enlightenment of Professor Caritat is in the generic tradition of utopian fiction that stretches back at least as far as Thomas More's *Utopia* of 1516 and it recalls Christian's quest for the Celestial City in John Bunyan's *The Pilgrim's Progress* of 1678. Plato's *Republic*, written 400 years BC, is the ancient precursor of such speculation about the good society as well as western social and political theory in general. Utopian writing was greatly revived in the nineteenth century under the influence of socialism, culminating in William Morris's *News from Nowhere* in the 1890s. In the twentieth century the most notable contributions to the genre were dystopian rather than utopian, such as Zamyatin's *We*, Huxley's *Brave New World* and Orwell's *Nineteen Eighty-Four* (see Kumar 1987). The dialectic between utopia and dystopia is of great significance (Williams 1980). This was already present during the eighteenth century Enlightenment, which was less concerned with the fictional delineation of an ideal society than exploring the range of conceivable possibility with a sceptical eye, as in Voltaire's *Candide* in which the perfect society is not to be found. This is very self-consciously the model for *Professor Caritat*. The hero's alias, Pangloss, is taken from *Candide* but his actual name derives from Caritat's and apparently Lukes's own favourite Enlightenment philosopher, the Marquis Jean-Marie-Antoine Nicolas Caritat de Condorcet, author of *Sketch for a Historical Picture of the Progress of the Human Mind*. The character Caritat is in constant dialogue with the philosophers of the Enlightenment, consulting them in the night whenever he is presented with an intellectual puzzle to solve on his travels. Caritat tries to keep an open mind when confronted with the different versions of the good life that he personally finds troubling and is always put straight on what to think by his philosophical forebears.

For Lukes, it seems clear that it is the crisis of socialism towards the end of the twentieth century rather than counter-Enlightenment reasoning as such which motivates his novelistic disquisition. On only one occasion does he directly address poststructuralism, in the figure of Globulus on his visit to Caritat before the latter's escape from the Militarian gaol. The authorities have previously offered Caritat the prospect of replacing Globulus as chief ideologist for the regime. Globulus is described in no uncertain terms: 'an arch-opportunist, superficial to the core, a psychiatrist who pretended to be a "philosopher", a man who had once flirted with Handism but was now the government's most loyal and – it seemed – trusted apologist and ideologist' (Lukes 1995: 25). Globulus says to Caritat, 'We . . . know that this whole illusion of Progress is, as our French philosophical friends – Foucault, Lyotard, Baudrillard, Kristeva – say, an exhausted "meta-narrative"' (Lukes 1995: 37). He also cites Rorty on history's lack of direction. Significantly, Globulus follows a priest into Caritat's cell who has spoken in 'the unmistakable words and accents of Joseph de Maistre, bitter and implacable enemy of the Enlightenment and the French Revolution' (Lukes 1995: 34). In Militaria, then, Caritat was denied his freedom and his beliefs in critical reason and the possibility of historical progress were challenged by proponents of the counter-Enlightenment old and new. The trouble is that on Caritat's subsequent travels things do not get much better.

In Utilitaria everything is reduced to the crudest forms of calculation and meaning is evacuated, following the Benthamite variant of Enlightenment to a logical and absurd conclusion. For instance, once people have grown too old to be useful they are dispatched to FAREWELL HOUSE for compulsory euthanasia. There are internal tensions, however, between the ruling party, the Rulers, who trust in expert judgement and the populism of the oppositional Actors. There are also Bigotarians around who wallow in a mythical past and abduct Caritat because they believe he is an ideologist for Utilitarianism. Caritat is eventually abandoned to his captors by the Utilitarian government, led by one version of Margaret Thatcher, Hilda Juggernaut, because he is no longer deemed useful. Also, in an appeal court case of Bigotarian terrorists, which is based upon the notorious Birmingham Six case, Utilitarian 'justice' is seen not to have much to do with the validity of evidence but, rather, with the management of public opinion and confidence in the Law.

Caritat is saved from the Bigotarians by the Communitarian emissary, Goddington Thwaite (Terry Waite), and spirited away to Communitaria, which at first seems rather more promising than Utilitaria. In Communitaria, belief does matter but perhaps too much. Communitaria is presented as a thoroughly multicultural society where respectful coexistence between ethnic and religious groups is assiduously cultivated and safeguarded. That rules out 'satire', however, because one group must not be deemed to offend another group. The Communitarians are a distinctly humourless bunch who are constantly sensitive to offence being given deliberately or otherwise, which is the one thing they share in common. There is also the suspicion that the whole elaborate superstructure of multiculturalism is there to conceal and preserve the hegemony of the dominant group, the Bees. This is what, at the Unidiversity, the young lecturer Philomena Bodkin thinks and Nicholas Caritat is inclined to agree with her. He is also keen, however, to defend the Enlightenment legacy from Bodkin's assumption that it is bound up with Bee hegemony over Indigens and women like herself. That is what gets Caritat into trouble. He is accused of attacking her sexually and of casting a slur on her Indigen ethnicity. Yet again, Caritat has to flee. In Communitaria, as in Militaria and Utilitaria, there is also an underground movement, the Miscreants, who believe in hybridity and individual freedom. Getting drunk with them in the student hall of residence where Bodkin is warden leads to the incident from which Caritat is wrongly accused. He catches a train to Freedom.

On the train, Caritat falls asleep. When he awakens the train has stopped at an out-of-the-way country station. Caritat alights from the train and comes across a couple of ageing men in riding gear who are fishing in a pond. Their names are Fred and Karl. They are putting into practice their youthful ideal of communist society against capitalism's alienating division of labour, described by them in *The German Ideology* in the 1840s:

> as soon as the distribution of labour comes into being, each man has a particular, exclusive sphere of activity, which is forced upon him and from which he cannot escape. He is a hunter, a fisherman, a shepherd, or a critical critic, and must remain so if he does not want to lose his means of livelihood; while in communist society, where nobody has one exclusive sphere of activity but each can become accomplished in any branch he wishes, society regulates the general production and thus makes it possible for me to do one thing today and another tomorrow, to hunt in the morning, fish in the afternoon, rear cattle in the evening, criticise after dinner, just as I have a mind, without ever becoming hunter, fisherman, shepherd or critic.
>
> (Marx and Engels 1970: 53)

And, that is exactly what Fred and Karl are up to in Proletaria. They have been out hunting (no mention of political incorrectness). They are now fishing, from which they will break off for a spot of cattle-rearing before dinner, after which they will get down to some serious criticizing with their old revolutionary comrades and their guest, Nicholas Caritat. He is assured that 'The government of men has been replaced by the administration of things'

(Lukes 1995: 185). The separation of mental and manual labour is no more. Caritat, however, cannot quite understand how they have been able to dispense with the market mechanism of distribution and he has difficulty fathoming Fred and Karl's circular reasoning about wants and needs. They speak from a position of absolute rationality and can see very well why Caritat was dissatisfied with the different forms of one-sidedness in Utilitaria and Communitaria. The following day Caritat is given a guided tour of a textile factory, the architecture of which is curiously reminiscent of the Reading Room at the British Museum. Here he is treated to a harmonious combination of music and work where the workers are beautiful and healthy and are not alienated. Working there is only one among the many things they do for productive and pleasurable purposes.

Before he can write his letter to Justin announcing 'MISSION COMPLETE', Caritat wakes up. Proletaria was a dream. He arrives in Libertaria, which is not a dream. It is ruled by money. On meeting Leon, his guide to the free market, Caritat describes himself as 'a scholar of the Enlightenment'. 'Oh Lord', the young man replies, 'Another producer of useless graduates' (Lukes 1995: 199). Caritat's adventures in Libertaria include pretending to be Globulus in order to get a job as a psychiatrist in the university hospital, working there as a porter, being sacked for letting three patients back in following their liberation to care in the community, and taking the advice of Professor Tipster to invest all his money in the privatization of the National Library, which turns out to have been a lucrative move once the books are sold off. Caritat comes across a second manifestation of Margaret Thatcher in the figure of Libertaria's Prime Minister, Jugular Hildebrand. She declares:

> With each day that passes under our Government, individual freedom has grown wider and deeper and the so-called social doctrines and policies that used to threaten it have been exorcised. I am glad to say that the very word 'social' has been expunged from our vocabulary. No more social this and social that! No more social justice or social welfare or social policy or social problems or social safety nets! No more social class! No more social engineering! As I have often said, there is no such thing as society. Only individual persons exist, and their freedom grows daily.
>
> (Lukes 1995: 213)

Having been reduced to sleeping in cardboard boxes out in the street with the three mental patients, Caritat divides up his winnings from the National Library privatization between them and takes flight yet again, this time in search of a place called Egalitaria on the Northern border of Libertaria. He winds up at Minerva in the north of Libertaria where he meets Hegel's owl, 'walking forwards with its head swivelled backwards . . . Grasping the meaning of things past' (Lukes 1995: 254, 256). The owl leads Caritat into a forest where young people are up in the branches resisting Hildebrand's latest privatization programme. He is sympathetic but unable to climb a tree to join them. The owl has some wisdom to impart. Human beings can see only one thing at a time and that is a problem shared by all the societies Caritat has visited. They are committed to just one goal to the exclusion of all others:

> 'What,' Nicholas asked, 'is the alternative?'
> 'Only connect!' replied the owl. 'The alternative is to see that none of these ideals is worth anything without the others. Only then will you create a world fit for humans, and also,' he added as if as an afterthought, 'for owls.'
>
> (Lukes 1995: 257)

Dusk falls and the owl flies off without answering Caritat's question about whether apparently irreconcilable principles can actually be reconciled together and if this may be so in Egalitaria. Caritat writes his final letter to Julian, saying that his journey remains unfinished. At the crossroads, where there are several roads to take, Caritat is uncertain in which direction to go but thinks he can see the light of a hostelry in the distance. Maybe he will go on to find what he is looking for or suffer the tragic fate of his inspiration, Condorcet, victim of French Revolutionary Terror.

Conclusion

Although not a utopia, *The Curious Enlightenment of Professor Caritat* can be seen as a contribution to 'the education of desire', a notion which E.P. Thompson (1976) derived from Miguel Abensour and used to justify the value of the utopian writing of William Morris. Utopia, as a fiction genre, articulates imaginable possibility. Where does *Professor Caritat* stand, then, in relation to the Enlightenment project and the contradictions of intellectual modernity? Utilitarianism, communitarianism and economic libertarianism can all be seen as offshoots of the Enlightenment and each represents a particular limitation and indeed fanaticism. That Proletaria, another variant of the Enlightenment project, can be conjured up only in a dream is a poignant reminder of the collapse of Marxist confidence and socialist conviction which turned much political radicalism postmodern towards the end of the twentieth century. Yet, Caritat's critical reasonableness is also a resilient version of the Enlightenment and it is interesting in the novel that it always seems to connect with the forces of opposition in closed forms of culture and society, with the exception of Bigotarianism, representing the residual though popular category of old conservative opposition to modernity, of which there are several instances in the contemporary world.

In this chapter I have not felt it necessary to disagree with Habermas's judgement that the Nietzschean tradition which is such a driving force for poststructuralism and intellectual postmodernism is 'neo-conservative' in that these strands of thought are fundamentally doubtful and, indeed on occasion, utterly dismissive of rational projects for social emancipation. However, it would be mistaken not to recognize that many critical and radical political positions are now articulated in terms of the 'post': so we have, for instance, postmodern feminism and a ubiquitous identity politics that actually favour hybridity more noticeably than extreme communitarianism, as we shall see in Chapter 4. Moreover, such currents of thought, at their best, are concerned with a messy reality; and, in this, their suspicions of totalizing philosophy and utopian aspiration are reasonable. They may even be considered another variant of the latterday Enlightenment's critical reason in spite of their professed hostility to the modern project.

3 | SCRAMBLED IMAGES

Introduction

Postmodern culture, for some, constitutes a crisis of representation because it is associated with a detachment of the sign from the referent, the signifier from the signified, representation from reality, image from truth. At the deepest philosophical level this involves a dethronement of logocentrism (Derrida 1976 [1967]), which is not so much a happening as the revelation of a fault at the heart of the western episteme. As Jonathan Culler (1976: 109) defines it, 'logocentrism involves the belief that sounds are simply a representation of meanings which are present in the consciousness of the speaker'. According to Jacques Derrida, logocentrism privileges speech over writing and supports an untenable logic of identity (Lechte 1994). Writing itself is an act of meaning production and not just the transcription of word-thoughts. Moreover, it deploys various rhetorical devices, especially metaphors, to convey or, rather, construct meanings that are not demon-strably identical to their referent: the signified perpetually slides under the signifier. Thus, it is a significatory practice – and a slippery one at that – which brings into being, say, logical distinctions between, for example, what is inscribed as true or false. Any attempt to fix meaning and truth once and for all is in this way destabilized by Derridean deconstruction. Norris (1987), however, insists that it is mistaken to infer that Derrida believes truth claims are impossible. Instead, such claims should be treated pro-visionally and the ruses of language must be reflexively understood. So, for Norris, then, deconstruction is not necessarily at odds with a realist episte-mology, which assumes, putting it simply, that there is a knowable real world and there are grounds for adjudicating truth claims. If this is so, Derrida differs from other poststructuralist thinkers, such as Jean Baudrillard, who seek to refute any possibility of realist knowledge, however provisional and self-consciously methodological.

Derrida emphasizes writing yet it has become increasingly pronounced in contemporary discourse to stress the visual image over the word. There may be a realist warrant for doing so: for instance, since the invention of photography, as Susan Sontag (1979: 3) remarks, 'there are a great many more images around'. It is commonplace to say that we live in a predominantly 'visual culture' (Jenks 1995). And, as Roland Barthes taught, images, including the iconic images of photography, can be read like a language (Heath 1977). Technologies of vision with enormous powers of image manipulation that are nowadays so much enhanced by digitalization are a privileged object for a great deal of postmodern cultural theory. The great theorists of modernity – the likes of Marx, Weber, Durkheim and Simmel – neglected the rise of technological media, the communicative apparatus of modern formations (Murdock 1993). Although, in latterday theorizing, this neglect has met with some correction (for instance, J.B. Thompson 1995), poststructuralism and postmodernism have attained a commanding position in the theoretical study of recent developments in communications media, especially computer-mediated communications.

There has also been, however, something of an 'anti-ocular' bias hitherto in French theory (Jay 1986); for example, in Michel Foucault's (1977) treatment of surveillance and in Guy Debord's (1995) critique of 'the society of the spectacle', which was originally published in 1967. For Foucault, Enlightenment vision became a means of oppressive power through the institutionalized panopticon, from prisons, to schools and workplaces. Clear-sightedness is indeed closely associated with modern reason but not inevitably for oppressive purposes (it is only too significant that when the eponymous hero of *The Curious Enlightenment of Professor Caritat* is arrested by Militarian soldiers his spectacles are smashed: Lukes 1995). For critics of modernity, though, it is Cartesian perspectivalism, the belief in all-knowing and all-seeing, that is objectionable. Yet, as Martin Jay (1992) argues cogently, there was more than just one 'scopic regime of modernity'. He identifies two further regimes in addition to Cartesian perspectivalism: Baconian description and Baroque vision. In Cartesian perspectivalism, the light of God, the *a priori* truths of mathematics and Renaissance rules of perspective, were the all-revealing lenses of accurate vision. This excessive rationalism was countered, historically, by the Baconian tradition of empirical description, exemplified in Jay's account by the photographic precision of Dutch painting. These were two sides of modern science and visualization, the Cartesian and the Baconian, the rational-deductive and the empirical-inductive. Still, they were not the only scopic regimes in the formation of European modernity: 'In opposition to the lucid, linear, solid, fixed, planimetric, closed form of the Renaissance . . . the baroque was painterly, recessional, soft-focused, multiple and open' (Jay 1992: 187). Its philosophical affinities were with 'Leibniz's pluralism of monadic viewpoints, Pascal's meditations on paradox, and the Counter-Reformation mystics' submission to vertiginous experiences of rapture' (Jay 1992: 188).

Jay notes that from a postmodern point of view, although he does not name it as such, the hierarchy of the scopic regimes of modernity is altered: Cartesian perspectivalism and Baconian descriptivism are downgraded and the Baroque's 'madness of vision' rises to the top. This is most evident in the shift from modern to postmodern urban design. He further remarks, however, that there may be a historical connection between the absence of Cartesian perspectivalism and Baconian description in eastern cultures and 'their lack of indigenous scientific revolutions' (Jay 1992: 189). In this sense, these two scopic regimes do indeed represent the sway of western modernity and are manifestly still doing so in recently modernizing cities around the world.

Scopic regimes are not just about imagery and theories of knowledge: they are also about technologies. Paul Virilio (1994 [1988]) insists upon this point in giving an historical sketch of successive logics in relation to 'visual and audio-visual prostheses' (1994: 6) and the emergence of the 'vision machine'. The age of 'formal logic' is associated with drawing and painting. The age of 'dialectical logic' is associated with photography and film. The age of 'paradoxical logic' is associated with video recording, holography and computers (Virilio 1994: 63). In that history, the relationship between the human being and the machine has reversed. Whereas earlier technologies extended the human being's capacities of sight and representation, later technologies are able to see and represent for themselves. This involves 'the *automation of perception*' and 'the new *industrialization of vision*' (Virilio 1994: 59). Synthetic images can now even be created by machines for machines. Virilio thus invokes a nightmare of dehumanization but with none of the glee of his 'theoretical anti-humanist' philosophical compatriots, like Baudrillard. His is a grim view indeed. For Virilio, the development of the vision machine is closely connected to the conduct of war and, in modern communications, speed is of the essence, instantaneous communication accompanying the dissolution of the human(e) subject, something which happened in the conduct of the 1991 Persian Gulf War and was written about controversially by Jean Baudrillard.

Dissimulating

It is often remarked that Baudrillard is a 'provocative' thinker. This goes for both his earlier neo-Marxist phase and his later 'postmodern' phase (see Kellner 1989a and Poster 1988, the latter for extracts from Baudrillard's many writings). Baudrillard initially came to prominence in the intellectual context of 1960s Parisian Leftism and was associated with such critics as Barthes and Debord. He participated in the critical analysis of 'consumer society'. Whereas classical Marxism had evoked a politics of production, neo-Marxism opened up a politics of consumption. The situation of the working class was radically altered under the conditions of monopoly capitalism and mass consumerism. In one way or another, it was felt or argued in the French neo-Marxist *milieu*, the working class had been 'bought off' by affluence. The experience of exploitation and struggle at 'the point of production' was being displaced in significance by ideological processes associated with commodification and specularization. It was not just that working people had access to more commodities, such as domestic labour-saving devices, mass-produced fashion and motorcars, but that these objects were bearers of glittering meanings, signs of the good life, promising to satisfy popular desires here and now. The socialist promise of 'a better society' somewhere else or sometime in the future that would fulfil 'real needs' and release human potential was much less palpable than the ways in which 'false needs' induced by the 'false consciousness' of consumer capitalism were being met on a daily basis. Baudrillard himself, however, moved rapidly beyond any distinction between 'real' and 'false', as did French theory in general. The economy of signs was not epiphenomenal, mere ideology masking reality, simply effacing use value beyond even the effacement wrought by exchange value. Baudrillard sought at first to supplement neo-Marxism with a semiology of consumption (most notably in *Le Système des objets*, published in 1968), a theory of sign value and the coding of commodities, but soon his 'political economy of the sign' came to replace any vestige of a Marxist problematic. In *Le Miroir de la production* of 1973, Marxism was finally dismissed as outmoded, part of the system rather than part of its radical subversion.

L'Echange symbolique et la mort (1976), published in English as *Symbolic Exchange and Death* (Baudrillard 1993), is said by both Douglas Kellner and Mike Gane to be a definitive text in the development of Baudrillard's thought. For Kellner (1994), it is where Baudrillard's postmodernism crystallized. Gane (1991, 1993) claims, however, that Baudrillard is not a 'postmodernist'. There has been a certain rancour in the difference of opinion between these two commentators on Baudrillard. The label itself does not matter so much as grasping the specificity of the theoretical viewpoint that Baudrillard ('Baudrillard'?) came to represent. Baudrillard announced a sharp break between prevailing forms of sociality and representation: this can indeed be regarded as a postmodern declaration, different in detail no doubt but not in general tenor from Lyotard's declaration of 'the postmodern condition'. For both Baudrillard and Lyotard, an entirely new way of thinking is required, though one not actually so new when its historical precursors are considered, Nietzsche in particular. Kellner's position is that Baudrillard has something of genuine insight to say on a host of different topics concerning communications media and culture, yet his perspective is too all-engulfing to be adopted as a whole. To put it mildly, it overstates the case and leaves too much out of the reckoning:

> Baudrillard exaggerates the break between the modern and the postmodern, takes future possibilities as existing realities and provides a futuristic perspective on the present, much like the tradition of dystopic science fiction, ranging from Huxley to some versions of cyberpunk. Indeed, I prefer to read Baudrillard's work as a science fiction, which anticipates the future by exaggerating present tendencies and thus provides early warnings about what might happen if present trends continue. It is not an accident that Baudrillard is an avicienado of science fiction, who has himself influenced a large number of contemporary science fiction writers.
>
> (Kellner 1994: 13)

In his public commentary on late modern society and culture, Baudrillard started out as a kind of sociologist and wound up as a kind of science fiction writer. Such a depiction would not trouble him. He even remarked that his writings on the Gulf War would in the due course of time be read as science fiction. Baudrillard presents himself with irony and his popularity has something to do with a certain literary flair, most strikingly in his Nietzschean-style aphorisms, for instance, just taken at random, 'We are at the end of production' (Poster 1988: 129), 'labour is no longer productive' (ibid.: 130), 'We live in the mode of the *referendum*, and this is precisely because there are no more referentials' (ibid.: 142), 'Everything is seduction and nothing but seduction' (ibid.: 162), 'the model is more real than the real' (ibid.: 186) – aphorisms, when quoted, that are guaranteed in some quarters to add a spurious profundity to student essays. Most shocking of all: just before the bombing started, 'the gulf war will not take place'; while it was going on, 'the gulf war – is it really taking place?'; and afterwards, 'the gulf war did not take place' (Baudrillard 1995). It is reasonable to assume, in spite of the ironic intent or post-ironic result, that Baudrillard is serious and that he adopts such shock tactics because he believes this is the only way of being heard above the meaningless babble of postmodern culture. The 'fatal strategy' – and the death wish it implies – is the means of silencing the noise. You have to take Baudrillard seriously: otherwise, why bother with him at all. He is not just another cultural theorist on the syllabus to be studied, an erstwhile sociologist who became dissatisfied with staying inside disciplinary boundaries. He is not only, if at all, concerned with breaking bounds but, instead, with wreaking havoc over any modern project of rational deliberation. Teaching Baudrillard on a sociology course is rather like inviting Hitler to a bar mitzvah: he may fascinate but he's out to kill.

Two essays, 'The Order of Simulacra' (originally published in 1976 as part of *L'Echange symbolique et la mort*) and 'The Precession of Simulacra' (originally published in 1978), are especially nodal in Baudrillard's *oeuvre*. His three orders of simulacra are: first, 'the counterfeit' of nature, from Renaissance art to the Industrial Revolution; second, 'production', determined by market value under industrial capitalism; third, 'simulation', which is dominant in 'the current code-governed phase' (Baudrillard 1993: 50). None of them are reflections: they are all constructions. The stucco angel stands for the counterfeit, the one-off work of art in an artificial material. Industrialization brings about a multiplication of images and representations, Benjamin's (1973b) 'work of art in the age of mechanical reproduction'. Under conditions of electronic reproduction, a new phase is ushered in: 'Cybernetic control, generation through models, differential modulation, feedback, question/answer, etc. . . . the new *operational* configuration (industrial simulacra being *mere operations*)' (Baudrillard 1993: 57). Leibniz, Voltaire's adversary, discovered the binary principle which is realized in the twentieth century by structural linguistics and information technology. This takes meaning beyond 'representation' into a field with a logic of its own. Baudrillard happily acknowledges his inspirations, in addition to McLuhan, the prophet of electronic media, he demonstrates his deeper philosophical affiliation by remarking, 'As Nietzsche said: "Down with all hypotheses that have allowed belief in a real world" ' (Baudrillard 1993: 61).

Baudrillard goes on to illustrate his point with a discussion of 'public opinion', which he sees as a simulation constructed by polling rather than representing what people think or, alternatively, functioning to manipulate popular consciousness. Politics, and in the two-party system of liberal democracy, its dependence on the warrant of 'public opinion', is a self-referring world of its own, a world towards which the masses are sublimely indifferent. It is not just that people are simply bemused and fooled by entertaining spectacle and turned off by the remoteness of official politics. Reality itself has imploded. The simulacrum has become hyperreal, more real than the real, no longer to be measured by its assumed modalities; and, this transition derives from a particular technological capability: 'Binarity and digitality constitute the true generative formula which encompasses all the others and is, in a way, the stabilized form of the code' (Baudrillard 1993: 73).

Representations that precede reality cease to be representations and become simulations instead. This is the fundamental message of Baudrillard's essay, 'The Precession of Simulacra', where he begins by referring to Jorge Luis Borges's parable of the cartographers who produce a map so detailed that it covers the whole of the empire. As the map frays at the edges so does the imperial territory start to shrink away. This is 'the map that precedes the territory – *precession of simulacra*' (Baudrillard 1994a: 1). For him, a simulation is not quite the same as dissimulation since the latter leaves reality intact by pretending that something is absent which is not. Simulation, in contrast, invokes a presence that is absent. The hyperreality of simulation arises at the endpoint of a historical succession of image-making techniques:

> Such would be the successive phases of the image:
> it is the reflection of a profound reality;
> it masks and denatures a profound reality;
> it masks the *absence* of a profound reality;
> it has no relation to any reality whatsoever: it is its own pure simulacrum.
>
> (Baudrillard 1994a: 6)

Baudrillard famously illustrates his case with reference to the fabulations and imaginary environments of Disney which, for him, do not represent or distort American reality but, instead, provide the desert, the empty space which is America, with a sense of plenitudinous reality. Yet more significant than this proposition, however, is what Baudrillard has to say about US politics and military strategy. For instance, in Baudrillard's estimation, the 'scandal' of Watergate, which led to President Nixon's downfall after the revelation of his wrongdoing, was the 'same scenario as in Disneyland' (Baudrillard 1994a: 14). It dramatized a moral crisis in politics, thereby distracting attention from the absence of morality in the American polity. At this point Baudrillard's judgement is indistinguishable from what still remained of ultra-Marxism in the late 1970s and suggests why his ideas could be so influential on the postmodern Left:

> *Watergate is not a scandal*, that is what must be said at all costs, because it is what everybody is busy concealing, this dissimulation masking a

strengthening of morality, of a moral panic as one approaches the primitive *(mise en) scene* of capital: its instantaneous cruelty, its incomprehensible ferocity, its fundamental immorality – that is what is scandalous, unacceptable to the system of moral and economic equivalence that is the axiom of leftist thought, from theories of the Enlightenment up to Communism. One imputes this thinking to the contract of capital, but it doesn't give a damn – it is a monstrous unprincipled enterprise, nothing more. It is 'enlightened' thought that seeks to control it by imposing rules on it.

(Baudrillard 1994a: 15)

This passage indicates why the debate over Baudrillard is not so much to do with a tension between postmodernism and Marxism but, rather, to do with differences between intellectual modernity and postmodern thought. The official Leftism of organized communism had been denounced on the Far Left as cant long before as well as during the events of 1968: so, in this respect, Baudrillard was not saying anything previously unheard. Similarly, his argument concerning nuclear 'deterrence' during the Cold War, as to do with sustaining a military-industrial complex on both sides in the absence of 'real' war, was credible enough a view even on the Western Left in spite of popular campaigning for nuclear disarmament. There were plenty of hot wars, however, during the Cold War, not least of which was Vietnam. For both sides in the Cold War, according to Baudrillard, the historical aim was to suppress 'tribal, communitarian, precapitalist structures' (1994a: 37) rather than to defeat one another comprehensively, an observation which is prophetic of the New World Order's enemy *after* the collapse of communism and symptomatic of Baudrillard's anti-modern sympathies. That western capitalism did eventually defeat eastern communism to a significant extent by wearing it down in the arms race is a realist proposition, the possibility of which is not entertained by Baudrillard in 'The precession of simulacra'. Nevertheless, he was essaying an account of how the world works with a smattering of realism. Baudrillard was also, however, very keen to distance himself from a critical realist or modernist theory of knowledge: 'It is the whole traditional world of causality that is in question: the perspectival, determinist mode, the "active", critical mode; the analytic mode – the distinction between cause and effect, between active and passive, between subject and object, between the end and the means' (Baudrillard 1994a: 30).

Baudrillard realized that he was taking a risk with his original Gulf War article, which was published in *Liberation* and reprinted in the *Guardian* days before Desert Storm and the aerial assault on Iraq commenced in January 1991. But, as he made clear in concluding that article, it was difficult to resist applying his theory of simulation to the conflict between the USA and its United Nations' 'allies' with Saddam Hussein over Iraq's occupation of Kuwait when the evidence so much called for it. In the propaganda build-up to the military attack 'the war' had indeed been modelled on television and from beginning to end the mediation of events obscured, to say the least, what was happening. Baudrillard dramatized his own 'take' on these matters with the outrageous claim that war could not possibly occur. Christopher Norris was so incensed by Baudrillard's sophistry that he immediately set about writing a book examining how this 'purveyor of the silliest ideas yet to gain a hearing among disciples of French intellectual fashion' (Norris 1992: 1) should have ended up making such an outrageous statement. In *Uncritical Theory: Postmodernism, Intellectuals and the Gulf War*, Norris tracked back into Baudrillard's position within the formation of poststructuralist theory, identifying how its epistemological **relativism**, which undermines truth claims and the possibility of real world knowledge ('the current fashion for attacking Enlightenment reason and all its works': Norris 1992: 30), lay behind Baudrillard's greatest provocation to date. Although written at speed in order to intervene in current political debate, Norris's critical book carefully dissects the philosophical issues at stake. Several commentators have derided Norris's failure, however, to appreciate Baudrillardian irony. More seriously, the editor of the book version of Baudrillard's three articles on the Persian Gulf War, Paul Patton, accuses Norris of irresponsibly seizing the opportunity to ride a philosophical hobby horse rather than appreciating the seriousness of Baudrillard's argument:

> epistemological scepticism founded upon the logic of representation is not part of Baudrillard's argument: not only does he make truth-claims about what happened, his interrogation of the reality of the media Gulf War presupposes that this is a very different kind of event from those which occurred in the desert, a simulacrum rather than a distorted or misleading representation. These essays advance no universal claims about the collapse of the real into its forms of representation, but rather make specific ontological claims about aspects of present social reality, such as the virtual war which results from the strategy of deterrence and the virtual international war which we experienced through the media.
>
> (Patton 1995: 17)

Furthermore, Patton suggests that Baudrillard's position was not so very different from that of Noam Chomsky, a figure of the latterday Enlightenment and implacable critic of American foreign policy. In the collection of dissenting essays, *Triumph of the Image* (Mowlana *et al.* 1992), Chomsky himself asked, 'What war?' And, replying to his own question, Chomsky

(1992: 51) said, 'This was slaughter, not war'. The Iraqi forces were no match at all for the firepower of the USA and its allies. They inflicted negligible casualties whereas Iraqi deaths were, at the very most conservative estimate, in excess of 150,000, half of them civilian, a figure which was increased subsequently by the yet harder to calculate postwar effects of the western bombardment and blockade. In reality, the bombing was saturation, not the much trumpeted 'surgical strikes', wiping out, most notoriously, children at a nursery and Iraqi soldiers on the Basra retreat as well as 'taking out' military installations. Concern for the sovereignty of Kuwait was hypocritical in the light of, among other actions, the USA's invasion of Panama and its hegemonic interest in Gulf oil and its price. The adversaries, for Baudrillard, were an 'arms salesman' and, in a questionable piece of Orientalism, a 'rugs salesman'. Baudrillard did, however, stress the otherness of the Arab for western identity (1995: 37) and 'the consensual reduction of Islam to the global order' (1995: 83).

Baudrillard, it must be said, caused offence by displaying no evident concern for the victims of American overkill and anti-war campaigners in the USA and elsewhere, who struggled without much success to contest the official line and challenged the self-righteousness of President Bush's cynical war. His essays need also to be seen in comparison with the range of detailed research and critical argument in a publication like *Triumph of the Image*, which presents material for a more complex and much less deterministic account of the Persian Gulf War than Baudrillard with all his sophistication provided. Similarly, Kellner's (1992) research, summarized in *Media Culture* (Kellner 1995), demonstrates the value of his 'model of a multiperspectival cultural studies, which combines 1) analysis of the production and political economy of texts with 2) textual analysis and interpretation and 3) analysis of audience reception and use of media culture' (Kellner 1995: 199). By looking at a problem from different angles, its multiple dimensions can be illuminated, including the operations of the Baudrillardian code in an era of simulation. In contrast, Baudrillard's approach is reductionist and, in the case of the Persian Gulf War, failed to grasp the spaces of contestation and, quite specifically, ended up simply deriding the reasoned arguments and campaigns against it in the west. Baudrillard's subsequent articles on Bosnia, it should be registered in fairness, were more responsible in their observations (see Mestrovic 1998).

An opponent of both Saddam Hussein and American militarism at the time of the Gulf War, Edward Said was dissatisfied with the scale of opposition in the west and the near closure of mainstream media to dissenting voices when there was such widespread popular ambivalence towards 'the war', however sanitized its presentation. As to Baudrillard's view of it as a hyperreal non-event, however, Said did not even express anger. 'Good old Baudrillard! For that I think he should be sent there. With a toothbrush and a can of Evian, or whatever it is he drinks' (Said 1993: 32).

Representing Capital

The great Latvian film director and admirer of Walt Disney, Sergei Eisenstein, once planned to make a film of Karl Marx's *Das Kapital*. Images of exploited workers and top-hatted capitalists were common enough in the Soviet films of the 1920s and 1930s that were meant to represent the inexorable reasons for revolution in 1917. Still, even had the resources and opportunity been made available by the Soviet State, to actually represent the circulation of the commodity and its fetishization might have proven a difficult task for Eisenstein. He was, of course, a modernist rather than a realist so the film would not necessarily have taken the form of a character-based story which runs the risk of reducing a collective process of exploitation and struggle to a drama of conflicting individuals set against the backdrop of an ultimately inviolable system, as in Oliver Stone's *Wall Street* (see Denzin 1991). Yet, the representation of capitalism does occur on a daily basis, not so much in particular artworks but, rather, in the general field of cultural production and circulation in homologous relation to the field of commodity production and circulation. This is the message of Fredric Jameson's 'Postmodernism, or, the cultural logic of late capitalism', originally published as an article in 1984 and reprinted as the first chapter of Jameson's major book of the same title, published in 1991.

In his introduction to the book, Jameson reflects upon why he had thought it necessary to theorize postmodernism in the early 1980s. Fundamentally, it was an attempt to make sense of history in a period when a sense of history had been lost. Modernism, in always focusing upon what was new, had been concerned with change, most particularly the culturalization of nature. Postmodernism arises when the world has become fully culturalized or 'humanized', when, in Jameson's (1991: ix) words, 'nature has gone for good'. By attending to culture, we can see the implications of this apparent completion of the modern project. There we find

> an immense dilation of its sphere (the sphere of commodities), an immense and historically original acculturation of the Real, a quantum leap in what Benjamin still called the 'aestheticization' of reality (he thought it meant fascism, but we know it's only fun: a prodigious exhilaration with the new order of things, a commodity rush, our

'representation' of things tending to arouse an enthusiasm and a mood swing not necessarily inspired by the things themselves).

(Jameson 1991: x)

In addition to subsuming nature, culture itself has become fully commodified: 'Postmodernism is the consumption of sheer commodification as a process' (Jameson 1991: x). Thus, culture is no longer the romantic or modernist resistance to capitalist civilization, the refusal of commodification. It has, instead, become integrated thoroughly into the system of commodity production and circulation. Culture is commodity; commodity is culture. Alongside this ubiquitous process something has appeared in intellectual discourse, namely theoretical postmodernism, which has two especially distinctive characteristics. 'First,' says Jameson (1991: xi), 'the theory seems necessarily imperfect or impure', by which he means it is contradictory. Jameson is quite happy to use a notion of contradiction since he is philosophically dialectical materialist rather than poststructuralist or postmodernist. Postmodern theory attacks all foundations of knowledge, all essential concepts, dissolving them into an endless play of shifting signifiers. Yet, in practice, it cannot actually sustain such a position. Its very claim that culture and society have been utterly transformed, which includes the absorption of the social into the cultural, the assertion that all social relations are only significations, in effect, the claim that sociology cannot be anything other than cultural studies, is a foundational assumption.

Second, postmodern theory is peculiarly depthless. It eschews explanation of a phenomenon by recourse to something behind it or beneath it. Baudrillard's treatment of the Gulf War as exclusively a media event is a perfect example. He deliberately refuses to give a rational account of this media event as propaganda or ideological distortion generated by real interests and processes that are absent from the television screen. That also indicates why postmodern thinking is so difficult to pin down, to summarize or to evaluate. It is always moving on, chasing the flow of signifiers. For Jameson, then, the crunch comes with 'the decision as to whether one faces a break or a continuity – whether the present is to be seen as a historical originality or as the simple prolongation of more of the same under different sheep's clothing' (1991: xii–xiii). Jameson's answer is dialectical: it is a bit of both. Postmodern culture is novel but this is not inexplicable in relation to historical formations. Capitalist civilization has transformed itself in such a way that the culture in general has become reconfigured. Postmodernism is the cultural logic of late or multinational capitalism. Postmodern culture is best understood, in Raymond Williams's (1977) formulation, as a 'structure of feeling'. In sum, then:

The fundamental ideological task of the new concept . . . must remain that of coordinating new forms of practice and social and mental habits (this is finally what I take Williams to have in mind by the notion of a 'structure of feeling') with the new forms of economic production and organization thrown up by the modification of capitalism – the new global division of labour – in recent years.

(Jameson 1991: xiv)

Analytical attention is not confined to the relations between an economic and political system, on the one hand, and a cultural system or general configuration of culture, on the other hand. That said, it is necessary to grasp systemic relations in Jameson's account of postmodernism. The task is also existential, to do with understanding how people experience their lives and act under such conditions: 'the "postmodern" is to be seen as the production of postmodern people capable of functioning in a very peculiar socioeconomic world indeed' (Jameson 1991: xv).

In his introduction to *Postmodernism, or, the Cultural Logic of Late Capitalism*, Jameson explains that the reason why the original essay, serving as the book's first chapter, was not revised since the position enunciated some years previously is because the reality it discusses has not changed significantly. Jameson had, in fact, received considerable criticism (see Kellner 1989b), not all of which did he reject. For instance, Jameson appreciated critical insights into his neglect of agency in stressing systemic forces in an excessively totalizing fashion. He also, subsequently, felt it necessary to clarify his position in relation to and in contrast with various combinations of modern and postmodern thought (Chapter 2). The bulk of the book is made up with a number of additional studies that elaborate upon specific aspects of postmodern culture: for instance, Jameson's belief that video is a distinctly postmodern form since it transcends the individual artwork and authorial signature is erased. It is curious that Jameson should have fixed in this way upon a comparatively obscure avant-garde practice which has appropriated a popular medium within an art context, producing a new genre of video art. This runs counter to what I believe to be one of the great strengths of Jameson's original argument about postmodern culture, that it is not reducible to a style or to form but should, instead, be apprehended as a 'cultural dominant', a reconfiguration of the field in general and in which developments within mass-popular culture are more telling signs of the time than what happens in specialized arts practice. I realize, however, that I am here extending the implication of Jameson's argument to conform rather more with my own point of view. Jameson probably does hold out greater hope for the resistant force of a postmodern avant-garde than I do, in spite of what Nicholas Zurbrugg (1993) says. From my point of view, mass-popular culture is the primary terrain of cultural struggle and, I believe, there is more space there for a cultural politics than, perhaps, Jameson would allow. To illustrate the argument, I would suggest that a mass-popular genre such as television situation comedy is at least as likely to articulate progressive possibility and disturb a prevailing sense of 'reality' as that which often seems to function as research and development for future advertising discourse in video art.

According to Jameson, postmodernism is about much more than the exhaustion of high modernism in the arts and the critical irrelevance of the avant-garde. Noting the aesthetic populism of Venturi, he goes on to outline the intellectual reorientation towards the popular, framed by 'the effacement . . . of the older (essentially high-modernist) frontier between high culture and so-called mass or commercial culture' and resulting in 'the emergence of new kinds of texts infused with the forms, categories, and contents of the very culture industry so passionately denounced by all the ideologues of the modern, from Leavis and the American New Criticism all the way to Adorno and the Frankfurt School' (Jameson 1991: 2). There is an intellectual fascination with a 'whole "degraded" landscape of schlock and kitsch, of TV series and *Reader's Digest* culture, of advertising and motels, of the late show and the grade-B Hollywood film, so-called paraliterature, with its airport paperback categories of the gothic and the romance, the popular biography, the murder mystery, and the science fiction or fantasy novel' (Jameson 1991: 2–3). High art forms cease to distinguish themselves sharply from such mass-popular forms when drawing upon them, as was so in the past: the aesthetic deployment of mass-popular devices has become not just quotation but, instead, represents a coalescence between two circuits of culture that were hitherto ranked very differently. Yet more significant is the possibility, though only implicit and perhaps unintended in Jameson's own discussions of mass-popular culture, that the mass-popular has become the key site for newer representational modes, progressively displacing high art at the cutting edges of experimentation. To argue thus is not necessarily to deny that much and, indeed, most mass-popular cultural product is standardized and cliché-ridden. Jameson himself displays a kind of cultural democracy by discussing examples of special interest from both high art and mass-popular culture in developing his theoretical arguments. Evident in many of his particular judgements, however, is Jameson's own residual preference for 'real' culture even when he is talking about Hollywood.

Questions of cultural evaluation are not so crucial in the argument as Jameson's claim that there is a correspondence between emergent configurations in the cultural field and transformations in capitalism, which had been described by conservative theorists such as in Daniel Bell's 'post-industrialism'. Left-wing critics, since the 1960s, had denounced such theorizing as ideological. Jameson, however, influenced by Ernest Mandel (1975), insists upon the need to rethink capitalism in line with real developments in the economy, most particularly the rise of what others have called an 'informational mode of production', facilitated by electronics and computing. Following Mandel's use of 'long wave' theory of economic development, Jameson proposes a set of cultural and economic correspondences: realism associated with nineteenth century and largely national pockets of market capitalism, modernism associated with the early twentieth century's monopoly capitalism and imperialism, and postmodernism associated with the late twentieth century's global capitalism, each mediated by particular forces of production: steam power, electricity and combustion, and electronics and nuclear power.

Jameson's periodizing hypothesis is vulnerable to criticisms of economic and technological reductionism and on a number of other grounds as well (see Homer 1998). Whatever its virtues, it is far too schematic. There are more nuanced versions of how to theorize the relations between recent cultural and socio-economic change in the work of David Harvey (1989) most notably and, also, in the work of Scott Lash and John Urry (1994). Harvey's central thesis in *The Condition of Postmodernity* is that postmodern culture can be seen in relation to the recomposition of capitalism that was hastened by the OPEC (Organization of Petroleum-Exporting Countries) crisis of 1973. Quite specifically, the Fordist system (**Fordism**) of American capital had become vulnerable due to its inflexibility in terms of the assembly line system of serial production and the labour bargain with strong unions and welfare provision. It became necessary to enter into a more flexible, post-Fordist, regime of capital accumulation, a faster construction of and response to market demand with much less security for workers and, in effect, the destruction of much industrial capacity in what were 'expensive' labour markets and the seeking out of cheaper labour markets elsewhere. Rapid turnover and stylistic differentiation in commodity production and circulation are resonant in many ways with the sheer pace of postmodern cultural turnover, and not only in fashion. Harvey, a geographer, particularly stresses the material and mental reconfigurations of space, the mobility of capital and the speed of communications across the world. He says, 'we have been experiencing, these last two decades, an intense phase of time-space compression that has a disorienting and disruptive impact upon political-economic practices, the balance of class power, as well as upon cultural and social life' (Harvey 1989: 284). In *Economies of Signs and Space*, Lash and Urry (1994) further develop the insights of Harvey and others to examine complex commodity and symbolic flows in a globalizing economy and in relation to the postmodernization of culture that Jameson did so much in the first instance to delineate. Discussion of these issues will be resumed in Chapter 5 with reference to Manuel Castells's (1996, 1997a, 1998) monumental work on 'the information age'.

Jameson's original periodizing hypothesis shed light on the significance of postmodernism in spite of its weaknesses with regard to the specific linkages of economy and culture. The hypothesis suggested that postmodernism is not simply to be understood as an intellectual mode or set of aesthetic styles. It may more usefully be comprehended as signifying a moment in history, the moment at which Marx's prediction that capitalism transforms everything, that no practice or place is safe from its reach, was coming true. It is Jameson's contention that postmodernism is the 'cultural dominant' of the present, understood in Williams's (1977) framework of dominant, residual and emergent cultures which coexist at any one moment in time. Although totalizing in its ambition and in need of greater refinement, such a claim never suggested that all contemporary culture is necessarily to be understood as postmodernist. In fact, the coexistence of different cultures is a feature of the field. Postmodernism, in this sense, represents the 'force field' of contemporary culture and enunciates the prevailing 'structure of feeling', led and disseminated abroad by the USA, the most powerful nation in the world.

Another correspondence drawn by Jameson is with contemporary 'theory'. He lists this along with a number of related aspects of postmodernism:

> the following constitutive features of the postmodern: a new depthlessness, which finds its prolongation both in contemporary 'theory' and in a whole culture of the image or the simulacrum; a consequent weakening of historicity, both in our relation to public History and in the new forms of our private temporality, whose 'schizophrenic' structure (following Lacan) will determine new types of syntax or syntagmatic relationships in the more temporal arts; a whole new type of emotional ground tone – what I will call 'intensities' – which can be grasped by a return to older theories of the sublime; the deep constitutive relationships of all this to a whole new technology, which is itself a figure for a whole new economic world system.
>
> (Jameson 1991: 6)

To give a graphic illustration of his initial take on the aesthetics of postmodernism, which he sees as exemplary of a wider cultural configuration, Jameson compares two works of visual art: Vincent Van Gogh's *A Pair of Boots* and Andy Warhol's *Diamond Dust Shoes*. The Van Gogh work is a painting, a classic example of modern art which confers artistry on mundane objects, the footwear of a peasant. By representing these boots in pure colour, Van Gogh's picture articulates a utopian vision, the autonomous and transformative capacity of art. In contrast, 'Andy Warhol's *Diamond Dust Shoes* evidently no longer speaks to us with any of the immediacy of Van Gogh's footgear; indeed, I am tempted to say that it does not really speak to us at all' (Jameson 1991: 8). It is a multiply reproducible photographic image that is manipulated into existence by someone schooled in advertising, Warhol, whose 'work in fact turns centrally around commodification' (Jameson 1991: 9). There is a flatness in the image, offering no meaning to be interpreted, quite different from Van Gogh's celebration of labour.

Jameson contends that in postmodern culture there is a 'waning of affect', which I take to be a decline of emotional identification and human sympathy. He goes on to discuss another famous modern painting, Edvard Munch's *The Scream*, 'a canonical expression of the great modernist thematics of alienation, anomie, solitude, social fragmentation, and isolation, a virtual programmatic emblem of what used to be called the age of anxiety' (Jameson 1991: 11). Such Expressionist art assumes there is an inside to be expressed outside, an externalization of emotion. This is an hermeneutic model of surface and depth, a model disavowed by postmodernism's refusal to countenance the possibility of a profound meaning, in this case emotional, inscribed in the image. There are other depth models, each depending upon a binary opposition, that have been similarly deconstructed and disavowed in contemporary 'theory': dialectics (essence/appearance), Freudianism (latent/manifest), existentialism (authenticity/inauthenticity) and semiotics (signified/signifier). The specific point about Expressionism, however, is that alienation requires a human subject to be alienated. With the dissolution of the unified subject, a cardinal tenet of poststructuralism, how can one be alienated from one's true self? The flatness of postmodern culture is further illustrated by Wells Fargo Court at the top of Bunker Hill in Los Angeles, appearing, in Jameson's (1991: 12) words, as 'a surface which seems unsupported by any volume'.

There is a similar issue at stake in Jameson's discussion of parody and pastiche. For him, pastiche has replaced parody in postmodern culture. Parody requires something to parody in order to achieve its satirical effect. That which is parodied must, then, in some sense be a normal state of discourse. The intended effect of parody is critical comment. In postmodern culture, discursive styles are borrowed with no intent to achieve such an effect: there is no object of criticism in pastiche. Images and styles are endlessly recycled for consumption and, because they have no referential depth, they are quickly discarded in the next recyclement. These arguments link up with Jameson's famous discussion of nostalgia films and, in particular, Lawrence Kasdan's *Body Heat*, a remake of the 1940s classic, *Double Indemnity*. Although the film is set in the present of the 1980s it carefully obscures the signs of that decade and evokes an earlier fortyish feel and noirish look. Without actually being set in the past, it vaguely yet deliberately signifies 'pastness'. Moreover, its leading actor, William Hurt, Jameson notes, is a departure from the personality filled stars of the past. He does not, however, comment upon the leading actress, Kathleen Turner, an emergent star at that time whose strength of personality, as represented in publicity and films, would not so readily confirm Jameson's point about the flattening out of representational discourse in postmodern culture.

To return to Jameson's original motive for commenting upon postmodernism: he sees the present as characterized by a 'crisis of historicity'. Curiously, the obsession with the past in public culture is a feature of this crisis: 'the past' merely becomes a set of manipulable signs which give little sense of the actual shapes and forces of material history. This flattening out of history not only occurs in public but also is experienced subjectively in a schizophrenic loss of temporality. Jameson draws on Jacques Lacan's account of schizophrenia as a 'breakdown in the signifying chain'. The syntagmatic or diachronic logic of meaning in the succession of signifiers is disrupted by an unrelated synchronicity of signs: something like a kind of generalized zapping between television channels. This schizophrenic condition has been observed clinically but Jameson's point is not strictly to do with psychopathology. Similarly to Gilles Deleuze and Felix Guattari (1984 [1972]), he is making a point about the culture, although with a rather different judgemental inflection. Schizo-culture is trapped in a succession of perpetual presents in a scrambling of signifiers and images.

Another aspect of Jameson's argument is to do with the return of the sublime, the object which resists representation and invokes awe and intensity of feeling. In eighteenth century aesthetics, this was seen as a question of nature, the overwhelming excess of certain landscapes and seascapes, for instance, mountainous regions and stormy seas. These sights contrasted with the domesticated pleasures of the picturesque scene, so beloved of the nineteenth century bourgeoisie. Under postmodern conditions, according to Jameson, the major representational problem is to depict the space of global capitalism and its communicational networks, actual space and virtual space. A typical mode is 'high-tech paranoia' in thriller movies that depict power as conspiracy when, in fact, it is better understood as systemic. Jameson (1991: 37) writes, 'our faulty representations of an immense communicational and computer network are themselves but a distorted figuration of something even deeper, namely, the whole world system of present-day multinational capitalism'.

Cognitive mapping

A crucial move in Jameson's argument comes with his analysis of 'a full-blown postmodern building' (1991: 38), John Portman's Westin Bonaventure Hotel in downtown Los Angeles. This allows him to introduce the theme of a peculiarly postmodern disorientation in space. The Bonaventure is described as a total, all-absorbing space with three understated entrances at different levels which may prove difficult to find again once one has been inside the hotel for a while. It is closed off subtly rather than abruptly from the 'real world' outside by a reflective glass skin. There are four identical towers and a huge atrium that may be ascended and descended by either elevator or escalator. Visitors are moved up and down by these kinetic sculptures and in such a way that any sense of bearing in relation to the structure of the building as a whole is abandoned, willingly or otherwise. Jameson notes that shopkeepers on the second floor were desperate for customers who had apparently lost themselves dreamily in hyperspace. Directional colour-coding had been introduced but did not help much. The Bonaventure is popular and pleasurable, albeit disorienting, while representing both concretely and metaphorically, according to Jameson, a 'postmodern hyperspace' that 'has finally succeeded in transcending the capacities of the human body to locate itself, to organize its immediate surroundings perceptually and cognitively to map its position in a mappable external world' (1991: 44). Whatever the hyperbole specifically with regard to the Bonaventure, Jameson's general argument is clear enough, that postmodernism brings about a spatial disorientation by superseding an older, modernist and, in Kevin Lynch's (1960: 2) term, 'legible' urban space.

Jameson insists that his argument is not a moralizing one. He is not denouncing postmodernism, nor is he applauding it. Like Marx's analysis of capitalism itself, the postmodern has to be grasped both 'positively *and* negatively': 'postmodern (or multinational space) is not merely a cultural ideology or fantasy but has genuine historical (and socioeconomic) reality as a third great original expansion of capitalism around the globe' (Jameson 1991: 49). The autonomy of culture, that which had been its critical force, has finally been eroded while simultaneously, however, the cultural has proliferated to an extent never before witnessed. It both speaks the spatial and significatory powers of capital and disorients the human subject. In response, Jameson calls for a new aesthetic, equally inspired by the old adversaries,

Bertolt Brecht and Georg Lukács (see Bloch *et al.* 1980). This would be an 'aesthetic of **cognitive mapping**', a pedagogic realism in a new representational mode. In his major article on postmodernism, Jameson does not specify the formal characteristics of the new aesthetic, though cognitive mapping is a key principle of his subsequent research presented in *The Geopolitical Aesthetic* (1992). The notion of cognitive mapping, derived initially from the urban theorist Lynch, is further conceptualized in the terms of Louis Althusser's (1984) Lacanian theory of ideology, which suggests that the function of ideology is to hail and position the subject. The issue, then, is not just one of spatial orientation but also of psychic and social identity, how the subject understands itself and makes sense of its place in a seemingly opaque yet ultimately, it is hoped by Jameson, intelligible world. It is worth quoting Jameson at length on his preliminary formulation of cognitive mapping:

> An aesthetic of cognitive mapping – a pedagogical political culture which seeks to endow the individual subject with some new heightened sense of its place in the global system – will necessarily have to respect this enormously complex representational dialectic and invent radical new forms to do it justice. This is not then, clearly, a call for a return to an older kind of machinery, some older and more transparent national space, or some more traditional and reassuring perspectival or mimetic enclave: the new political art (if its possible at all) will have to hold to the truth of postmodernism, that is to say, its fundamental object – the world space of multinational capital – at the same time at which it achieves a breakthrough to some as yet unimaginable new mode of representing this last, which is at present neutralized by our spatial as well as our social confusion. The political form of postmodernism, if there ever is any, will have its vocation the invention and projection of a global cognitive mapping, on a social as well as a spatial scale.
>
> (Jameson 1991: 54)

Jameson's concluding observation in the book version of *Postmodernism, or, the Cultural Logic of Late Capitalism* that 'cognitive mapping' was meant only as a code word for 'class consciousness' is unnecessarily reductive and does not do justice to the problem that he posed in the original essay and went on to explore fruitfully in later writings. The problem is that of self-understanding and spatial awareness in a culturally fluid and economically all-consuming system. So, the subjectivities and identities involved are multiple, including those of ethnicity and 'race', gender and sexuality, as well as class. Moreover, the issues of space, incorporating both actual and virtual spaces, physical geography and mental geography, are extremely complex and various. On this latter point Jameson subsequently observed:

the new space involves the suppression of distance (in the sense of Benjamin's aura) and the relentless saturation of any remaining voids and empty places, to a point where the postmodern body – whether wandering through a postmodern hotel, locked into rock sounds by means of headphones, or undergoing the multiple shocks and bombardments of the Vietnam War as Michael Herr conveys it to us – is now exposed in a perpetual barrage of immediacy from which all sheltering layers and intervening mediations have been removed.

(Jameson 1988: 351)

It would be reasonable to interpret Jameson's invocation of cognitive mapping as amounting to a call for a sociology of identity and space, which are indeed major themes in contemporary social science, for instance, in 'postmodern geography' (Soja 1989, 1996). Jameson himself, however, has argued that social science is incapable of achieving quite what he means in terms of connecting the social totality sensuously to personal experience (1988: 358). Only art and ideology can do that satisfactorily in his opinion, though others may wish to disagree (see, for instance, Pickering 1997).

In *The Geopolitical Aesthetic* (1992: 1), Jameson has attempted what he calls 'an unsystematic mapping or scanning of the world system itself' by analysing 'the political unconscious' (Jameson 1981) of a selection of films from the west and the east. At the heart of late or multinational capitalism are information and communication technologies, which Jameson argues are less graphically representable than, say, the transport technologies, the automobiles and airplanes of the second stage of capitalism. However, these technologies are themselves representational vehicles, bearers of signification and coded imagery. Jameson's reading of David Cronenberg's 1982 film, *Videodrome*, offers an illustrative sketch of an aesthetic of cognitive mapping. The film figures within a generic trope of totality as conspiracy, characteristic of a whole wave of paranoia thrillers in western cinema. Interestingly, *Videodrome* is not a typical 'Hollywood' product, coming from the comparative margin of Toronto and featuring an oblique Canadian take on media society. Jameson describes:

the unique status of David Cronenberg's *Videodrome* . . . within our paradigm, a film which owes its canonical, well-nigh classical position to its triumphant evasion of virtually all high cultural qualities, from technical perfection to the discrimination of taste and the organon of beauty. In it, the owner of a porno television channel in Toronto (James Woods), while exploring the possibility of acquiring genuine snuff films, discovers that the product in question (produced by an outfit called Videodrome) contains a subliminal signal that causes hallucinations and

eventually fatal brain damage. This turns out to be a right-wing conspiracy against the degeneration of moral values for which pornography
and television alike are held responsible. Woods' discovery then brings
into view a counter-conspiracy of a more pro-television, religious type,
in which the cathode ray is used as therapy and an instrument of regener-
ation. But by that time, the Philip K. Dick-like reality-loops and halluci-
natory after-effects are so complex as to relieve the viewer of any further
narrative responsibility, who can only passively witness the manipulation of the hapless James Woods by both sides, as he becomes assassin-
avenger, duped suicidal victim and sacrifice all at once.

(Jameson 1992: 23)

Videodrome is very knowing, a media reflection on the media. The televisual
character Brian Oblivion is dead, a victim of the subliminal signal, but 'lives'
in the videotapes that are stored away and shown on appropriate occasions
by his daughter. Oblivion is based upon Marshall McLuhan, the late Canadian media guru and inspiration for Baudrillard's extreme statements
about the implosion of the social in the media (see Ferguson 1991). The
'snuff movies' received by satellite dish ostensibly from Malaysia, it is
revealed, have actually been made and transmitted in Pittsburg by the right-
wing conspirators. Throbbing videotapes are inserted into the stomach of
the hallucinating character played by James Woods. He and the character
played by Deborah Harry both die in 'real life' yet continue to exist in some
virtual sense on the television into which they have been sucked or suckered.
For Jameson, '*Videodrome* is a kind of realism', allowing us to 'glimpse the
grain of postmodern urban life more vividly than any documentary or social
drama' and representing the social totality of late modern and media capitalism in the popularly available transcoding of 'conspiracy' (Jameson 1992:
32–3).

It could be argued, however, that Jameson's film analyses, his searching
out of instances of cognitive mapping on celluloid, constitute rather a
limited application of his own argument concerning the representational
features of the 'Third Machine Age', the age of the computer and digitalization, which results in the technological convergence of all communications
media and a burgeoning of screen culture (see, for instance, Hayward and
Wollen 1993; Winston 1996). Sherry Turkle, commenting on William
Gibson's *Neuromancer* (1984), the novel in which the term 'cyberspace' was
coined, observes:

Prefigured by *Neuromancer*'s matrix of informational space, postmodernism's objects now exist outside science fiction. They exist in the
information and connections of the Internet and the Worldwide Web,

and in the windows, icons, and layers of personal computing. They exist in the creatures on Simlife computer game, and in the simulations of the quantum world that are routinely used in introductory physics course. All of these are life on screen. And with these objects, the abstract ideas in Jameson's account of postmodernism become newly accessible.

(Turkle 1997: 45)

Similarly to Nicholas Negroponte (1995), the Massachusetts Institute of Technology (MIT) guru of digitalization's wondrous bounty, Turkle stresses the navigational powers of the on-line computer, its capacity for individual orientation in spaces that are constructed between the real and the imaginary, as well as its tremendous though frequently mundane calculative uses. While some are carried away by the new image culture and communication in cyberspace that are frequently given philosophical warrant by the McLuhanite and Baudrillardian strands of thought (such as Taylor and Saarinen 1994), others are sceptical about the techno-hype. One such sceptic and, indeed, fierce critic of unqualified enthusiasm for 'postmodern' vision is Kevin Robins. In his book, *Into the Image*, he carefully dissects the assumptions underlying the enthusiasm in relation to the actual uses of the technologies and their social and psychological implications. He recognizes the technological advance but doubts the valuation normally put upon it. With regard to technology:

> New vision technologies have made it possible to expand the range of photographic seeing – 'beyond vision' – through the remote sensing of micro-wave, infra-red, ultra-violet and short-wave radar imagery . . . If there have been notable developments in the way of seeing, there has also been a significant breakthrough in the recording and handling of images. New image technologies, based on digital electronics, have also changed what we mean by photography. We can say that these new vision and image technologies are post-photographic.
>
> (Robins 1996: 37)

Digitalization enables the transcoding of images and sounds across media and, specifically in photography, the relation of the image to reality can be rendered entirely arbitrary: total artifice is possible. But, as Robins asks, 'The capacities of these new image technologies are certainly impressive but just *how* significant are these developments? And, indeed, *what* is the real nature of their significance?' (1996: 38). In actual fact, they are a further extension of the Enlightenment's aspiration to total control through vision, 'the recycling of old fantasies of technological mastery and transcendence'

(Robins 1996: 4), which is best exemplified, for him, and similarly to Virilio, by military simulations and the use of photographic guidance in smart bombs. In fact, these technologies were developed in the first instance for such purposes. More generally, fantasies of order and control are built into the design of information and image technologies, resulting in a separation of the human subject from palpable reality and the difficult problems of lived experience. The invitation to inhabit a virtual space is an invitation to escape the chaotic social space of the real world.

Robins particularly stresses how the sense of sight is the most distancing of the senses and he extols the more humane and connective sense of touch. The appeal of the new technologies has to be understood with regard to the psychic investments they encourage, especially functioning as a means of warding off fear and anxiety. While this is of general significance, the Gulf War represented a test case for the screening out of reality, both for publics at large and military personnel. Discussing the pilots who unleashed the bombs on Iraq to devastating effect, Robins contends that their actions were facilitated by 'a splitting process that differentiates a spectator-self from an actor-self' (1996: 78). This, for him, has become a widespread phenomenon in the late modern culture of the west where the self can divide and coexist in many ways, in this case, between humane civility and barbaric violence, either in lived behaviour or imaginary identification with actions on screen. There is, in this sense, a crisis of self-identity, which is celebrated as the dissolution of the unified subject and the essential self in poststructuralist and postmodernist thought. Yet, it can also be questioned on ethical and political grounds, as does Robins.

Conclusion

In this chapter, I have explored a number of questions concerning image and reality, which are both epistemological and ethico-political questions. They are epistemological because there is an issue at stake to do with whether representational imagery and discourse entirely construct reality or in some sense, at least, are motivated by structures and processes in the 'real world'. Poststructuralists and postmodernists have called into question any realist account of meaning as referential. Clearly, they are right to refuse a reflective notion of meaning, such as which holds that, for example, television is merely a 'window on the world'. The coverage of the Gulf War finally put that notion to rest. Yet, the question remains regarding how imagery and meaning are constructed socially and not only in an entirely autonomous discursive space. While Baudrillard would contend that reality has been absorbed by discourse so that we now have only virtual wars, Jameson alternatively argues that the postmodern scrambling of images and meanings is in a relation of correspondence with globalizing capitalism and, as others have argued further, this now happens at great speed so that time is less and less constrained by space. We can watch the war occurring on television and, as Baudrillard suggests provocatively, this takes place not even necessarily during the event but quite possibly prior to its actual occurrence.

Jameson's major contention is that the cultural field is reconfigured by the globalization of capital, that older national forms, distinctions and hierarchies are cast into doubt and confusion by this greatly extended space which is so difficult to represent. Many of the issues turn on the significance and use of newer communicational technologies facilitated by computerization. It is not simply a question of being for or against such technology and contemporary cultural and spatial reconfigurations. It is, rather, a question of understanding these phenomena and intervening in their representational modes, seeking out possibilities for a return to reality. Robins, likewise, insists upon a distinction between the real and the imaginary, the actual and the virtual. And, while zealous poststructuralists and postmodernists might see this as reductionist, it is they who are reductionist by reducing everything to the free play of discourse. The alternative position is to try and grasp the interrelations of a set of different determinations, economic, political, ideological and aesthetic. This is a matter not only of explanation but also of ethics in a world of cultural differences *and* shared spaces.

4 | FRACTURED IDENTITIES

Introduction

Fredric Jameson (1991: 37) remarks that 'our faulty representations of some immense communicational and computer network are themselves but a faulty figuration of something even deeper, namely the whole world system of present day multinational capitalism'. Electronic and digital technologies, with their immense information-processing, communicative and representational properties are not only significant, however, from the point of view of political economy. They have come to mediate identity as well, producing metaphors of deconstruction and reconstruction of the self in the organism/machine interface (Turkle 1997).

In Brett Leonard's 1992 film, *The Lawnmower Man*, when a chimpanzee runs amok in the virtual reality laboratory and is killed, Dr Lawrence Angelo turns to a human subject to experiment upon instead. Jobe, the lawnmower man, described by Philip Hayward (1993: 186) as 'an intellectually disadvantaged male', becomes so smart through Angelo's programme of intelligence enhancement that he eventually decides to dematerialize himself on the Net and seize control of world communications. Angelo's own motives for conducting such research were framed by the utopian modernist wish to bring about human improvement by deploying advanced technology for educational and ameliorative ends. But Angelo's research at Virtual Reality Industries has been paid for by the US government in order to enhance the conduct of war. Jobe's treatment is interfered with by Angelo's boss, Timmins. He restores the Project 5 abstract, the aggression factor, to the drug that is taken by the experimental subject so as to facilitate virtual reality treatment.

The Lawnmower Man, combining the genres of science fiction and horror, is a compendium of cyberspace ideas, special effects and political paranoia. Its central motif is the transformative power of technology over subjectivity and identity, graphically depicted in simulations of what is already a simulatory mode, virtual reality, and in which the genius who was once feeble minded turns into an uncontrollable monster. Science, again, is seen to unleash extraordinary powers and, at the same time, stirs up fear and anxiety. It recalls an old yet modern story, Mary Shelley's *Frankenstein*, re-engineered for postmodern times. *The Lawnmower Man* is not especially unusual among the Hollywood movies that have explored issues concerning the technological subject and the destabilization of identity, with their profusion of cyborgs and replicants, in the later part of the twentieth century. Following Jameson's lead, it is worth considering the possibility that this is not just about technology. Nor, however, is it only about capitalism. It may also be about variously generated reconfigurations of identity in a period of intensive social and cultural change, a period when identity itself, as Kobena Mercer (1994) observes, has become a problem. Eric Hobsbawm (1996) points out that 'identity' has emerged as a major category of political debate only since the 1960s. The prime locus of identity politics is the USA, a country made up historically of different ethnicities and where the late modern women's movement and the gay and lesbian movements have flourished comparatively, giving a controversial lead in this respect, as in so many other respects, to the rest of the world.

Deconstructing identity

Although cyborgs, like the deconstructed/reconstructed Jobe, are prominent figures in contemporary science fiction, they are also a figment of science, as conjured up by Donna Haraway's (1991) superb conceit, 'The cyborg manifesto', originally published in 1985. In defining the cyborg as 'a hybrid creature, composed of organism and machine' (1991: 1), Haraway explains her use of this 'myth' in order to come to terms with the dispersal and hybridization of identities in the late modern world.

Haraway had, in her early work, traced how biological research and sociobiology could be read ideologically, as constructed by cultural narratives mapped out across 'nature'. Research on apes, monkeys and lemurs, primate cousins of the human being, was supposed to provide inferences about the biological bases of social behaviour, 'man the hunter' and so forth. Yet, the knowledge thus produced frequently went the other way, making sense of the 'lower' primates in terms of currently prevailing social codes and conventions. During the 1930s, domination and subordination were studied in order to explore the relative strength of processes of competition and cooperation in nature and, by implication, society. Since then, stress has become a major concern of sociobiology. Such themes can be readily seen as refractions of life problems in a capitalist economy and the ideological imperative to naturalize what is, in reality, cultural. There has also been a paradigm shift from study of the organism to study of cybernetic systems, inter- and intra-communication networks, in correspondence with the bodily work of an earlier scientific management and the latterday shift towards managing an information society.

Subsequently, Haraway fixed upon the cyborg as 'an ironic political myth faithful to feminism, socialism, and materialism' (1991: 149). This may be seen as a switch from a Marxist to a postmodernist problematic, but one which subsumes the former into the latter. As Haraway observes:

> In the tradition of 'Western' science and politics – the tradition of racist, male-dominated capitalism; the tradition of progress; the tradition of the appropriation of nature as resource for the production of culture; the tradition of the reproduction of the self from the reflection of the other – the relation between organism and machine has been a border war.
>
> (Haraway 1991: 150)

Similarly to Judith Butler (1990, 1993), Haraway sees the theoretical and practical task as being one of 'imagining a world without gender' (1991: 150), of refusing the fixed identities, including the sexual, prescribed by modern systems of domination: 'The cyborg is a creature in a post-gender world' (Haraway 1991: 150). This is not, she insists, specifically a call for bisexuality but, instead, involves the dissolution of any polarity. 'The cyborg is resolutely committed to partiality, irony, intimacy, and perversity. It is oppositional, utopian, and completely without innocence' (1991: 151). She acknowledges the cyborg's origins in militarism and patriarchal capitalism but this should not hamper its appropriation for a radically alternative political myth.

The myth of the cyborg derives, according to Haraway, from three 'boundary breakdowns'. The first breakdown is between human and animal. Research in biology is a factor here, as is the politics of animal rights, challenging cruelty and human arrogance. The second breakdown is between organism and machine. Smart machines have increasingly put the distinctiveness of human mental and physical capacities into question, and, indeed, have also extended such capacities. The third breakdown is between physical and non-physical. Miniaturized technology is everywhere, often functioning as the invisible machinery of our calculations and intellectual processes. One can also add to Haraway's point here by referring to interactions between virtual and actual realities. When we visit the library on computer screen, are we visiting the library or not?

Haraway is interested in the transgression of boundaries of any kind. This relates to the general critique of essentialism in poststructuralist thought. Nothing exists in splendid isolation as a thing in itself, a self, a nation, any kind of identity. The signification of identity exists only in relation to something else. It is called into being by the binary code of language, albeit creating binaries that need to be deconstructed from the point of view of postmodern thinkers like Haraway. In this framework and in these conditions, Haraway argues, all identities are fractured. There are no essential identities of class, ethnicity, gender or sexuality: everything is potentially fluid and transformable into something else. Fixed identities are kept in place only by systems of domination. Difference, then, is the principle of radical alterity, the refusal of dominative modes of thought. Haraway insists, 'one must not think in terms of essential properties, but in terms of design, boundary constraints, rates of flows, systems logics, costs of lowering constraints' (1991: 162). This requires going with the flow of a new paradigm, the paradigm of networking and becoming rather than of separation and essential being. In this context, 'The cyborg is a kind of disassembled and reassembled, postmodern collective and personal self' (Haraway 1991: 163).

Commenting on the 'New Industrial Revolution', Haraway points to the rise of the 'the homework economy . . . a world capitalist structure . . . made possible by the new technologies' (1991: 166). The enhanced role of women in the information society's workforce, doing the actual work productively and not just reproductively servicing male workers, is of immense significance; and one which was seriously neglected in Jameson's three stages scheme. In fact, Haraway chooses to adopt and modify Jameson's (1991) scheme by gendering the categories of social and cultural analysis. This calls for a recognition of the 'patriarchal nuclear family' in the earlier stage of market capitalism, the 'modern family mediated (or reinforced) by the welfare state and institutions like the family wage' under monopoly capitalism, and 'the "family" of the homework economy with its oxymoronic structure of women-headed households and its explosion of feminisms' under conditions of globalizing and multinational capitalism (Haraway 1991: 167).

It is worth quoting Haraway at length here:

> If it was ever possible ideologically to characterize women's lives by the distinction of public and private domains – suggested by images of the division of working-class life into factory and home, of bourgeois life

into market and home, and of gender existence into personal and political realms – it is now a totally misleading ideology, even to show how both terms of these dichotomies construct each other in practice and in theory. I prefer a network ideological image, suggesting the profusion of spaces and identities and the permeability of boundaries in the personal body and in the body politic. 'Networking' is both a feminist practice and a multinational corporate strategy – weaving is for oppositional cyborgs.

> (Haraway 1991: 170)

Haraway is very well aware of the costs as well as the gains of economic 'postmodernization'. There is 'a massive intensification of insecurity and cultural impoverishment, with common failure of subsistence networks for the most vulnerable' (Haraway 1991: 172). In addition to the dislocations and fractures wrought on a global scale, Haraway believes, however, that there are grounds for hope in the dissolution of older boundaries and identities and, also, in the search for new solidarities to be forged across classes, genders and races. Hence, the postmodern political myth and metaphor of the indeterminate, multivalent and transformative cyborg.

The great strength in Haraway's position is how she combines a post-structuralist deconstruction of modern categories with a fine sense of material reality, exploitation and injustice. She is also keen to distance her epistemological position from anything goes relativism. Similarly to Chris Shilling (1997), in his work on the sociology of the body, Haraway wants to retrieve some notion of 'objectivity' in relation to the materiality of the body from a thoroughgoing social constructionism. 'Feminists have to insist on a better account of the world; it is not enough to show radical historical contingency and modes of construction for everything' (Haraway 1991: 187). Haraway is, however, sceptical and indeed hostile towards universal science, although she does not automatically assume that clarity of vision is an illusion. Knowledge, in her view, is necessarily situated and particular but potentially objective. You can get it right and you can get it wrong. 'The alternative to relativism', Haraway argues, 'is partial, locatable, critical knowledges sustaining the possibility of webs of connection called solidarity in politics and shared conversations in epistemology'. For her, '[r]elativism is a way of being nowhere while claiming to be everywhere' (1991: 191).

More recently, the British cyberfeminist, Sadie Plant (1996, 1997), has made out a case for the peculiarly female qualities of computer-mediated communications. If this once apparently masculine technological mix was previously a turn off for women, no longer is that so. In the early 1990s, a digitalized billboard on a Sydney thoroughfare appeared, declaring 'A cyberfeminist manifesto for the 21st century':

We are the virus of a new world disorder
disrupting the symbolic from within
saboteurs of big daddy mainframe
the clitoris is a direct line to the matrix.

(quoted by Plant 1996: 171)

The development of computing from the centrally controlled mainframe computers to the popularly accessible desktops and laptops since the 1980s, plus entry to the decentred Internet, provided women with opportunities to break into the masculine preserve and to feminize the matrix, which was, in any case, already to some extent potentially feminist. Ada Lovelace had written the programme for Charles Babbage's Analytic Engine in the 1840s and, when it was constructed one hundred years later, the programming language for the first mainframe computer was written by Grace Murray Hopper. Babbage and Lovelace were inspired by the Jacquard loom, a machine that was 'crucial to the processes of automation integral to the industrial revolution, and the emergence of the modern computer' (Plant 1996: 178). As Plant further observes, 'Weaving is the exemplary case of a denigrated female craft which now turns out to be intimately connected to the history of computing and the digital technologies' (1996: 178). Inter-connectedness and intuitive leaps of the imagination, characteristic of com-puter-mediated communications, break with the linear logic of a patriarchal order, according to Plant. Moreover, the future which has hitherto always been deferred is now with us:

Once upon a time, tomorrow never came. Safely projected into the reaches of distant times and faraway galaxies, the future was science fic-tion and belonged to another world. Now, it is here, breaking through the endless deferral of human horizons, short-circuiting history, down-loading its images into today.

(Plant 1996: 181)

Plant also comments upon a pervasive crisis of masculine identity, including the undermining of the father's authority in the home, changes in working patterns that favour female labour and girls' greater educational success than boys. As she says, 'These crises of masculine identity are fatal cor-rosions of everyone: every unified, centralized containment, and every system which keeps them secure' (Plant 1996: 181). However, she does not see a new 'authentic or essential' womanhood arising from the masculine crisis of identity. That idea of a perfectible, coherent and unified self is gone forever: such a judgement is integral to the optimistic appraisal that Plant makes of present technocultural developments. Plant's argument here is, to an extent, consistent with Judith Butler's (1990: ix) 'radical critique of the categories of identity'.

Butler is renowned for having deconstructed the binary opposition between sex and gender in her *Gender Trouble* (1990). It was politically useful for feminism to confine sex to biology and to treat gender as entirely cultural so that femaleness and femininity are not simply equated. From this point of view, it is possible to be female without being 'feminine' in a patriarchal sense. Moreover, in mainstream feminism, it has been important to deconstruct patriarchal identities and struggle for new, liberated identities. Once the deconstruction has started, however, there is potentially no end to it, as Butler has demonstrated rigorously. She wanted to argue, from a Foucauldian perspective, that sex and sexuality are entirely the products of discursivity. Biology is so deeply culturalized that the distinction fundamental to mainstream feminism is no longer tenable. Butler posed some provocative questions from a position that was later to be named 'queer theory':

> Is drag the imitation of gender, or does it dramatize the signifying gestures through which gender itself is established? Does being female constitute a 'natural fact' or a cultural performance, or is 'naturalness' constituted through discursively constrained performative acts that produce the body within the categories of sex.
>
> (Butler 1990: viii)

From this point of view, the figure of the drag artist in a licensed space of transgression may not be so much 'other' as a particular dramatization of how sexual identity works in general. Sex, according to Butler, thus seemed to be pure performativity. Butler herself has subsequently insisted that she was misunderstood as arguing a case for the complete freedom to perform one's sex and sexuality (see Osborne and Segal 1994) and in her later book, *Bodies that Matter* (Butler 1993), greater emphasis is placed upon bodily and material constraints. The example of the drag artist was meant to be an extreme instance of performativity, not a paradigm for sex and sexuality as such.

What is at stake is usefully illuminated by Stuart Hall's (1996) commentary on the effects of deconstruction. The Derridean procedure of deconstructing a word-concept, say 'identity', does not result in its utter rejection but, instead, puts the term under erasure, graphically depicted by a cross or a line through the word. More commonly, however, the problematized concept is put in quotation marks, as is my practice in this book. The concept still has to be used – there is nothing to put in its place – yet there has to be a necessary reflexivity in its use, a recognition that it represents an analytical problem as well as a fallible solution. As Hall notes, there have been several different theoretical currents at work to deconstruct the modern subject and essential identity: the philosophical attack on the Cartesian subject of knowledgeability, the Lacanian stress on the splitting and decentring of the psychological subject and the effectivity of the unconscious, the Foucauldian genealogies of the discursive technologies of selfhood, the performativity of queer theory, and the various critiques of essentialisms of ethnicity, nationhood and 'race'. Taking all this on board and linking identity to identification, Hall says:

> I use 'identity' to refer to the meeting point, the point of *suture*, between on the one hand the discourse and practices which attempt to 'interpellate', speak to us or hail us into place as the social subjects and particular discourses, and on the other hand, the processes which produce subjectivities, which construct us as subjects which can be 'spoken'.
>
> (Hall 1996: 5–6)

Hall himself, however, is sceptical of simply grafting such theorizing onto the analysis of 'the racialized and ethnicized body' that occurs within a discourse of 'compulsive Eurocentrism' (Hall 1996: 16). Yet, although he raises this matter, Hall fails to consider the many problems and dilemmas that arise from the theoretical deconstruction of identity, so keen is he to stress the positive rather than the negative consequences. Most importantly, there is the question of how the politics of identity sponsors an enormous proliferation of particularisms that are prone, in some cases, to replicate, though much more explicitly, the kind of particularistic indifference to others that is concealed in the fake universalisms of dominant discourse. In this respect, for instance, queer theory abjures an understanding of heterosexuality, suggesting at best, as does Butler (Osborne and Segal 1994), that it is vaguely ridiculous and founded oppressively upon the suppression of other sexualities.

Lynne Segal has posed some important questions concerning the limits of queer theory with regard to both homosexuality and heterosexuality. First, the celebration of exuberant performativity is apt to disregard the problems of

> lesbian and gay men who, like single mothers, battered and burdened women everywhere (in ways overdetermined by 'race' and ethnicity) are already too much submerged by economic and social disadvantage or endangered by media hate campaigns and a hostile world, to feel empowered by subversive gender or sexual performance.
>
> (Segal 1997: 219)

Second, 'Whilst it may go against the grain of some feminist writing, it seems important to note the diversity of women's and men's actual sexual activities, which suggest that "straight sex" may be no more affirmative of normative gender positions than its gay and lesbian alternatives' (Segal 1997: 221). More generally, a set of questions arise concerning the commitment of identity politics to equality (see Sarup 1996) and, indeed, solidarity across different marginal and subordinate social positions, questions that are much too easily dismissed as illegitimately 'universalistic'.

Without denying the vital importance of difference as a subversive principle, it is also important to appreciate some of the tensions that arise in Left politics when 'identity' and 'difference' displace 'universalistic' identifications and considerations. Hobsbawm (1996), in defending an older Left tradition, usefully summarizes the key aspects of 'collective identity'. First, 'collective identities are defined negatively; that is to say against others' (1996: 40). Second, 'it follows that in real life identities, like garments, are interchangeable or wearable in combination rather than unique and, as it were, stuck to the body' (1996: 41). Third, 'Identities, or their expression, are not fixed, even supposing you have opted for one of your many potential selves' (1996: 41). And, 'The fourth and last thing to say about identity is that it depends on the context, which may change' (1996: 43). If we accept this as a satisfactory outline of how 'identity' functions, it is quite clear that identity politics is difficult to reconcile with modern Leftism, which is not something that would much trouble postmodernists but may concern others. Hobsbawm insists, 'The political project of the Left is universalist: it is for *all* human beings' (1996: 43). On the other hand, 'Identity groups are about themselves, for themselves and nobody else' (1996: 44).

Denying the other

Postmodern rhetoric places great stress on difference and otherness while constantly denouncing modern attitudes for ethnocentric universalism. Contrasts between the modern and the postmodern seem very sharp indeed in the context of, say, a North American university, the context in which such differences are perhaps most keenly felt intellectually. Yet, in a wider context, say, that of the world as a whole, these intellectual differences are likely to pale into insignificance. Postmodernism may thus appear as the latest chapter in the cultural history of western modernity rather than something completely different. This is the view expressed powerfully and with great cogency by Ziauddin Sardar in his polemical work, *Postmodernism and the Other: The New Imperialism of Western Culture* (1998).

According to Sardar (1998: 13), 'far from being a new theory of liberation, postmodernism, particularly from the perspective of the Other, the non-western cultures, is simply a new wave of domination riding on the crest of colonialism and modernity'. There is a cruel irony in the postmodern celebration of alterity, the binary opposite, the different. In fact, 'by suddenly discovering Otherness everywhere', paradoxically, postmodernism denies genuine Otherness, the incommensurable differences between western and non-western cultures. Its fascination and championing of non-western otherness is a further oppression of the non-western Other, who is yet again consumed by the voracious appetite of the west:

> Colonialism was about the physical occupation of non-western cultures. Modernity was about displacing the present and occupying the minds of non-western cultures. Postmodernism is about appropriating the history and identity of non-western cultures as an integral facet of itself, colonising their future and occupying their being.
>
> (Sardar 1998: 13)

The declaration that modernity is *passé*, that its beliefs and assumptions have suddenly become invalid, as I have sought to show in this book, is a peculiarly modernist attitude. Yet, clearly there is something of a crisis in western modernity that is signalled by postmodernism. For instance, Sardar notes, theories of chaos and complexity call into question certainties of knowledge and scientifically rationalized control. As we saw in Chapter 3, postmodernism collapses the distinction between representation and reality. Images do not signify but, rather, conjure up a simulacrum of reality. There is a pervasive sense of meaninglessness. Everything is put in doubt. These features of postmodern/western culture, in Sardar's judgement, are all negative and they are only partly relieved by the more positive concern with 'variety, . . . multiplicities: . . . plurality of ethnicities, cultures, genders, truths, realities, sexualities, even reasons' (Sardar 1998: 10–11). But postmodern plurality should not be taken at its own estimation, Sardar insists, as a deconstruction of western selfhood in the face of the Other. He questions the postmodern 'we', which always refers to the westerner and never the non-westerner. Crises of identity and epistemology, the chronic choices of those freed of tradition and modern restraint, do not much concern the famine stricken and dying of Africa. These are specifically western problems that do not touch upon the material and cultural realities of the Rest. The west treats non-westerners with renewed barbarism yet a war like that in the Persian Gulf appeared unreal. The ethnic cleansing of the Bosnian War, an effect of western culture, and many other instances of suffering around the world, either instigated or overlooked diplomatically by western powers, contribute to, in Bob Geldof's phrase, 'compassion fatigue'. As Stanley Cohen (1996: 45) observes, in his study of the failures of western human rights

organizations, 'We need not accept the vanities and silliness of post-modern-
ist theory to understand that the issue is not the abstract right to know, but
what does it mean anymore "to know"'. What the west knows of the non-
western Other becomes especially complex under postmodern conditions.

Sardar's critique of an exemplary postmodern and mass-popular cultural
product, Disney's *Pocahontas*, illustrates perfectly the innoculatory effect of
modern myth making that was identified by Roland Barthes as long ago as
1957. Barthes (1973 [1957]: 150) remarked, 'One immunizes the contents
of the collective imagination by means of a small innoculation of acknowledged evil; one thus protects it against the risk of a generalized subversion'.
In the 1990s something like the *Pocahontas* cartoon had to be politically
correct, questioning the past stereotyping of 'native Americans' and show-
ing how European and especially English explorers were at fault in the
colonization of 'the New World'. The claim was made in Disney's publicity
material that the movie corrected history. *Pocahontas* ostentatiously displays, in Sardar's (1998: 90) words, 'awareness of difference and the recognition of ethnic and cultural diversity through stereotypes'. Both sides
stereotype the Other: 'savages' and 'white demons'. Through their love and
anticipation of late twentieth century sensibility, however, Pocahontas and
John Smith, 'The Native American "babe" and the spirit of the "all-Ameri-
can" he-man' (Sardar 1998: 92), transcend the limitations of their ancient
tribes and the demonization of the Other.

For Sardar, the key western values, associated with modernity and its
postmodern variant, are underpinned by a pervasive individualism whereas
the non-west puts much greater emphasis on collective and communal
values. In spite of the assault of western modernity and postmodernism
upon the Rest, these Other cultures have retained values of community,
belonging, morality and meaningfulness (Sardar 1998: 65). This relates, in
Sardar's very generalized argument, to non-western resistance to the western
discourse of human rights which can conceive of rights only in individualistic terms. Non-western cultures have a much broader conception of rights,
a conception of rights that is grounded characteristically and explicitly in
religion. The rights defended by non-western cultures are human in general,
not just individual, and also respectful of the non-human, animals and
nature. Rights, moreover, are attached to duties and obligations; and, they
are not discrete and atomistic but, instead, harmoniously interconnected by
traditional belief systems, according to Sardar (1998: 71–2).

As many commentators have argued, the moment of postmodern culture
is one of an accentuated consumerism where personal identity is constructed
by what one buys and intense commodification leaves no aspect of life
untouched. According to Sardar, non-western youth, more so than their

elders, are extremely vulnerable to the blandishments of postmodern consumerism. Late modern western societies typically have ageing populations while in the rest of the world youth is in comparative abundance. And, as Sardar notes in particular, 'the increasing spending power of east and southeast Asian youth . . . is the lodestar of postmodern marketing techniques and multinational merchandising concerns' (1998: 140). The economics of western television programmes, for instance, whereby the costs of production can be recouped in the home market, especially for US products, so that programmes are rented abroad much more cheaply than the costs of domestic production, means that young people in non-western countries are subjected to constant bombardment from western culture and especially the values of consumerism. Generational tensions open up and non-western identities become increasingly fractured due to the seduction of the young by western commercial culture. In this respect, Sardar reiterates an old cultural and media imperialist argument that has been much discredited, it must be said, in the west (see Tomlinson 1997) but, none the less, remains an argument of critical credibility for the Rest.

Sardar's own specialism is science policy; one area of 'postmodern' thought with which he shows most sympathy concerns the new theories of chaos and complexity. Deterministic and reductionist models of science, Sardar notes, have been called into question in the west. Chaos theory breaks with linear causality and focuses upon what is apparently random in nature. Complexity theory explores systems and equilibria that arise in what might otherwise seem like a chaotic universe. That which was rejected as irrational in the western scientific tradition and ideas that were once viewed as merely symptomatic of the backwardness of Other cultures in the modern world have now been reappropriated by these new theories. Sardar remarks, 'eastern philosophy has never seen the world in anything other than complex terms' (1998: 224). So, what had been denied as Other has suddenly become permissible and, indeed, fashionable in western culture. New Age spirituality, however faddish, is another feature of western doubt and the reappraisal of different ways of thought. Still, however, there is a fundamental gulf between western secularism and non-western religiosity. According to Sardar, religion and belief in God are necessary in order to discern good from evil. Furthermore, 'From the perspective of non-western societies, surviving postmodernism is all about moving forward to tradition' (1998: 273), which he insists is not an argument for a conservative traditionalism but, instead, a means of sustaining 'the values and axioms of a civilization' against the amorality, relativism and, ultimately, nihilism of postmodern western culture.

In describing Sardar's thesis, I have deliberately resisted criticism since I believe it is important to grasp his critique and, most importantly, his case that postmodernism is not so much a break with western modernity as its continuance. This confirms my own view, though I would disagree with many of Sardar's judgements specifically concerning non-western cultures, especially with regard to the role of religion and questions of human rights. Sardar himself concedes very little and, in this, I find that his argument lacks balance. He does, however, advocate multiple dialogues between non-western cultures and *with* western culture, albeit finding little to value in his reified depiction of western culture. Also, Sardar does, as if in an afterthought, mention what he calls the 'darker side' of non-western cultures and 'an undeniably authoritarian streak that needs to be checked' (1998: 287). A great deal more could have been said in this regard, for instance, on women's rights, although Sardar, one might infer, quite reasonably assumes that plenty is said already on such matters in western publications on the Rest.

The relations between the west and the Rest have become of increasing concern in American foreign policy discourse, as is exemplified by Francis Fukuyama's (1989, 1992) 'end of history' thesis and, yet more so, by Samuel Huntington's (1993, 1996) 'clash of civilizations' thesis. Even before the opening of the Berlin Wall, Fukuyama had announced the global victory of western liberal democracy and free market capitalism. Inspired by the French Hegelian, Alexandre Kojeve, Fukuyama was not arguing a case simply about the turn of world events but rather claiming that there was an Historical, with a capital H, logic which communism had failed to supersede and that not even the most theocratic of non-western societies could resist. Fukuyama was both very influential and widely criticized for his western triumphalism. The only criticisms he really took seriously, however, were from the western political Right, as he noted in the booklength version of the thesis (Fukuyama 1992). Following Hegel, he suggested that History is driven not only by economics but also by a 'politics of recognition' through which the slave is eventually recognized as equal to the master, which, in Fukuyama's estimation, is best exemplified by the freedoms of liberal democracy. However, also following Nietzsche, whom Fukuyama (1992: xxii) regards, in my opinion correctly, as the Right's 'most brilliant spokesman' in the history of European philosophy, there arises the problem of 'the last man', the mediocre individual of economic well-being and mass democracy, who is only interested in 'comfortable self-preservation'. Fukuyama wondered whether the Nietzschean *Ubermensch* might rise up against this dismal 'herd' mentality that is brought about by the democratic-egalitarian resolution of History.

In comparison with Fukuyama's thesis, Huntington's (1996) thesis on 'the clash of civilizations' is, up to a point, a much more insightful and somewhat less ethnocentric account of the complexities of world order following the collapse of soviet communism and the end of the Cold War. According to Huntington (1996: 20), 'culture and cultural identities, which at the broadest level are civilization identities, are shaping the patterns of cohesion, disintegration and conflict in the post-Cold War world'. We live now in a 'multipolar and multicivilizational world'. Huntington argues for the greater explanatory power of his 'civilizational paradigm' over the four extant paradigms of international relations. The 'One World' paradigm, of which Fukuyama's 'end of history' is a version, was popular around 1990 when the conflict between western capitalism and eastern communism apparently ceased. This harmonious view became unconvincing very quickly, however, especially in light of the rekindling of older conflicts between, most notably, Christendom and Islam, among a plethora of ethnic tensions in the world. It is tempting in the west, then, to resort to a second paradigm, that of 'Us and Them' but this is unsatisfactory as well since it unduly homogenizes the non-western. It is preferable to think in terms of 'the West and the Rest', in recognition of several different non-western civilizations (Huntington 1997). The civilizational paradigm also has virtues over the '184 States, More or Less' paradigm which reduces international relations to the relations between sovereign states and fails to appreciate spheres of influence and the power of identities that transcend the nation-state. The fourth unsatisfactory paradigm is that of 'Sheer Chaos' which views the world as an unaccountable mess.

For Huntington, the world is intelligible but complex. Civilizations are made up of a number of elements: religion, 'race', comprehensiveness, longevity, and cultural rather than political identity. The most important element, Huntington argues, is religion and this is uppermost, yet not always congruently so, in his identification of seven or eight civilizations currently in the world. The first is *Sinic* in which Confucianism is prominent. Although many scholars would include *Japanese* civilization in the Sinic category, Huntington does not. In his opinion, it is a distinctive offshoot of Chinese civilization, so distinctive historically that it must be seen as separate. The third civilization identified by Huntington is *Hindu*; the fourth, *Islamic*; the fifth, *Western*; the sixth, *Latin American*; the seventh, *Orthodox*. Finally, and eighth, somewhat reluctantly following Braudel, Huntington sees *African* as possibly a separate civilization in spite of its northern relation to Islam and southern relation to western Christendom.

Huntington's *The Clash of Civilizations and the Remaking of World Order* (1996) is a fascinating book, dealing with a wide range of questions and, in many cases, it is extremely informative about cultural differences in the world. His arguments and evidence on particular cases, however, whether he is discussing the role of 'core states' or 'torn nations', for instance, are no doubt contestable. In concluding this section, I do not so much want to discuss the details as bring out Huntington's domain assumptions and identify his questionable claims specifically regarding western civilization. His emphasis on values and their grounding in religion, whether as strength of belief or trace of belief, underplays the role of material interests; and, it is material interests, diffusely those of the west and, rather more concretely, those related to the USA that are implicit in his general argument. For instance, he seeks to resolve the problem of Europeanness by equating it with Christendom, thus demarcating Europe along the fault line with Islam and schismatic Eastern Orthodoxy, so that Turkey's claim to European community membership is questioned and even Greece, according to Huntington, cannot be regarded as properly European. The equation of Europe with historical Christendom, made by Huntington, is consistent with a critique of Europeanness from the point of view of the excluded and marginalized, say that of Turkish ethnicity in Germany, yet the implication of his argument is to justify exclusion. Huntington is much concerned with the problem of immigration. The influx of Muslims into Europe and Hispanics into the USA may give rise to 'cleft societies encompassing two distinct and largely separate communities from two different civilizations, which in turn depends on the numbers of immigrants and the extent to which they are assimilated into the Western cultures prevailing in Europe and America' (Huntington 1996: 204). That these are already cleft societies that need to be reconfigured in thoroughly multicultural ways is not Huntington's view: far from it. The problem is one of 'assimilation'; and, if not assimilation, then what? Exclusion?

The general position enunciated by Huntington is quite consistent with what has sometimes been called *cultural racism*. It is the kind of position that allowed Enoch Powell's apologists to deny that he was a racist. Apparently, Powell did not believe that Caribbean and Asian Commonwealth immigrants to Britain during the 1960s were necessarily lesser beings than the English; he just did not want them diluting Englishness. Similarly, Huntington makes no claims concerning the superiority of western culture and like a good poststructuralist or postmodernist he rejects any universalistic pretensions associated with its values, such as democracy or equality, or anything of that sort. In fact, he argues strenuously that the west should not interfere in other civilizations. The Rest should be left to deal with their own problems. The west may have instituted modernization but modernization and westernization are not the same. In the later phases of modernization among the Rest, it is common for anti-westernization to arise. At home, of course, it is important to protect the integrity of western culture and civilization, according to

Huntington, by fighting off the multiculturalists (see Goldberg 1994) who have done so much to undermine the American way of life. He is concerned about 'problems of moral decline, cultural suicide, and political disunity in the West' (Huntington 1996: 304). In fact, Huntington makes his position and concerns abundantly clear:

> Western culture is challenged by groups within Western societies. One such challenge comes from immigrants from other civilizations who reject assimilation and continue to adhere to and propagate the values, customs, and cultures of their home societies. The phenomenon is most notable among Muslims in Europe, who are, however, a small minority. It is also manifest, in lesser degree, among Hispanics in the United States, who are a large minority. If assimilationism fails in this case, the United States will become a cleft country, with all the potentials for internal strife and disunion that entails. In Europe, Western civilization could also be undermined by the weakening of its central component, Christianity.
>
> (Huntington 1996: 305)

Huntington wants to resist the 'siren calls of multiculturalism', which he sees as particularly characterized by the undermining of a culture of individual rights by the myriad calls for collective rights, not only to do with 'race' and ethnicity but also to do with sex and sexuality. However, Huntington's position, in spite of his arguments concerning non-interference, is not strictly speaking one of splendid isolationism and resistance to multiculturalism in the USA and the defence of Christianity in Europe. The USA has a much larger geopolitical role than that. In alliance with Europe, he argues, there should be more integration between western states, the Catholic countries of eastern Europe should be included in the west, Latin America should be westernized, China and Japan should be kept separate, Russia should be recognized as 'the core state of Orthodoxy' and 'Western technological and military superiority over other civilizations' should be maintained while, somehow, the west should avoid destabilization by refraining from interference in Other civilizations (Huntington 1996: 312).

Self-identifying

It was once assumed that modernization in non-western countries inevitably meant or resulted in westernization. Huntington (1996) has argued, however, that in the later phase of modernization a reaction typically sets in against western culture and there is a resurgence of indigenous culture, sometimes led by religious fundamentalism. Thus, the older west-ern concept of 'universal civilization' is resisted and, in Huntington's opin-ion, should not now be promoted abroad by the west in any case. One of the many difficulties with his position, though, is a fixed notion of western culture that is confined to home consumption and, indeed, represents a con-servative and questionably purist notion, albeit no longer deemed univer-salizing. A consequence of this position is that it neglects and, moreover, seeks to suppress actual changes occurring in the cultures of western societies, multiculturalism and also, more diffusely, the rise of what Ulrich Beck (1992a [1986]) calls 'reflexive modernity', a universalizing phenom-enon emerging at a late stage of western industrial capitalism. A similar position on recent social change is held by Anthony Giddens (Beck *et al.* 1994). The thesis of reflexive modernization can be seen, in general, as a critical response to excessive claims concerning postmodernization (see, for example, Crook *et al.* 1992). It is a thesis which still seeks to make sense of contemporary history in the broad framework of a persistent modernity while taking proper account of changes associated with 'postmodernity'. The thesis is examined in some detail in the final chapter of this book. Here, I shall concentrate specifically on Giddens's arguments concerning latterday modernity and self-identity.

As Giddens argued in *The Consequences of Modernity*, 'Rather than entering a period of post-modernity we are moving into one in which the consequences of modernity are becoming more radicalised and universalised than before' (1990: 3). Briefly, as noted earlier, Giddens identifies four rela-tively autonomous institutional dimensions of modernity that are being further extended around the world: *capitalism, industrialism, surveillance* and *control of the means of violence* (1990: 55–63). Capitalism is defined in terms of 'Capital accumulation in the context of competitive labour and product markets'; industrialism as 'Transformation of nature: development of the "created environment"'; surveillance as 'Control of information and social supervision'; and, finally, military power, under modern conditions, as 'Control of the means of violence in the context of the industrialisation of war' (1990: 59). Although Giddens quite rightly insists upon a relative autonomy for each dimension, I would tend to emphasize the priority of capitalist development as the driving force, something which has been especially borne out by the collapse of communism in eastern Europe and the turn to a 'capitalist road' in ostensibly communist China. Modernity can broadly be seen as capitalist civilization yet without necessarily undervalu-ing the power of other institutional dimensions. Such an argument has already been made earlier in this book and elaborated upon with detailed reference to Jameson's (1984) thesis on postmodernism as the cultural logic of late capitalism and qualified by Harvey's (1989) more refined account of the relations between culture and economy. Compared with Giddens, however, Jameson understates the significance of industrialism, surveillance and military power. In addition, Giddens connects questions of self-identity to the accentuation of institutionalized modernity, globalization and the further erosion of tradition, which he considers a western project that in one way or another is affecting every part of the world more intensively than ever before. Giddens actually has very little to say about non-western society and is open to criticism on this score (see Mestrovic 1998) yet, nevertheless, he provides an important characterization or typification of certain aspects of social existence in conditions of 'late', 'high' or 'radicalized' modernity, terms which he uses interchangeably.

Giddens believes, then, that the consequences of modernity have been accentuated and modernity has become reflexive. This involves the further dissolution of traditional forms of life, forms of life characterized by repetition, the cyclical reproduction of customs, habits and cherished assumptions across the generations. Tradition is comparatively static whereas modernity is dynamic. The basic parameters of life in conditions of high modernity have become much less fixed and predictable than they were even during the great upheavals of earlier phases of modernity. In effect, tradition had persisted as a counterpoint to the unsettling features of earlier modernity. Now, however, personal experiences of dislocation, uncertainty and choice, characteristic of modernity in general, are yet more pervasive and constitutive of identity. Global forces affect local circumstances and we are all caught up in the dynamics of a rapidly changing and unpredictable world on a daily basis. The global and the local intersect in complex ways and selfhood must be understood in reflexive relation to current institutional transformations. Giddens rejects the earlier and what he considers one-dimensional depictions of modernity by Max Weber as an iron cage of rationality and by Karl Marx as an exploitative monster. Instead, he favours the image of the juggernaut, 'a runaway engine of enormous power which, collectively as human beings, we can drive to some extent but which also threatens to rush out of our control and which could rend itself asunder' (Giddens 1990: 139). Resistance is crushed by the juggernaut. For those on the ride, however, it is both terrifying and exhilarating. There are risks and there are rewards. Although 'existential anxiety' is normalized, most hold on, protected by a sense of 'ontological security'.

In *Modernity and Self-Identity*, Giddens identifies three major dynamics of late modern life: '*separation of time and space*', '*disembedding* of social institutions' and 'intrinsic reflexivity' (1991: 16, 19). First, under pre-modern conditions, temporal and spatial arrangements are closely connected together through, for instance, the seasonal rhythms of agriculture in the local rural community. With the advent of modernity, time becomes abstracted from this form of life, eventually turning into a universal temporal scheme, a global calendar and clock, related to the growth of trade and international communications. Time is less and less constrained by space. Transport and communications speed up, overcoming what once were immense physical and natural barriers to generalized human concourse.

Second, 'the *disembedding* of social institutions' is described by Giddens as 'the "lifting out" of social relations from local contexts and their rearticulation across indefinite tracts of time and space' (1991: 18). Giddens identifies two kinds of 'abstract system' that facilitate such disembedding: 'symbolic tokens' and 'expert systems'. *Symbolic tokens* are 'media of exchange', most obviously money, which has become increasingly abstract. Everything, in principle, is reducible to a universal scale of exchange values, not always effectively so but *in principle*. Money even loses its physicality in coins and notes, at the extreme appearing as digits on a VDU (visual display unit). *Expert systems*, according to Giddens, 'bracket time and space through displaying modes of technical knowledge which have validity independent of the practitioners and clients who make use of them' (1991: 18). New forms of depersonalized expertise are constantly being produced alongside the older professions of, say, medicine and law. The growth and spread of management consultancy is a good example. The routine use of abstract systems depends upon trust, belief that the money has value and the experts really know what they are talking about.

'Intrinsic reflexivity' is the third major dynamic of late or high modernity. Intellectual monitoring of action, self-consciously using fallible knowledges, is routinely built into institutional and personal life. The modern constantly reflects upon itself and these reflections play back into the modern, keeping it in perpetual transformation. Yet, knowledge is not what it used to be: instead of the quest for certainty of earlier modern knowledge systems, late modern knowledge is characterized by 'radical doubt'. This is so of latter-day scientific and research practices but it is also there in the routine conduct of everyday life. As Giddens remarks, 'The integral relation between modernity and radical doubt is an issue which, when exposed to view, is not only disturbing to philosophers but is *existentially troubling* for individuals' (1991: 21).

In these late modern conditions, 'the interlacing of social events and social relations "at distance"' are experienced 'with local contextualities' (Giddens 1991: 21). The role of the modern media is crucial to this '*dialectic of the local and the global*', print in the formation of modernity and, since then, 'the electronic signal'. Contemporary experience is highly mediated experience, typified by the '*collage effect*' of modern communications, especially television, and what Giddens calls the '*intrusion of distant events into everyday consciousness*' (1991: 27). Giddens rejects a reflectionist model of the communications media but he is also sceptical of the notion that this is a new second-order reality, 'hyperreality', in the term popularized by Eco and Baudrillard. The modern media may have reality forming effects but these are variable empirically with regard to the unifications and disaggregations of popular knowledges and identifications.

Like Beck (1992a), Giddens stresses the pervasiveness of risk calculation for institutional practices and individual life courses where social existence is characterized by 'new parameters of risk and danger' (Giddens 1991: 28), resulting from the unintended consequences of modern technologies such as in the use of nuclear power, chemicals and information. The late modern self is continually presented with 'as if' scenarios and difficult choices, which at some level are between different 'possible worlds'. There is some reliance on specialist expertise to make these calculations as to risk and how to deal with it. When this is linked to the knowing imperfections of modern knowledge, for experts and lay people, it is clear that living with uncertainty – or what deconstructionists and postmodernists like to call 'undecidability' – captures something of the texture of late modern experience whether in the public realm of, for instance, economic decision making or in the private realm of the self and its significant others. In these circumstances, 'the self becomes a *reflexive project*' (Giddens 1991: 32).

Giddens's position on the self is existentialist rather than psychoanalytic, though he draws on ideas from object relations theory. The influence of poststructuralist, Lacanian psychoanalysis is slight indeed. For Giddens, the human subject is a knowing agent, though clearly not all knowing or free from the constraints of social institution. At the heart of his understanding of selfhood is the tension between *existential anxiety* and *ontological security*. Late modern existence is fragile: chaos is always likely to erupt in the lives of individuals and in the operations of society. Yet, late modern life is not characterized only by a sense of dread. Basic trust established in early childhood through parental care and the routines of everyday life typically creates a 'protective cocoon' for individuals: insecurity is warded off, or else ordinary social life would be difficult to sustain. That people are mostly secure ontologically, only momentarily troubled by existential anxiety, though more often than not unexpectedly, is evident when one considers what it really means to experience psychological breakdown, to be someone 'whose sense of self is fractured or disabled' (Giddens 1991: 53). Here, Giddens is particularly influenced by R.D. Laing's *The Divided Self* (1965 [1960]). For Laing, 'the ontologically insecure individual', in Giddens's

(1991: 53) words, 'lack[s] a consistent feeling of biographical continuity' and is 'obsessively preoccupied with apprehension of possible risks'. 'A normal sense of self-identity', which is on a continuum with the 'abnormal' when someone has, in colloquial terms, 'lost the plot', on the other hand, is facilitated by 'the capacity *to keep a particular narrative going*' (Giddens 1991: 54).

Similarly to Ken Plummer (1995), Giddens stresses the role of narrative in the construction and maintenance of self-identity. In telling stories about ourselves, making sense of the past, the present and future possibility, we reflexively produce a more or less coherent sense of self. Somehow, we manage to answer fundamental questions of existence in such a way that keeps us going. As Giddens says: 'What to do? How to act? Who to be? These are focal questions for everyone living in circumstances of late modernity – and ones which, on some level or another, all of us answer, either discursively or through day-to-day social behaviour' (1991: 70). These are not novel questions of modern life but, according to Giddens, they become more urgent for self-identity in late modernity where traditional supports are being further eroded: 'In a post-traditional social universe, reflexively organised, permeated by abstract systems, and in which the reordering of time and space realigns the local with the global, the self undergoes massive changes' (Giddens 1991: 80).

The late modern self is obliged to choose a 'lifestyle', a term which has been somewhat degraded in advertising and marketing discourse yet needs to be retained in a more substantial manner to refer to the actual crafting of social identity where ways of being are not prescribed by tradition. Experience is heavily mediated and life planning is a difficult and uncertain matter: it is hard to tell what is 'authentic' or to predict the outcomes of one's choices. Giddens remarks, 'To live in the universe of high modernity is to live in an environment of chance and risk, the inevitable concomitants of a system geared to the domination of nature and the reflexive making of history' (1991: 109). Individuals face 'fateful moments' in their lives when crossroads are reached and the decisions made are of particular consequence. It is not uncommon in these circumstances for individuals to seek expert advice regarding the risks involved in choosing a path to take.

Another feature of late modern existence identified by Giddens is the '*sequestration of experience*' (1991: 149). In order to sustain ontological security some fundamental aspects of life are in a sense privatized, hidden from public view. For example, this is especially evident in the treatment of death and dying. It is also evident in what Giddens calls the '*privatisation of passion*'. Giddens challenges Michel Foucault's (1981 [1976]) exclusive emphasis on the modern obsession with sexuality, giving rise to a proliferation of discourse and display, of which there is plenty of evidence. However, sexuality is also very much a personal matter and which becomes, under conditions of privatized living, less the object of public discipline, prescription and prohibition; and, more an affair of choice, albeit within certain situational constraints. Generally speaking, Giddens takes a Habermasian rather than a Foucauldian line on questions of self-identity and personal relationships by stressing communication over power. His idea of 'the pure relationship', most notably, is by definition a communicative rather than a power relationship. By 'pure relationship', Giddens does not mean purity in a moralizing sense but, instead, 'a social relationship which is internally referential, that is, depends fundamentally on satisfactions or rewards generic to that relation itself' (1991: 244).

In *The Transformation of Intimacy* (1992), Giddens explores the possibilities of the pure relationship. As Theodore Zeldin (1995) has documented and as Giddens (1992: 2) says, 'Modern societies have a covert emotional history, yet to be drawn fully into the open'. According to Giddens (1992: 15), '"Sexuality" today has been discovered, opened up and made accessible to the development of varying lifestyles'. Giddens acknowledges the plasticity of sexuality and what he has to say about the pure relationship, which he regards as becoming increasingly normalized, is meant to apply to both heterosexuality and homosexuality. It has, perhaps, been most pioneered by homosexuals, necessarily inventing ways of being and relating on the margins of predominantly heterosexual cultures. The pure relationship is about commitment. It 'has no external supports' (1992: 138). This is what makes it egalitarian and democratic. It is not only confined, however, to sexuality. Giddens also believes it is coming to characterize parent–child relationships in their opening up to negotiation, communication rather than power, authority and bitter resistance. In many ways, the pure relationship is like the old idea of friendship, reciprocal and freely chosen.

According to Giddens, the pure relationship of late modernity represents a 'democratisation of the private sphere' (1992: 184). It is the personal relationships version of Habermas's 'public sphere' (1989 [1962]) and 'ideal speech situation' (1979 [1976]). Says Giddens,

A forum for open debate has to be provided. Democracy means discussion, the chance for the 'force of the better argument' to count as against other means of determining decisions (of which the most important are policy decisions) . . . In the arena of personal life, autonomy means the successful realisation of the reflexive project of the self – the condition of relating to others in an egalitarian way.

(Giddens 1992: 186, 189)

The concept of the pure relationship is an ideal typification in a double sense, a tool for analysing actual relationships and, also, idealistic. Yet, Giddens would not have formulated the concept at all credibly if the phenomenon did not already exist to some extent in the conduct of personal relations under conditions of late modernity, though one can see how it might be criticized by some as ethnocentrically representative of a western, new *petit-bourgeois* ethics.

The pure relationship is part of the emergence of what Giddens calls 'life politics', which can flourish only in comparatively emancipatory circumstances where principles of justice, equality and participation are paramount. In *Modernity and Self-Identity*, Giddens lists the kind of existential questions that characterize life politics, associated with the human relation to nature, the control of biological reproduction, the conduct of international relations, the self and the body. Shilling (1993: 202) complains that Giddens 'effectively establishes a divide between nature and culture' by suggesting that nature has become entirely culturalized and by neglecting '*the interweaving of biological and social factors*'. While this is an important rejoinder to both postmodernist *and* late modernist exaggeration of the cultural malleability of nature and the body, Giddens is accurate in arguing that all sorts of questions concerning rights are raised by the advance of enculturation over nature and technological manipulation of biology, for instance, to do with genetic engineering.

Just before concluding this chapter, it is important to point out, in passing, that Giddens's work has been submitted to fierce criticism by Stjepan Mestrovic (1998), who dubs him 'the last modernist'. Roughly, Mestrovic's claim is that Giddens presents an overly optimistic, smug and inaccurate depiction of life in late modernity. Although Mestrovic does not consider himself to be a postmodernist, he prefers to extol the grim insights of Baudrillard against Giddens's latterday enlightenment. More important perhaps than this, however, is Mestrovic's argument that Giddens has no sense of the emotional and irrational aspects of social life: this, in spite of the fact that *The Transformation of Intimacy* is quite self-consciously an attempt to construct a sociology of the emotions. Mestrovic invokes the concept of *caritas*, Latin for love and clearly related to Christian charity, in contrast to Giddens's allegedly cool and mistaken attitude, which is odd since Mestrovic himself displays precious little *caritas* in the way he attacks Giddens. In fact, Giddens's concept of the pure relationship would seem to have an elective affinity with *caritas*. Mestrovic's critique of Giddens's sociological formalism may have come across as somewhat less contradictory and more convincing had he himself displayed a little intellectual *caritat* (fr. charity).

Conclusion

This chapter has considered various aspects of the transformation of identity in the late modern world, though not by any means exhaustively. Identity is a multi-accentual concept, mediating self and history in many complex ways. Poststructuralists and postmodernists have challenged essentialist notions of identity regarding gender and sexuality, for instance, but also 'race' and ethnicity. For them, the human subject is decentred, constantly in process of becoming and increasingly hybrid. There is much value in this view and it bears considerable resemblance to Anthony Giddens's treatment of self-identity, although he stresses the production of identity in radicalized modern conditions and is rather unsympathetic to the utter fluidity of postmodernism. Either way round, it has to be appreciated that these issues concerning the transformation of identity may just be the latest manifestation of western individualism. This is not particularly a problem for Giddens since he admits the 'western' qualities of modernity and insists that they are being globalized. The critique of western culture made by Sardar is much more damaging, in contrast, to postmodern thinking since it disputes claims to do with the deconstruction of westernness from within and the genuine opening out to cultural difference.

It is interesting to note how the kind of cultural relativism which tends to characterize postmodernism can be given a very conservative inflection indeed by the likes of Samuel Huntington, whose message seems to be, you can hang on to your own cultures and we will purify ours. The implications for the development of multiculturalism in western societies are clear: either assimilate to western ways or go away. Yet, whether from a postmodern point of view or a late modern point of view, it can be argued, Huntington is defending the indefensible or perhaps even the non-existent, a fixed western identity when, in fact, identity is in flux. It has to be said that Huntington's position on cultural identity has a certain resonance in non-western cultures where the project, for some, is to maintain tradition and restore indigenous identity against the ravages of modernization and westernization. The defence of cultural purity, however, is probably an impossible as well as a dangerous project whether in the West or in the Rest. And, while an accentuated modernity is in many respects destructive and on a number of counts needs to be questioned, it also potentially heralds greater democratization of life.

5

THE INFORMATION AGE

Introduction

This chapter is devoted to just one book, Manuel Castells's *The Information Age: Economy, Society and Culture*, published in three volumes towards the end of the twentieth century, *The Rise of the Network Society* (1996), *The Power of Identity* (1997) and *End of Millennium* (1998). Reviewing *The Rise of the Network Society*, Anthony Giddens (1996) compared Castells's three-volume project to Max Weber's classic *Economy and Society*. That was an apt comparison and one that is invited by Castells's subtitle, which adds, however, 'culture' to 'economy' and 'society'. In scope and ambition, Castells's *The Information Age* clearly does bear comparison to the greatest works in the history of social science. It was researched and written over twelve years, during which time Castells's own health broke down. The fruits of his arduous labour, inscribed in nearly 1500 pages, constitute a truly remarkable scholarly achievement, bringing together enormous amounts of data in a coherent analytical framework, and resulting in a book which is both tremendously educative and a pleasure to read. Unusually for an intellectual work on such scale, *The Information Age* is in a sense complete, structured and rounded off with elegant precision. Commentators will no doubt find plenty of lacunae and, in due course, various critiques of and constructive modifications to Castells's multilayered thesis are likely to be made as it inspires further research. This is not, however, only a work of scholarship but also, arguably, a political intervention of strategic importance. I would go further than Giddens, then, by suggesting that *The Information Age* may come to be seen as *Das Kapital* of our time.

The Information Age is concerned with the restructuring of capitalist civilization, its globalization and organizational change, since the 1960s, facilitated by the development and use of information technologies and the collapse of soviet communism and its claim to represent an alternative modern civilization. 'The Net', obviously referring specifically to the Internet but also, and more diffusely, the network model of society and culture in general which is transforming institutional realities and the conditions of everyday life around the world, is in binary relation, according to Castells, to 'the Self'. The relation between the Net and the Self is characterized by Castells as one of 'structural schizophrenia between structure and meaning' (1996: 3). The technical means of communication have become more sophisticated yet social communication has suffered, engendering widespread feelings of alienation and anxiety.

'Bewildered by the scale and scope of historical change', Castells observes, 'Postmodern culture, and theory, indulge in celebrating the end of history, and, to some extent, the end of Reason, giving up on our capacity to understand and make sense, even of nonsense' (1996: 4). Castells sets himself against what he calls 'intellectual nihilism, social scepticism, and political cynicism' and declares, 'I believe in rationality' (1996: 4). His cardinal proposition is that the major and empirically observable trends of a rapidly changing world – the spread of information technology, the globalization of capitalism, the rise of religious fundamentalism and other forms of identity politics, processes of inclusion and exclusion within cities and between geopolitical regions across the planet, most notably – are intelligible in their interrelatedness: they are aspects of a complex whole.

In this chapter I aim to explicate Castells's general thesis concerning 'the network society' and look specifically at what he has to say about time in 'a culture of real virtuality' and the building of resistant identities. These themes relate most closely to the themes of this book and for that reason are selected and highlighted. They mainly figure in the first two volumes – *The Rise of the Network Society* and *The Power of Identity* – of Castells's three-volume work. The third and final volume, *End of Millennium*, provides an account of the collapse of soviet statism, which stresses its structural incapacity to make the transition to the informational economy mode of production; the formation of what Castells calls a 'fourth world' of exclusion, represented by the greater part of a continent, Sub-Saharan Africa and, also, for instance, by the inner city ghettos of black America; the international criminal economy; the rise of Asian-Pacific economic power, and the integration of Europe. Castells (1997b) himself has written an admirably lucid introduction to the themes of *The Information Age*, which was published in the journal, *City*, in 1997.

Networking

At the heart of Castells's analysis is the transformation of capitalism in the closing decades of the second Christian millennium, including more flexible forms of management; decentred organization in networks of firms; increased power of capital over labour; individualization of work; much larger incorporation of women into the paid labour force yet continuing gender discrimination at work; the deregulation of markets and the undermining of the welfare state; and intensified global competition in conditions of high geographical and cultural differentiation. Although these changes can be seen, to a degree, as elements of a strategic response to the political challenges to capitalism in its heartlands from the 1960s and the economic crises that erupted in the 1970s, Castells places greater emphasis on how they have been facilitated by the development and implementation of new information technologies. Without this 'technological revolution', ushering in 'a new mode of development, informationalism' (1996: 14), the renewal and extension of capitalism globally, might not, and probably would not, have happened.

Castells's perspective is framed by the interaction of technology with relations of production, experience and power. *Production* refers to human action upon matter – in the first instance, nature – and the extraction of a surplus for investment from product yield. *Experience* is to do with human action upon the self, mediating biology and culture in social and natural environments. *Power* is the exercise of the will of some over others, giving rise to institutionalized dominance through physical and symbolic violence. In the network society, these relations are reconfigured by the use of information, computing and telecommunication technologies.

In defence of his position, Castells argues that the accusation of technological determinism (see Williams 1974, 1985 [1983]), that might be made against him, would be mistaken since he does not separate technology, as an independent force, from society but, instead, sees them as intertwined with one another. The new technological paradigm that emerged in the 1970s did so in a specific social and cultural context, that of a particular segment of society in the USA. The forms it took and its widespread ramifications are inextricably associated with this context, characterized by dynamic capitalist innovation and individualistic, lifestyle ideology. Technologies, however, have consequences that are not necessarily intended, as is the case with the Internet itself, originally sponsored by the federal state for defence purposes yet appropriated first for academic, then for both commercial and countercultural purposes.

The role of the state is vitally important for encouraging or inhibiting technological development. China's technological backwardness until recently and since around 1400 when it had been 'the most advanced technological nation in the world' (1996: 7) and 'the inability of Soviet statism to master the information technology revolution' (1996: 10) are the outstanding historical cases of state inhibition. The promotion of informationalism by the federal state in the USA and the Japanese government's organization of the post-Second World War technology-led manufacturing boom are major instances of positive state action, both of which cast into doubt assumptions concerning the market freed of state interference as the driving force of innovation.

According to Castells:

> What characterizes the current technological revolution is not the centrality of knowledge and information, but the application of such knowledge and information to knowledge generation and information processing/communication devices, in a cumulative feedback loop between innovation and the uses of information.
>
> (Castells 1996: 32)

The 'new socio-technical paradigm' becomes possible not only due to the invention of the microprocessor in 1971 but, most importantly, because microcomputers are networked together through switching devices and telecommunications. Castells stresses not only the social but also the geographical context of such technological innovation, describing California's Silicon Valley as 'a milieu of innovation' where 'autonomous dynamics of technological discovery and diffusion, including synergistic effects between various key technologies' took place, though flourishing there due to the 'strong, military-induced technological push of the 1960s' (1996: 51). In sum, 'It is . . . by this interface between macro-research programs and large markets developed by the state, on the one hand, and decentralized innovation stimulated by a culture of technological creativity and role models of fast personal success, on the other hand, that new information technologies came to blossom' (1996: 60).

The information technology or networking paradigm has five distinguishing characteristics (1996: 61–2). These technologies, first of all, in Castells's words, '*act on information*'. Second, their effects are '*pervasive*': no human activity remains unaffected by the potential applications of the technology. Third, there is a '*networking logic*' of complex interaction and patterns of development that are unpredictable. Fourth, 'the information technology paradigm is based on *flexibility*' (1996: 62). The systems of information processing and communication are infinitely reconfigurable. Finally, the power of the paradigm is secured by '*convergence of specific technologies into a highly integrated system*. Information systems now include microelectronics, telecommunications, optoelectronics and computers. There is also growing interaction between microelectronic technologies and biological engineering. 'Complexity' is the buzzword of the new paradigm and is its epistemological principle.

None of this is only to do with the technology as gadgetry but, rather, information technologies are deeply implicated in economic and other processes, most consequentially with regard to globalization: 'information itself' becomes 'the product of the production process' (1996: 67). Information technology greatly facilitates capital mobility and speed of transaction. In this respect, Castells makes a crucially important distinction between 'world economy' and a qualitatively different 'global economy':

> The informational economy is global. A global economy is a historically new reality, distinct from a world economy. A world economy, that is an economy in which capital accumulation proceeds throughout the world, has existed in the West at least since the sixteenth century, as Fernand Braudel and Immanuel Wallerstein have taught us. **A global economy is something different: it is an economy with the capacity to work as a unit in real time on a planetary scale.** While the capitalist mode of production is characterized by its relentless expansion, always trying to overcome limits of time and space, it is only in the late twentieth century that the world economy was able to become truly global on the basis of the new infrastructure provided by information and communication technologies. This globality concerns the core processes and elements of the economic system.
>
> (Castells 1996: 92–3)

Instantaneous communication across the globe breaks down barriers of time and space and is especially functional to the conduct of international business. Financial markets now operate in a single time frame. Castells's version of the globalization thesis is not just about the scale of trade, then, and so is less vulnerable to the critique made by Paul Hirst and Grahame Thompson (1996) than simpler versions of the thesis. He is also careful to point out that globalization is not an evenly distributed process: it is as much polarizing as unifying. The key question at stake with regard to international power, inequality and poverty, however, is no longer simply one of some parts of the world exploiting other parts of the world but has become, instead, to do with the structural irrelevance and exclusion from the global economy of certain parts of the world, such as most of Africa where information technologies are least developed. As Castells notes in the third volume of *The Information Age*, 'The rise of informational/global capitalism in the last quarter of the twentieth century has coincided with the collapse of Africa's economies, the disintegration of many of its states, and the breakdown of most of its societies' (1998: 82–3). Countries and international regions are differentially positioned in the global economy, with the USA and Africa the most extremely differentiated. Technological capacities, access to markets, price controls and political muscle result in a variety of differentiations and economic advantage and disadvantage. The global and informational economy exhibits 'an extraordinarily *variable geometry* that tends to dissolve historical, economic geography' (1996: 106).

The networking paradigm, in addition to information technology and the global economy, draws attention to organizational change in the later part of the twentieth century: 'the rise of the informational economy is characterized by the development of a new organizational logic which is related to the current process of technological change, but not dependent upon it' (1996: 152). In this respect, Castells is influenced by research on the shift from Fordist mass production to post-Fordist 'flexible specialization', a more versatile regime of capital accumulation and mode of social regulation. The large, tightly controlled organization is cumbersome in comparison with networks of smaller organizations that can respond more swiftly to changing market conditions. Also, the Japanese led the way in developing newer forms of management based on consensus building and teamworking. Castells himself suggests, however, that such organizational features are actually 'designed to reduce uncertainty rather than to encourage adaptability' (1996: 158).

He also distinguishes between two forms of network enterprise: '*the multidirectional network model enacted by small and medium businesses*' and '*the licensing-subcontracting model of production under an umbrella corporation*'. The first of these is exemplified by innovative firms of the 'Third Italy', which was viewed widely, during the 1980s, as the ideal model of flexible specialization, dynamic and creative small business networks in an integrated region. The second form of network organization is characteristic of large corporations offsetting risk through franchising, such as McDonald's, and vertically disintegrated arrangements in, for instance, the film and television businesses. Whatever the specific forms, Castells says more generally, 'Networks are the fundamental stuff of which new organizations are and will be made' (1996: 168). For him, 'the unit is the network' (1996: 198).

Of related significance are the transformations in working practices and forms of employment associated with the emergence of 'networkers' and 'flextimers'. Castells disagrees with theories of postindustrialism which overstate the shift from manufacturing to service work. Manufacturing still matters but it is being reconfigured by information technology, with atten-dant changes in occupational structures, especially the comparative decline of 'masculine' manual work and the rise of 'feminine' informational work. Also, in general, the problem of job loss has been much exaggerated with regard to the impact of the new technologies. Jobs are created as well as lost, which is not always appreciated when attention is focused exclusively upon the fate of heavy industries in North America and Europe. The collectivism of the traditional working class is indeed being displaced, however, by the individualization of work, part-time working and temporary contracts, in which there is little trade union protection. Great emphasis is now placed upon value-addedness through innovation that privileges a core labour force of '*networkers*', who make decisions, research, design and organize. Outside these charmed circles are the '*networked*', who are on-line but do not make decisions of consequence. Further out are 'the *switched-off* workers, tied to their own specific tasks, defined by non-interactive, one-way instructions' (1996: 244).

Networking, then, has a number of manifestations in Castells's new para-digm of an emergent modern society, facilitated and realized by the conver-gence of information technologies, economic globalization, organizational flexibility and occupational restructuring. As Castells defines it, a 'network is a set of interconnected nodes' and a 'node is the point at which a curve inter-sects itself' (1996: 470). Among the examples he gives are stock markets and political networks. Also included are

> coca fields and poppy fields, clandestine laboratories, secret landing strips, street gangs, and money-laundering financial institutions, in the network of drug traffic that penetrates economies, societies, and states throughout the world.
>
> (Castells 1996: 470)

Less informally,

> They are television systems, entertainment studios, computer graphics milieux, news teams, and mobile devices generating, transmitting, and receiving signals, in the global network of the new media at the roots of cultural expression and public opinion in the information age.
>
> (Castells 1996: 470)

They represent the social form of contemporary life, in many cases at an early stage of development and in other cases already highly developed by informationalism. In general:

> Networks are open structures, able to expand without limits, integrating new nodes as long as they are able to communicate within the network,

namely as long as they share the same communication codes (for example, values or performance goals). A network-based social structure is a highly dynamic, open system, susceptible to innovating without threatening its balance. Networks are appropriate instruments for a capitalist economy based on innovation, globalization, and decentralized concentration; for work, workers, and firms based on flexibility, and adaptability; for a culture of endless deconstruction, and reconstruction; for a polity geared towards the endless processing of new values and public moods; and for a social organization aiming at the supersession of space and the annihilation of time.

(Castells 1996: 470–1)

Globalizing time

The networking paradigm applies to both economic process and cultural process and draws attention to the interconnections between economy and culture without, however, reducing the latter to the former. Castells is particularly influenced by Marshall McLuhan (for example, 1964) in his treatment of cultural technology, seeing the development of computer mediation as the most important change in communications since the invention of the alphabet, though one which was already partly anticipated by the impact of television. Television heralded 'the end of the Gutenberg Galaxy, that is of a system of communication essentially dominated by the typographic mind and the phonetic alphabet' (Castells 1996: 331). Some see email as the revenge of the word against the image in electronic communications but not so Castells. Like McLuhan he stresses the visual and the non-linear.

The vital technological development is convergence in multimedia, resulting in the 'potential integration of text, images and sounds in the same system, interacting from multiple points, in chosen time (real or delayed) along a global network, in conditions of open and affordable access' (1996: 328). Crucially, computer-mediated communications (CMC) enable interactivity. A specific architecture characterizes network culture and which is unlikely to change in the foreseeable future: this is the very culture of networking itself, the multiple points of access and the cross-hatching of communication which no central authority can control. Castells is quite aware, however, that the actual operations of computer-mediated communications are far from utopian, when limitations of access and typical usage are taken into account. As he says, 'the most important cultural impact of CMC could be potentially the reinforcement of the culturally dominant social networks' (1996: 363). None the less, *a common cognitive pattern* is emerging and most forms of cultural expression are coming within the orbit of computer-mediated communications. This is the culture of what Castells calls

> real virtuality ... a system in which reality itself (that is, people's material/symbolic existence) is entirely captured, fully immersed in a virtual image setting, in a world of make believe, in which experiences are not just on the screen through which experience is communicated, but they become the experience.
>
> (Castells 1996: 374)

If the symbolic mediation of everything is admitted, then, it makes no sense to say that the screen culture of electronic and computer-mediated communications is 'unreal'.

The new communications media transform the fundamental coordinates of space and time as they are apprehended socially, giving rise to a '*space of flows*' and '*timeless time*'. In his earlier work, Castells had already distinguished between the '*space of flows*' and the '*space of places*'. We are all, to some extent, located within place-bound experience, where we live out our social positioning: the immediately tangible situations of everyday life. On the other hand, the operations of economy and culture, in terms of trade and the circulation of images, sounds and information, function in spaces of flow. Such spaces are of increasing importance with the extensive development of network economies and cultures. There is, as Doreen Massey (1997 [1991]) has termed it, a '*power geometry*' operating in the relations between situatedness in place and the space of flows:

> different social groups, and different individuals, are placed in very distinct ways in relation to these flows and interconnections ... some people are more in charge of it than others; some initiate flows and movement, others don't; some are more on the receiving end of it than others; some are effectively imprisoned by it.
>
> (Massey 1997 [1991]: 234)

Castells's own view is very similar yet, from his point of view, this is not simply a complaint about inequality. Command over the space of flows is integral to organizational practice in a globalizing economy and must be understood as such. Places of production are dispersed and simultaneously coordinated at nodal points, facilitated by telecommunications linkages. Castells observes,

> The development of electronic communications and information systems allows for an increasing disassociation between spatial proximity and the performance of everyday life's functions: work, shopping,

entertainment, healthcare, education, public services, governance, and the like . . . [Moreover] our society is constructed around flows: flows of capital, flows of information, flows of technology, flows of organizational interaction, flows of images, sounds, and symbols.

(Castells 1996: 394, 411–12)

Differential access to and command over the space of flows is the key source of power and social inequality in the network society. Professional-managerial groups are privileged spatially in two ways, by functioning in the abstracted space of flows, whether physically through travel or mentally through telecommunications and electronic networking, and by social segregation in the space of places. They form into 'symbolically secluded communities' with a 'lifestyle . . . aimed at unifying the symbolic environment of the elite around the world' (1996: 416–17). In fact, theirs is 'an increasingly homogeneous lifestyle', a lifestyle that is shared by such groups wherever they are to be found, among majority populations in, say, the USA and within a modernized minority in, for instance, India. Taste cultures and consumption patterns are similar; and, there is a common anxiety to separate and protect themselves spatially from the excluded, the underclass in rich countries and the peasant and urban masses in poorer countries. Castells notes that this homogeneous culture of class privilege is manifest in contemporary architectural fashion, the styles of which are increasingly placeless.

Time is also transformed in the network society which functions on a global scale. In *The Power of Identity*, Castells provides a concise summary of three kinds of temporality that are currently in operation. First, there is the '*clock time*' that is 'characteristic of industrialism' (1997a: 125), the importance of which E.P. Thompson (1993 [1967]) stressed for establishing work-discipline in the early factory system. Second, there is '*timeless time*', which 'occurs when the characteristics of a given context, namely, the informational paradigm and the network society, induce perturbation in the sequential order of phenomena performed in that context' (1997a: 125). And third, there is what Lash and Urry (1994) call '*glacial time*', referring to the *longue durée* of humanity's relation to nature.

A traditional sense of time was comparatively loose: the clock time of modernity is much more precise and exacting. Yet, it is clock time and its relentless linearity which declines in significance with the advent of the timeless time of the information age. As Castells argues, 'linear, irreversible, measurable, predictable time is being shattered in the network society' (1996: 433). The new timeless time involves

the mixing of tenses to create a forever universe, not self-expanding but self-maintaining, not cyclical but random, not recursive but incursive:

timeless time, using technology to escape from the contexts of its existence, and to appropriate selectively any value each context could offer to the ever present . . . Capitalism's freedom from time and culture's escape from the clock are decisively facilitated by new information technologies, and embedded in the structure of the network society.

(Castells 1996: 433)

Timeless time is the emerging kind of time. Its effects are already evident in instances of what David Harvey (1989) termed, 'time-space compression', especially a global economy working in temporal unison. Manifestations of the annihilation of time, however, are widespread and various, most evidently affecting work, the speed of operations, flexible working time and the length of the working life, which has been shortening dramatically in richer parts of the world. In effect, Castells observes, 'the network society is characterized by the breaking down of rhythmicity, either biological or social, associated with the lifecycle' (1996: 446). Early retirement and prolonged longevity for the professional-managerial class extend the 'third age' yet, also, birth control reduces the reproduction of the young. Thus, while time is compressed in work and communications, it is expanded for the lives of the comparatively privileged and great efforts are made to keep death at bay. Time dynamics are quite the opposite for the poor of the world, with high rates of reproduction as well as infant mortality, longer hours and years of work, and shorter lives.

Timeless time is not only a feature of global economics but also characteristic of the aesthetic cultures of the network society: 'The culture of real virtuality associated with an electronically integrated media system . . . contributes to the transformation of time in our society in two different forms: simultaneity and timelessness' (Castells 1996: 461). There is, as Castells puts it, 'a nonsequential time of cultural products available from the whole realm of human experience' (1996: 462). Anything can be downloaded any time, in principle, at the whim of the consumer. All culture is, in this way, eternally available, although at the same time it is curiously ephemeral. This erasure of time in cultural consumption connects to the ideology of the end of history, which Castells castigates at several points in his great work on the information age. His critical observations echo Jameson's (1984) concerns about the diminution of historical memory and the formation of a culture that is caught in a perpetual present, that is a postmodern culture of pick and mix, blurred boundaries and depthlessness. In summary, then, according to Castells:

The space of flows . . . dissolves time by disordering the sequence of events and making them simultaneous, thus installing society in eternal ephemerality. The multiple space of places, scattered, fragmented, and disconnected, displays diverse temporalities, from the most primitive domination of natural rhythms to the strictest tyranny of clock time. Selected functions and individuals transcend time, while downgraded activities and subordinate people endure life as time goes by. While the emerging logic of the new social structure aims at the relentless super-session of time as an ordered sequence of events, most of society, in a globally interdependent system, remains on the edge of the new universe. Timelessness sails in an ocean surrounded by time-bounded shores, from where still can be heard the laments of time-chained creatures.

(Castells 1996: 467)

This is the purest form of capitalist civilization yet known, currently in the making and whose cultural effects are applauded as liberatory by post-modernists who see no evident relation between economy and culture or, at least, do not believe that drawing the connections is a worthwhile analytical task. In that respect, the postmodern imaginary is peculiarly ethnocentric and sustainable in its blinkeredness only in the privileged spaces of the wealthier parts of the world, and most markedly in the USA. The trans-formation of capitalism through the mediation of information technologies and resulting in the emergent network society, analysed by Castells, provides a vital perspective on how postmodernism functions as the culture in gen-eral of a fresh phase of capitalist civilization. Capitalism's presence in the world is thus extended and deepened, thereby accentuating the most salient features of a modernity that postmodernists have erroneously declared *passé*.

Identity building

At the beginning of *The Power of Identity*, Castells summarizes the thesis of *The Rise of the Network Society*:

> Our world, and our lives, are being shaped by the conflicting trends of globalization and identity. The information technology revolution, and the restructuring of capitalism, have induced a new form of society, the network society. It is characterized by the globalization of strategically decisive economic activities. By the networking form of organization. By flexibility and instability of work, and the individualization of labor. By a culture of real virtuality constructed by a pervasive, interconnected and diverse media system. And, by the material foundations of life, space and time, as expressions of dominant activities and controlling elites.

(Castells 1997a: 1)

In this second volume of *The Information Age*, Castells proceeds to examine questions of identity and, in so doing, he spells out what he considers to be the key sources of political resistance to the dominating powers of global capital, social movements that are obliged to conduct their politics, like other political forces, through the communications media. In this, information technologies are seen not only to enhance the power of capital but also to provide essential tools for opposition. Castells's typical way of proceeding is not to set out a complexly elaborate conceptual framework in abstraction but, rather, as he says, his method 'aims at communicating theory by analysing practice' (1997a: 3). *The Power of Identity*, as with the other two volumes of the trilogy, is made up of a rich body of empirical data, the details of which are fascinating, much of it organized as a series of case studies for comparison. Through the accumulation and interpretation of the empirical data and case study material, Castells is able to formulate a general and well substantiated argument concerning the ascendant forms of political struggle in the network society.

Castells defines identity as 'people's source of meaning and experience' (1997a: 6). Social actors form identities from cultural attributes that are especially salient to them. They identify symbolically and, therefore, meaningfully with collectivities: accordingly, identity is never just an individual matter. Identities are socially constructed rather than naturally given. The question for Castells, then, is how are these identities constructed in power relations within specific circumstances? Castells distinguishes between three types of identity: '*legitimizing identity*', '*resistant identity*' and '*project identity*'. In the book, he is mainly concerned with the second of these three types of identity. Legitimizing identity is to do with citizenship and rights associated with the nation-state. As Castells argues, however, it is no longer satisfactory to understand political identity only in terms of nations. The dialectic of globalization and identity cuts across the nation-state both economically and culturally. Resistant identity, in contrast, is less to do with nationhood than with communal identification, illustrated, for instance, by the various kinds of religious fundamentalism active in the contemporary world. Project identity is closest to Giddens's (1991) understanding of reflexive identity, which was discussed in Chapter 4. Castells does not fundamentally disagree with that conception of the desiring individual living under conditions of high modernity but he does stress a further qualitative development of modernity occurring with the rise of the network society. In effect, Giddens's reasoning on identity is insufficiently political for Castells, who proposes, 'the hypothesis that the constitution of subjects, at the heart of the process of social change, takes a different route to the one we knew during modernity: namely, *subjects, if and when constructed, are not built any longer on the basis of civil societies, that are in the process of disintegration, but as prolongation of communal resistance*' (1997a: 11).

These resistant identities are not necessarily 'progressive' in a left-wing sense. For instance, they include the Christian fundamentalist backlash against feminism, lesbian and gay movements in the USA. As Castells discusses at length in *The Power of Identity*, the patriarchal family is profoundly challenged by women's work and feminist consciousness: this is what has given rise to a deeply conservative form of resistant identity, in the case of Christian familialism. None the less, it is indeed resistance to a dominant trend in the network society. And, although Castells himself favours more progressive forms of resistant identity, for instance, in the urban movements that have fought for local autonomy and democracy, it would be mistaken not to appreciate the various kinds of inversion that are also manifest in struggles between dominance and opposition. Progressive and conservative identities of communal resistance, moreover, share characteristics in common:

> Cultural communes are characterized by three main features. They appear as reactions to prevailing social trends, which are resisted on behalf of autonomous sources of meaning. They are, at their outset, defensive identities that function as refuge and solidarity, to protect against a hostile, outside world. They are culturally constituted; that is, organized around a specific set of values whose meaning and sharing are marked by specific codes of self-identification: the community of believers, the icons of nationalism, the geography of locality.
>
> (Castells 1997a: 65)

Throughout the world there is 'a small elite of *globapolitans* (half beings, half flows)' (1997a: 69) but most people live in places where struggle is fairly local. Castells analyses and compares three social movements from this point of view: the Mexican *Zapatistas*, the *Patriots* of the USA and Japan's *Aum Shinrikyo*, all of which have constructed resistant identities to cultural globalization and, especially in the case of the *Zapatistas*, economic globalization. In each case he is concerned with understanding the social movement within its own terms. Castells adopts Alain Touraine's model for studying social movements with regard to '*identity*', '*adversary*' and '*societal goal*'.

At the inauguration of the North American Free Trade Agreement (NAFTA) on 1 January 1994, 3000 men and women of the *Ejercito Zapatista de Liberacion National* took armed control of a number of municipalities in the state of Chiapas, southern Mexico. The leaders were urban

intellectuals wearing ski masks. Their spokesperson, Marcos, it later tran-
spired, was a graduate in sociology and communications. The followers
were mainly local Indian peasants, descendants of those who had been
driven into the rainforests from the land they had cultivated by ranchers in
the 1940s. When the Mexican army attacked, the insurgents withdrew to the
rainforests. Several dozen were killed until the ceasefire of 12 January,
ordered by the Mexican president in response to public sympathy for the
Zapatistas. The cause of the revolt was the economic liberalization policy of
the governing *Partido Revolucionario Institucional* (PRI), which had ended
protection against corn imports and of the coffee crop price and the law on
communal ownership of occupied land, in preparation for NAFTA, thus
destroying the fragile peasant economy of Chiapas.

Castells examines how the resistant identity of the *Zapatistas* was formed:
first, in memory of past struggle led by the agrarian revolutionary, Emiliano
Zapatista; and second, against the new global order, further denying the historical rights of local peasants and Indians. After the collapse of communism, furthermore, Marcos articulated an ironic socialism with a certain
resilience in a *communiqué* quoted by Castells:

> There is nothing to fight for any longer. Socialism is dead. Long life to
> conformism, to reform, to modernity, to capitalism and all kind of cruel
> etceteras. Let's be reasonable. That nothing happens in the city, or in the
> countryside, that everything continues the same. Socialism is dead.
> Long life to capital. Radio, press, and television repeat it. Some social-
> ists, now reasonably, repentant, also repeat the same.
>
> (Castells 1997a: 77)

According to Castells, Indian ethnicity was not the most prevalent feature of
the movement's identity: instead, the tradition of peasant resistance to brutal
modernization, revived under globalizing conditions, characterized the *Zapatistas*. In addition, the main site of battle, for them, was not so much the
forest as the communications media, including the Internet, their own videos
and mainstream television:

> The success of the *Zapatistas* was largely due to their communication
> strategy, to the point that they can be called the *first informational guer-
> rilla movement*. They created a media event in order to diffuse their mes-
> sage, while desperately trying not to be brought into a bloody war. There
> were, of course, real deaths, and real weapons, and Marcos, and his
> comrades, were ready to die. Yet, actual warfare was not their strategy.
> The *Zapatistas* used arms to make a statement, then parlayed the possi-
> bility of their sacrifice in front of the world media to force a negotiation

and advance a number of reasonable demands which, as opinion polls seem to indicate, found widespread support in Mexican society at large.
(Castells 1997a: 79)

While the *Zapatistas* may be seen as romantic revolutionaries, recalling a history of popular insurgency and grassroots socialism, the American militias present the much darker visage of bigoted terrorism. Yet, there are similarities: the atrocious Oklahoma bombing of 1995 brought their version of populist politics to global public attention. The militias' common enemy is the American federal government, which they perceive as failing, among other things, in its duty to preserve 'the American way' and the prerogatives of the gun-toting, patriotic patriarch. Similarly, the murder of twelve people on the Tokyo subway by the young priests of *Aum Shinrikyo* in the same year as the Oklahoma bombing represented a revolt on behalf of 'tradition' against globalizing modernity. As Castells comments:

> the three movements analyzed here coincide in the identification of their adversary: it is the new global order, designated by the *Zapatistas* as the conjunction of American imperialism and corrupt, illegitimate PRI government in NAFTA; incarnated by international institutions, most notably the United Nations, and the US federal government in the view of American militia; while for *Aum* the global threat comes from the unified world government representing the interests of multinational corporations, US imperialism and Japanese police.
>
> (Castells 1997a: 105)

In each of these cases of resistant identity, there is a stress on 'authenticity', albeit in terms of very different identifications, and keen use of 'new communications technologies', networking support and, also, engagement with the mainstream media. Castells sees their actions in this respect as a particular variant of the necessarily 'informational politics' of the network society in general: 'outside the media sphere there is only political marginality' (1997a: 312). Dominant political practice exemplifies this well enough: so must oppositional politics. For dominant politics, Castells stresses the importance of scandal in particular, with its manifestly entertaining features, over earnest revelations of corruption. For oppositional politics, he stresses 'the recreation of local democracy', 'the opportunity offered by electronic communication to enhance political participation and horizontal communication among citizens' and the 'development of symbolic politics and of political mobilization around "non-political" causes' (1997a: 350–2). In *The Power of Identity*, Castells also analyses environmental and ecological politics (particularly, Greenpeace) and gender and sexual politics (most notably, lesbian politics in Tapei) from this perspective. Castells insists that in the network society political battles are cultural battles and must, realistically, be waged as such.

Conclusion

In the conclusion to the third volume of his trilogy, *End of Millennium*, which is the conclusion to the whole of *The Information Age*, Manuel Castells states summarily:

> A new world is taking shape in this end of millennium. It originated in the historical coincidence, around the late 1960s and mid-1970s, of three *independent* processes: the information technology revolution: the economic crisis of both capitalism and statism, and their subsequent restructuring; and the blooming of cultural social movements, such as libertarianism, human rights, feminism, and environmentalism. The interaction between these processes, and the reactions they triggered, brought into being a new dominant social structure, the network society; a new economy, the informational/global economy; and a new culture, the culture of real virtuality. The logic embedded in this economy, this society, and this culture underlies social action and institutions throughout an interdependent world.
>
> (Castells 1998: 336)

This new phase of capitalist civilization, facilitated by information technologies, brings with it transformations in relations of production, power and experience. With regard to relations of production, the old division between capitalists and workers, *bourgeoisie* and *proletariat*, is too simple a model for understanding the cleavages of the network society. Among the wealthiest and most powerful, there are significant differences between international finance, property holding and management: that is, the capitalist class itself is internally differentiated and hierarchized. There is also an 'internal fragmentation of labor', particularly around access to knowledge and decision making and, fundamentally, between core information workers and generalized labour that is hired and fired at will (1998: 346). A Weberian model of inclusion and exclusion, in general, provides a more accurate depiction than the two class model of exploitation, for Castells. Neo-Marxists have, in fact, held to more or less such a view for some time. Exclusion is the fundamental political problem of the network society on a global scale and with acute local manifestations. In terms of the transformation of power relations, the crisis of the nation-state and its association with representative democracy, now cut across by globalizing and localizing forces, is of utmost importance. Power is increasingly inscribed in cultural codes rather than in the institutions of an earlier phase of modernity, according to Castells. Moreover, politics is conducted through the media of communication, which are not themselves the sources of power but, rather, the mediation of power and, therefore, open to tactical negotiation. Relations of experience are being transformed most fundamentally by the crisis of patriarchalism, which, among other things, calls for new ways for men and women to relate to one another. Identities are no longer securely place-bound but are displaced and reconstituted through the space of a culture of real virtuality. Primary identification with, say, an ethnic group is rendered fragile and identity building becomes a complicated process.

Castells is reluctant to engage in futurology, though he does succumb a little to forecasting towards the end of *The Information Age*. He had mistakenly predicted, in *The Power of Identity*, that Tony Blair would meet with immediate character assassination by the news media on the election of New Labour in Britain. The Blair government, on coming into office, was very successful, in fact, at managing the news media and manipulating symbolic politics, which in itself became a source of complaint inside and outside the media (McGuigan 1998a). Unsurprisingly, in *The End of Millennium*, Castells predicts that current trends bringing about a network society, that he had analysed throughout the trilogy, would develop much further into the twenty-first century. Startling prediction, then, is not the strength of the work, which is, instead, in the complex and multiperspectival analysis of interweaving forces in a non-reductive and holistic framework. His claims are empirically founded and open to empirical testing: they are not infallible. Most importantly, Castells offers a way of making sense of social and cultural change which should contribute to future work in what is an endless task of analysis. He concludes, finally, by suggesting, deliberately against the tide of western intellectual fashion, that the 'dream of the Enlightenment, that reason and science would solve the problems of humankind, is within reach' (1998: 359), while noting the enduring horrors of the contemporary world. No outcome, good or bad, is inevitable and, Castells insists, 'There is nothing that cannot be changed' (1998: 360).

6

REFLEXIVE MODERNITY

Introduction

We live in a social world where change is endemic, in effect, a post-traditional world, which is not to deny the existence of various projects dedicated to restoring or inventing tradition so as to resist '[c]onstant revolutionising of production, uninterrupted disturbance of all social conditions, everlasting uncertainty and agitation' (Marx and Engels 1967 [1848]: 83). To characterize modernity as a condition in which '[a]ll that is solid melts into air' is a cliché yet, none the less, true. Towards the end of the twentieth century, similar claims were made for *post*modernization as had been made in the past for modernization. Modernity now took on the guise of tradition: postmodernists, like their modernist predecessors, were against traditional ways and solid foundations. The signs of change were all around, including dissolving boundaries between cultural forms and social identities. The modern but relatively short lived, in any longish historical perspective, hierarchies of elite and mass, serious and popular culture, for instance, were apparently collapsing. Aspects of popular culture even took on some of the characteristics of the avant-garde while serious culture came increasingly under the rule of the market. These developments, at one time so striking for cultural critics, were as nothing compared with the pervasive emergence of what Manuel Castells (1996) dubs 'a culture of real virtuality' where the distinction between representation and reality is put into question. To label such cultural change and related manifestations of epistemological uncertainty 'postmodern' makes descriptive sense, but does it necessarily signify an epochal shift from one civilizational principle to another, from modernity to postmodernity?

In fact, postmodernist writing is typically coy about societal transformation, preferring to emphasize the cultural and very often exclusively the textual, occasionally supplemented by the claim that the social has been subsumed in the cultural; which is one definition of postmodernism. While the distinction between social and cultural is categorical in a Kantian sense, it is reasonable to assume that in 'reality' they are inseparable. For analytical purposes, it might be considered a category error, however, to conflate the social and the cultural. The interplay of culture and society, signification and social relation, is the object of analysis from such a perspective, one which facilitates the argument of this book that the postmodernization of culture does not transcend historical modernity though it is a powerful challenge to intellectual modernity. Modernist thought is obliged to offer some response: the thesis of reflexive modernization is one such response. It has to be considered, however, whether or not the issue is only one of nomenclature. Are the theorists of reflexive modernity merely hanging on to a redundant term while conceding the debate to the postmodernists? The concept of reflexive modernity is similar in certain respects to the unusually explicit postmodernization of society thesis propounded by Stephen Crook, Jan Pakulski and Malcolm Waters (1992), regarding such observable phenomena as the diminishing centrality of class, the weakening of the nation-state in the global economy, the rise of new social movements and the crisis of scientism. Yet, on both substantive and philosophical grounds, the thesis of reflexive modernization remains modernist: substantive in the sense of Giddens's argument that contemporary perturbation results from accentuated and globalizing modernity: and, philosophical in the sense of an enduring commitment to critical reason in the interests of emancipation. Extreme postmodernists particularly reject the modern project's principle of emancipatory, universalizing knowledge, if only for purposes of 'provocation'. That is not necessarily so, however, for Crook *et al.*'s version of postmodernization.

For Crook *et al.* (1992: 2), 'postmodernization is an increased level of cultural effectivity'. Modernity, according to them, is characterized by a differentiation of spheres, for example, the cultural and the social. Postmodernity is not to be understood simply, as some have argued, as *de*differentiation (Lash 1990). Rather, postmodernization is best characterized by a 'dialectic of differentiation' (Crook *et al.* 1992: 47). For instance, the breakdown of the elite/mass culture divide is accompanied by a proliferation of taste publics. This connects with the social in terms of the emergence of a consumer society underpinned by an economy that awards primacy to sovereign consumption. That is now a very familiar and one-dimensional argument of cultural studies and it is curiously homologous with neo-classical economics, the recently ascendant ideology of globalizing capitalism (see

McGuigan 1997). In effect, Crook, Pakulski and Waters's postmodernization thesis is a variant of social theory as market speak, as though the cus-
tomer really was King or Queen. They call, moreover, for a postmodern
sociology to make sense of the new radically changed condition, a sociology
involving 'the endless pragmatic task of responding to uncertainty and
change' (Crook *et al.* 1992: 239). This is an agenda that is strangely reminiscent of modern(ist) sociology as such, a discipline charged historically
with making sense of modernization, the advent of, in Ulrich Beck's (1995a
[1991]: 22) words, 'Modernity, which introduces uncertainty into all niches
of existence'.

In the preface to their collaborative book on reflexive modernity, Ulrich
Beck, Anthony Giddens and Scott Lash (1994: vii) remark, 'The social and
cultural worlds today are thoroughly infused with reflexive knowledge'. The
two key thinkers here, Beck and Giddens, however, do not see the role of
reflexive knowledge in quite the same way. Giddens is less critical of intellectual expertise than Beck. For Giddens, modern institutions engage inces-
santly in reflexive self-monitoring. Beck would not deny that, but his
emphasis on 'risk' suggests a definitional conflict and struggle between
expert and lay knowledges. It is scientific, expert knowledge which frequently alerts the public to risk yet it is the actual or near catastrophe which
casts doubt on official risk calculation for the public. The contest of opinion
between experts on such occasions further highlights the clash of knowledges. The authors of *Reflexive Modernization* observe, 'The notion of
"risk" is central to modern culture today precisely because so much of our
thinking has to be of "as-if" kind' (Beck *et al.* 1994: vii). Life is unpredictable and it is difficult to be sure of anything. More than anyone else it is
Beck who has theorized the centrality of risk, though similar arguments
about its cultural significance have been made by others (such as Douglas
and Wildavsky 1983). It is also Beck who formulated the notion of reflexive
modernity, an idea that resonates with Giddens's initially independent thinking on latterday modernization processes.

Beck is a thinker who has one big idea which he endlessly worries: this is
that industrial society threatens its own existence and, more consequentially,
that of the planet by the risks it takes, particularly with regard to the environment. The side-effects of industrial society – pollution, radiation and so forth
– bring about a different kind of modernity, a risk-conscious society in which
there is a debate and indeed battle over the conditions of progress. The sense
of risk and attendant feelings of insecurity and uncertainty not only are
associated with potential ecological catastrophe, in Beck's argument, but also
are a feature of individual conduct and everyday life. This latter point is
clarified by Giddens's emphasis on detraditionalization. Giddens is a thinker

with several smaller though, nevertheless, substantial ideas than Beck's big one. For Giddens, tradition is rooted in collective memory and obligations that prescribe codes of practice at institutional and personal levels. Earlier modernity involved a collaboration between the modern and the traditional. Later modernity breaks free of tradition. Institutions become reflexively changeable and individuals experience what existentialists called 'freedom', that is, abandonment without guidance and choice without guarantees.

Risking everything

Ulrich Beck's book published in former West Germany in 1986, *Risikoge-sellschaft: Auf dem Weg in ein andere Moderne*, published in English in 1992 as *Risk Society: Towards a New Modernity*, is the *locus classicus* for the thesis of reflexive modernization. It is not just a work of abstract social theory but a significant intervention in the public sphere of the Federal Republic, a bestseller and required reading for the chattering class. Germany has had, of course, the most successful green political movement in the world in terms of electoral politics and, also, widespread popular consciousness. In the opening paragraph, Beck introduces his perspective in relation to postmodernism:

> The theme of this book is the unremarkable prefix 'post'. It is the key word of our times. Everything is 'post'. We have become used to *post*-industrialism now for some time, and we can still more or less make sense of it. With *post*-modernism things begin to get blurred. The concept of *post*-Enlightenment is so dark even a cat would hesitate to venture in. It hints at a 'beyond' which it cannot name, and in the substantive elements that it names *and* negates it remains tied to the familiar. *Past plus post* – that is the basic recipe with which we confront a reality that is out of joint.
>
> (Beck 1992a: 9)

Less ruefully, Beck (1995a: 47) observed subsequently, 'In social theory, helplessness is easy to recognize: it carries the prefix "post" like a blind man's cane: postindustrialism, postmodernism, postmaterialism, and so forth'. Beck is not just concerned with defending a past tradition of rational critique against quietistic irrationalism but with renewing enlightened thought and practice under radically changed conditions. The prospect of doing so is the bright side of risk society since the dark side is so universally perilous. Beck was working with a preliminary distinction between *simple* modernity and *reflexive* modernity, a distinction he later elaborated upon.

Reflexivity in Beck's discourse is not a coming to awareness but, rather, the outcome of structural contradictions in modern industrial society, which in turn result not so much from 'crises' but, instead, 'triumphs' (Beck 1997 [1996]: 25).

Reflexive modernity dis-embeds and re-embeds social relations, leading to an *individualization* of identity in place of class identification. The society becomes less functionally differentiated institutionally and more functionally coordinated. Yet, the rationalization process of an ever-progressive industrialism declines in credibility. The *side-effects* of modern industrialism become, in effect, uncontrollable and globalized, as in the case of nuclear fallout from the Chernobyl reactor. Modern industrialism produces '*circular, cumulative and boomerang effects*' (1997: 31). The individual experiences a socially produced insecurity and scientific reassurances are rendered dubious. Beck (1997: 38) identifies six contrasting features of simple and reflexive modernity. First, linear models of development are superseded by multi-layered and spiral reasoning due to enhanced recognition of uncertainty. Second, to quote Beck, 'while simple modernization ultimately situates the motor of social change in categories of instrumental rationality (reflection), "reflexive" modernization conceptualizes the motive power of social change in categories of the side-effect (reflexivity)'. Third, modernity begins to break with the logic of an industrialism that is negligent of its unintended consequences. Fourth, social life becomes de-collectivized and individualized. Fifth, as already noted, differentiation is replaced by coordination. Sixth, Beck says, 'beyond distinctions of left and right . . . political, ideological and theoretical conflicts are beginning that can be outlined with axes and dichotomies such as safe-unsafe, inside-outside, political-apolitical'.

Beck points out what is distinctive about contemporary risks:

> Human dramas – plagues, famines and natural disasters, the looming power of gods and demons – may or may not quantifiably equal the destructive potential of modern mega-technologies in hazardousness. They differ essentially from 'risks' in my sense since they are not based on decisions, or more specifically, decisions that focus on techno-economic advantages and opportunities and accept hazards as simply the dark side of progress.
>
> (Beck 1992b: 98)

A risk, then, is deliberately taken. The domestic use of nuclear energy, for instance, is a risk that is taken in the expectation that accidents will not occur and that the afterlife of waste materials, stretching for thousands of years, can be safely contained. Strenuous measures are deployed to ensure safety. They have to be, particularly in the case of nuclear power, because it is impossible to insure against catastrophe. Modern industrialism sought to cover itself with insurance in a 'calculus of risk' but this has broken down. It is impossible to make 'the incalculable calculable'. In less potentially cataclysmic risk technologies than nuclear power, and more mundanely, there is also a problem in attributing blame and seeking recompense from the perpetrators. Elderly sufferers from lung cancer have successfully sued tobacco manufacturers and compensation for damaging medication is routinely sought. The fact is, however, that in most cases risk is fundamentally incalculable and uninsurable. Culpability is, in practice, often unattributable due to unequal power between parties in dispute and, besides, there is epistemological uncertainty as to evidence and proof. Who is to blame for premature ill-health and early death? Where is compensation or retribution to be sought?

The world has been turned into a huge laboratory (Beck 1995a: 104) in which there is a 'reversal of experiment and application'. Findings are the result of real life experiments on the public. The effects cannot, in practice, be ascertained ahead of their eventuality. To most intents and purposes, then, 'risk calculations are a kind of bankruptcy declaration of technical rationality'. Those who wind up playing the game of proof with the perpetrators are caught in a Kafkaesque trial of evidence, counter-evidence and chronic undecideability. If risks were not taken there would be no problem but the fact of the matter is that they are taken routinely to supply consumers with products and services. As Beck says (1992a: 65), 'If people could agree to the not totally absurd premise of *not* poisoning *at all* then there would not be any problems'. The ordinary citizen's powers to approve or object are inherently limited, however, partly but not just because of a democratic deficit. It has to be said, unquestioning consent is given more often than not, whether out of sheer ignorance or lack of foresight, to risk taking that produces potentially devastating hazards which may remain invisible and mysterious until too late, when the real damage is finally revealed. In any event, the experts may be no more knowledgeable about the eventual costs of risk than the public.

It is important to appreciate that, for Beck, environmental damage and degradation are not threats of nature or even simply the unforeseen downside of technological advance: they are socially produced as the consequences of deliberate and calculated risk taking. He attributes primacy to the social dynamics of risk:

> natural destruction and large-scale technological hazards can and must be apprehended and deciphered as mystified modes of social self-encounter, twisted outwards and reified. They are objectified memories

of suppressed, social-human imperfection and responsibility, projected onto nature and technology. It is not something external but itself that society encounters in the hazards that convulse it; and the reigning paralysis can only be overcome in so far as society apprehends the hazards as signposts to its own history, and to its corrigibility.

(Beck 1995b [1988]: 158–9)

Ubiquitous side-effects signal the demise of industrial society as classically understood and the shift into a reflexive modernity that is beset by counter-modern movements, including, for example, 'deep ecology', which in its imagination would revert to a pre-industrial and pre-modern condition. Reflexively modern society continues to seek economic growth but its logic of risk distribution is not equivalent to the logic of wealth distribution which had hitherto been contested along class lines. The poor are still the most vulnerable actual or potential casualties of the 'organized irresponsibility' of risk taking and they are spatially disadvantaged, as in the siting of hazardous industry, such as chemical plants. The wealthy are keenest to protect their 'environment' in spite of their comparative advantages and protection from manifest hazard. There is, nevertheless, something peculiarly democratic about risk society: '*poverty is hierarchic, smog is democratic*' (Beck 1992a: 36). Nobody, in the end, is safe: the beneficiaries are also the victims. Thus, environmental politics are not fundamentally about class conflict, although it does tend to be the comparatively affluent who display the greatest concern about risks to their own health and safety that result from wealth creation and, specifically, a comfortable and high-tech lifestyle. There is no necessary revolutionary subject of environmental politics, however, because everyone is more or less vulnerable. Risk society is, therefore, both individualizing and universalizing. To quote Beck again:

> The driving force in the class society can be summarized in the phrase: *I am hungry!* The movement set in motion by the risk society, on the other hand, is expressed in the statement: *I am afraid!* The *commonality of anxiety* takes the place of the *commonality of need*. The type of the risk society makes in this sense a social epoch in which *solidarity from anxiety* arises and becomes a political force.
>
> (Beck 1992a: 49)

According to Beck there is a cultural 'overlap' between anxieties to do with ecological hazard and the anxieties of routine sociality, both generated by a society in which security is undermined:

> Traditional and institutional forms of coping with fear and insecurity in the family, in marriage, sex roles, and class consciousness, as well as in

the parties related to them, lose meaning. In equal measure it comes to be demanded of the individuals that they cope with fear and anxiety. Sooner or later, new demands on social institutions in education, therapy and politics are bound to arise from these increasing demands to work out insecurity by oneself . . . In the risk society, therefore, handling fear and insecurity becomes an *essential cultural qualification*, and the cultivation of the abilities demanded for it becomes an essential mission of pedagogical institutions.

(Beck 1992a: 76)

Individualization is socially and culturally produced under conditions of reflexive modernity, bringing into actual existence a social subjectivity long canvassed by bourgeois ideology, yet in the past restrained by class and tradition. In such a society individuals expect to control their fates, to spend their money and time as they wish, to be in command of their bodies and their living spaces. These are increasingly common expectations, though with the highly educated leading the way in authoring their own biographies, determining career paths, accepting and rejecting social obligations, and so forth. Older fixities of class and status are less acceptable. It is a kind of Americanization of the self.

The 'nuclear family' was a cornerstone of industrial capitalism and simple modernity, reproducing labour power, sustaining patriarchy and serving, ideally, as a safe haven for the individual. Feminism and rising rates of divorce have undermined that institution's stability for many members of a reflexively modern society. As Ulrich Beck and Elizabeth Beck-Gernsheim state:

Individualization means that men and women are released from the gender roles prescribed by industrial society for life in the nuclear family. At the same time, and this aggravates the situation, they find themselves forced, under pain of material disadvantage, to build up a *life of their own* by way of the labour market, training and mobility, and if need be to pursue this life at the cost of their commitments to family, relations and friends.

(Beck and Beck-Gernsheim 1995 [1990]: 6)

What we find, then, are a set of *'personalized contradictions'* (Beck 1992a: 105) in individual conduct and primary social relationships. No role can simply be prescribed. Women, in particular, struggle with contradictory aspirations and expectations in work, partnership and childcare. At the same time, men are disabused of the taken-for-granted support of women in terms of wifing, mothering and housework. Singlehood, serial monogamy, multiplex families arising from divorce and remarriage – in none of these arrangements are rules and conventions reliably established. Yet, they are increasingly common features of life in a reflexively modern society. We are all existentialists now. Beck comments:

> Individualization of life situations and processes thus means that biographies become *self-reflexive*; socially prescribed biography is transformed into biography that is self-produced and continues to be produced. Decisions on education, profession, job, place of residence, spouse, number of children and so forth, with all the secondary decisions implied, no longer can be, they must be made. Even where the word 'decisions' is too grandiose, because neither consciousness or alternatives are present, the individual will have to 'pay for' the consequences of decisions not taken.
>
> (Beck 1992a: 135)

So, in personal life, and not only in wealth creation, science, technology and official politics, risky decisions have to be taken with no guarantees as to outcome or, normally, sufficient insurance cover. Which is not to say there is no guidance or insurance on offer: it is just that they are unreliable in a complex and chancy social world. These are, in global terms, the problems of comparative wealth and affluence. They are likely to arise wherever the process of late or reflexive modernization is underway, for instance, in the middle-class enclaves of post-colonial countries.

Reflexive modernization also has a transformative effect on politics. What was hitherto considered unpolitical is politicized. Environmental and personal politics constitute a '*sub-politics*' of public opinion and definitional conflict in which social movements and the modern media are crucial actors. Simon Cottle (1998) has argued that Beck is too vague on the mediation of risk politics. This partly relates to a deficiency in his general social theory where there is a tendency to slide between ontological insecurity and epistemological uncertainty, between being and knowing. Such inconsistency is explicable with regard to Beck's overly rationalistic and cognitive understanding of culture, involving the assumption that people only feel insecure when they do not know what to think. According to Cottle, Beck's risk society paradigm needs to be explored with empirical research on how the politics of risk is actually mediated in specific cases, some examples of which are given later in this chapter.

Another criticism of Beck's general thesis is the marginal role he ascribes to capitalism. His more or less exclusive attention to *industrialism* and environmental hazard is very much marked by the divided history of Germany from the late 1940s until 1990, split between the capitalist west and the communist east. For Beck (1995b), however, the Chernobyl disaster was clearly as much an indictment of soviet communism as of industrialism in general. Yet, still, it is odd that he rarely refers to the role of corporate business and capital accumulation in the construction of a risky world. While acknowledging Beck's reflexive modernity as 'a valid defence of the idea of a "rational" society against postmodern critics', Michael Rustin (1994: 7) questions the idealism of his perspective and its neglect of capitalism. Under the influence of Jurgen Habermas and in a Weberian tradition, Beck places much more emphasis on 'norms and ideas' than on 'other agencies and powers', observes Rustin. He goes on to argue:

> Another interpretation can be made of this whole development. According to this, it is not abstract rationality which is its driving force, but rather the instrumental rationality of capital. It is the commodification of everything which is transforming the world, desacralising what was formerly sacred (the family, the natural world), breaking up those institutions (welfare states, trade unions, entrenched employment rights) which offered resistance to capital accumulation, instrumentalising even knowledge itself. The fundamental right on which this system is based, which Beck hardly refers to, is the right to property. It is 'shareholder democracy' – one share one vote – not citizen democracy – 'one person one vote' – which rules our world, and reason and science are deployed mainly as its instruments.
>
> (Rustin 1994: 11)

Rustin's critical comment on Beck's risk society thesis is resonant of the tone and analytical acuity of *The Communist Manifesto* but without anything like the same political optimism. Perhaps Marx and Engels were right all along: it is capitalism that changes the world; and, by implication, latterday risk consciousness and a 'postmodernist' reflexivity in all aspects of life are best understood in relation to the renewed dynamism of globalizing capitalism. That, however, is a very general though indispensable thesis, requiring local analyses of the precise determinations and mediations in play a century and a half after *The Communist Manifesto* was written.

Bad timing

In spite of its neglect of the specifically capitalist dynamics of a risky world, the thesis of reflexive modernization presents a revised understanding of the social and cultural present that must be taken seriously; and, one which makes sense of a great many current trends. It breaks with simple modernist assumptions about inevitable progress yet, simultaneously, stands against postmodernism's rejection of the emancipatory project of modernity. Inevitably, contemporary debates over the constitution of the present, including the relative balance between persistence and change, raise questions concerning time, occurring coincidentally with a popular interest in time at the turn of a millennium (Gould 1997). Is this a moment of fundamental transition from one time to another? What is time in any case? Two models of time are deeply embedded in western culture, as Stephen Jay Gould (1988 [1987]) has argued, time as an 'arrow' and time as a 'cycle'. 'Time's arrow' conceives of history, natural and social, as linear, as in geology and in the succession of societal epochs. In contrast, 'time's cycle', indicates repetition and recurrence, as in the seasons, birth, death and renewal, and also in allegedly millennial panics and, more frequently, *fin-de-siècle* anxieties.

Linear and cyclical time, deep seated though they be, are not the only time frames. There is also the question of speed. Time can be very fast, most notably in the annihilation of space by time, as in telecommunications. It can be very slow, 'glacial or evolutionary' (Macnaghten and Urry 1998: 147), the time of geological change and Darwinian natural selection. The long-term effects of the misuse of nature come into this slower time frame which is difficult to measure in life's time since the consequences are most severe for future generations. Many of the hazards, however, are slow but not that slow, for example, in the passage of BSE (bovine spongiform encephalopathy) to CJD (Creutzfeldt-Jacob disease), from cows to human beings; say, a decade. Delayed effects give rise to disputes over time, causation and meaning. This is not just a matter of time-scale but to do with what we can know and how we can know it, the tensions between science and common sense, the tensions within science and common sense. Ulrich Beck has warned of the futile game of proof that environmental activists are obliged to play with official authorities and big business. 'Proof' itself becomes a weapon in the conflict over hazards, in defence of the system against life. Incontrovertible proof is hard to come by, especially when time frames are out of sync. John Maynard Keynes, the economist, once remarked that in the long run we are all dead, thereby enunciating an underlying attitude that sustains economistic and instrumental reason against other modes of reasoning.

Since the Brundtland Report of 1987, and confirmed by the Rio Summit of 1992, environmentalism has become mainstream and is largely figured in terms of a discourse of 'sustainability'. Rather than seeing this as a public breakthrough for ecological sanity, however, many critics are concerned about discursive management of 'the problem' by governments and corporations within what has been called 'the dominant "technological" paradigm in environmental knowledge' (Lash *et al.* 1996: 3). Beck himself is criticized for not having broken sufficiently with this paradigm. For Scott Lash, Bronislaw Szerszynski and Brian Wynne (1996: 1), Beck's reasoning is, in effect, consistent with the 'epistemologically "realist", positivistic, disembedded, technological and cognitivist' reasoning of mainstream environmental discourse in corporate and governmental circles. Mainstream environmental discourse, they say, 'tends to mask important cultural, social and existential dimensions of the contemporary "environmental crisis"' (Lash *et al.* 1996: 1).

In arguing the case here for understanding environmental 'problems' as socially and culturally produced, as a matter of discursivity and not hard fact, Lash *et al.* (1996) conflate together a number of issues, not least of which is their equation of epistemological realism with empiricism and positivism. Beck himself is clearly not an empiricist, as his questioning of the discourse of 'proof' demonstrates. That sufficient evidence cannot always be adduced and the extent of future or even current damage quantified precisely for many of the hazards that are unleashed by modern industrialism does not mean that they do not exist. Their existence may just be a figment of the imagination, but that is not what Beck means. Rather, we have to theorize the unforeseen consequences of current actions, hypothesize the implications, thus deploying a mode of reasoning that is derived from analysis of social and institutional processes. Such a mode of reasoning assumes that risks are taken with the environment and people's lives, in order to sustain high levels of consumption, which are incalculable scientifically and beyond the instrumental comprehension of cost-benefit analysis. This is a realist argument, drawing upon theoretical analysis of subterranean and not so subterranean tendencies that are not in themselves entirely mysterious, and evinced according to an emancipatory knowledge interest (Bhaskar 1989). To equate such reasoning with empiricist fact grubbing and positivistic law making in social science only confuses the analytical and interpretative questions at stake in any debate over risk.

Bryan Wynne's work is very important in this respect. He criticizes Beck's 'overly realist account' (Wynne 1996: 44) and says, 'I agree with Lash' (1996: 45). What he seems to be agreeing with, in this instance, is a thoroughgoing social constructionism in the study of environmental risk which bears no family resemblance to a **critical realism** that seeks to combine 'objectivity', in some sense, with an appreciation of discursivity and subjectivity. Yet, Wynne also claims, and with good reason, that such an approach is not anti-scientific. In effect, what he actually studies is a conflict between expert and lay knowledges. He remarks,

vernacular, informal knowledge which lay people may well have about the validity of expert assumptions about real-world conditions – say, about the production, use or maintenance of a technology – is . . . an important general category of lay knowledge that is usually systematically under-recognized.

(Wynne 1996: 59)

Wynne proceeds to tell the story of his own research on sheep farming in Cumbria in the wake of the Chernobyl disaster of 1986.

Following governmental denials that radioactive fallout from Chernobyl would cause any problems in Britain, the Ministry of Agriculture suddenly imposed a three-week ban on the sale of sheep from hill regions such as around the Lake District in June 1986. This was obviously alarming for local farmers but they were reassured by scientists on behalf of the ministry that the half-life for caesium in sheep was twenty days and so business would soon be allowed to return to normal. When the three weeks had elapsed, however, the ban was not lifted. The scientists had revised their predictions due to belated awareness of local soil characteristics that had not been taken into account in the earlier calculation. In the first instance they had made an unwarrantedly universalistic assumption about the persistence of radiocaesium. Farmers were permitted to sell off their sheep but not for food. Questions then began to arise about radioactivity in the area where the Sellafield nuclear power plant is located. Under its earlier name of Windscale, this plant had caught fire in 1957. Local belief in persistent contamination from the 1957 accident and leakages since gave rise to a suspicion that Chernobyl was now being used to cover up an old scandal. Revisions of scientific prediction and a history of governmental secrecy fuelled scepticism in the area. Trust in scientists and the government reached a low ebb in the locality, unsurprisingly. Scientists insisted on the superiority of their knowledge, in spite of ignorance of local conditions, the use of general models that might not apply in particular cases and their association with clumsy and short-termist governmental manipulation of public opinion in a fraught situation.

What Wynne is most keen to demonstrate is that science does not operate in a vacuum: it is socially situated and apparent irrationalities in scientific practice may issue from human foibles and institutional imperatives. In effect, he provides a socially realist account of the imbrications of knowledge and power in a specific case study. This enables him to question Giddens's distinction between expert and lay knowledges in which expertise, scientific and otherwise, remains uninterrogated. One of the practical implications is that scientists should be much more reflexive about their own practices, recognizing their social situatedness and the fallibility of their judgements. No critical realist would disagree.

Technocratic expertise must not go unquestioned and the lessons of emancipatory modes of social and cultural analysis are needed in contribution to halting the madness that is frequently given a scientific and now even an ecologically 'responsible' imprimatur. This is of vital importance when environmentalism has ceased to be primarily an object of anti-systemic campaigning and has become incorporated into the rhetoric of dominant powers around the world. In his contribution to the Lash, Szerszynski and Wynne book, Robin Grove-White sums up what is at stake on a global scale very well:

> The interpretation of ecological modernisation as a technocratic project holds that the ecological crisis requires more than social learning by existing social organisations. Its structuring principle is that not nature but technology is out of control. In this context it draws upon the dichotomies dominant-peripheral and material-symbolic. It holds that ecological modernisation is propelled by an elite of policy makers, experts and scientists that imposes its definition of problems and solutions on the debate. An empirical example is the UN Brundtland Report. It is a 'nice try' but, as the Rio Conference and its aftermath show so dramatically, it falters because it is only able to generate global support by going along with the main institutional interests of national and international elites as expressed by nation states, global managerial organisations like the World Bank or the IMF, and the various industrial interests that hide behind these actors. Hence ecological modernisation is a case of 'real problems' and 'false solutions'. The material-symbolic dichotomy surfaces in the conviction that there is a deeper reality behind all the window dressing. Behind the official 'rhetoric' of ecological modernisation one can discern the silhouette of technocracy in a new guise that stands in the way of implementing 'real solutions' for what are very 'real problems'.
>
> (Grove-White 1996: 253)

Problems of knowledge and action with regard to environmental risk are usefully considered in the 'timescape perspective' proposed by Barbara Adam (1998). She is interested in 'the combination of existential threat, scientific uncertainty and governmental bungling' (1998: 3). Yet, like similar social critics of environmental politics, Adam (1998: 8) stresses 'the futility of the quest for objectivity and static truth'. Still, the aims would seem to be to achieve a more satisfactory explanation than is routinely provided by systemic power and to obtain some popular guidance for what to do. Adam describes her approach:

> I focus on the conflicts that arise within the industrial modes of life from
> a) the complexity and interpenetration of rhythms: cosmic, natural and
> cultural; b) the imposition of industrial time on the rhythmicity and
> pace of ecosystems; and c) the prevailing emphasis on visible materiality
> and quantity at the expense of that which is hidden from view or latent.
>
> (Adam 1998: 9)

Fundamental here is how industrial cycles of production, distribution and
investment, 'machine, economic and laboratory time' (Adam 1998: 11) conflict with the time of 'nature' and cyclical renewal of natural resources. Also,
we cannot always see and quantify what is going on in a way that suits
empirical science and liberal-democratic procedure. Radiation is a perfect
example for the timescape perspective:

> Radiation works silently and invisibly from within. It is known only to
> our cells. As such, it proceeds outside the everyday reach of our senses.
> Its materiality extending beyond the capacity of human perception and
> sensibility (except where extended by scientific instruments), radiation
> affects the collective present and long-term future, our own and other
> species' daughters and sons of a thousand years hence. It permeates all
> life forms to varying degrees and it disregards boundaries: skin, clothes
> and walls, cities and nations, the demarcation between the elements. It
> is a fate that we share with a global community of beings. Unbounded,
> it is dispersed in time and space and marked by complex temporalities
> and time–space configurations. Its lifecycles of decay span from
> nanoseconds to millennia. This means its time horizon too exceeds
> human capacity and concern. Thus, at the level of everyday life, outside
> conceptions where real means material and where this in turn is defined
> by its accessibility to the senses. Invisibility, vast, incredibly fast, and
> variable spans of decay, networked interdependence and the fact that
> effects are not tied to the time and place of emission, therefore, make
> radiation a cultural phenomenon that poses problems for traditional
> ways of knowing and relating to the material world.
>
> (Adam 1998: 10)

In addition to her general discussion of timescapes, Adam provides specific
case studies such as one concerning the BSE crisis in Britain which demonstrates the interlocking forces of government, media and science in misman-
aging food hazard and befuddling public opinion through time. In March
1996 the British Conservative government announced a causal connection
between BSE in cattle, brought about by feeding these herbivorous creatures
meat, and the contraction of CJD by humans, with a number of cases

already notified. This overturned previous governmental assurances that there was no such possible connection and resulted in a ban on British beef in mainland Europe and great popular uncertainty in Britain as to whether home produced beef was safe to eat or not. The government persistently contradicted itself in public pronouncements and quite contrary scientific opinion was available and reported upon in the news media. As a citizen, apart from her role as a student of such processes, Adam declared herself confused, confronted with a plethora of information, none of which could be relied upon. The BSE crisis illustrated, among other things, the pressure on science to claim certitude. As Adam (1998: 166–7) notes acutely, 'Where scientists are resistant to come up with quantifications and facts, journalists and politicians tend to do their job for them: the vague and propositional language of science gets translated into politically and economically accept-able certainties and assurances'. The fact of the matter is, however, that '[i]ndeterminacy and uncertainty stare us in the face wherever we look and search for reliable information' (Adam 1998: 188). In the BSE crisis, the time of news and opinion management had nothing to do with the time of the hazard, incubating for several years previously unbeknown to the public. Once the story had fallen out of the news the hazard had not necessarily gone away nor was it unavailable for a renewed spate of reporting and calls upon scientific expertise to make unreliable claims.

Commenting on Adam's case study of the BSE crisis, Macnaghten and Urry (1998) draw out four general inferences from the research. First, the risks of beef eating in Britain illustrate open-endedness, uncertainty, contin-gency and 'multiple assumptions of the social world' (1998: 259). Second, public trust in the state and in science is undermined by such cases. Third, the nation-state is ill equipped to deal with these problems in a 'globalized world' not least because 'reductionist science-based methodologies' cannot help governments to 'assess adequately wider social and moral dimensions of risk associated with new innovations and practices' (1998: 262). Fourth, 'the BSE saga particularly highlights the timed and sensed dimensions of risk . . . Such risks associated with eating beef well illustrate how an everyday and taken-for-granted social practice can have unknown, unsensed and indeterminate effects in the barely imaginable future' (1998: 262). In Mac-naghten and Urry's opinion, BSE is not so much a risk in Beck's sense of calculated decision making but, rather, one of the hazards of a civilization that is committed to 'short-term economic gain' (1998: 265).

From the point of view of social and cultural analysis, the task is not so much to contest the validity of natural science as such, although some critics of a postmodern persuasion seem to wish to do so. Instead, it is necessary to draw critical attention to the emplacement of scientific research, application and technology in actual economic and political contexts, in effect, focusing upon the contested role of science in system reproduction. This leads to the questioning of certitudes that only bad science would circulate unproblematically, though the pressures to do so are great. Science is also of much broader social and cultural significance, as a sign of modern civilization. When science is called into question, doubt is reasonably cast upon modernity itself, which can give succour to all sorts of counter-modern prejudice as well as to developing reflexively modern understanding and practice. In a highly mediated society, science is brought before the court of the public on a daily basis, frequently in distorted ways, due to its astonishing capacity to tinker with nature, most controversially in genetic engineering and routinely when things go manifestly wrong. Nowadays, a great deal is 'known' about public opinion through a polling culture which has burgeoned in the interests of managing potentially volatile popular consciousness.

In *Contested Natures*, Macnaghten and Urry (1998) have identified the limitations of polling culture when it comes to public understanding of risk and environmental concern. There is a simplistic view that the efficacy of public information and the extent of public awareness can be tested satisfactorily by opinion polls. As with all survey research, however, such polling typically reduces complex matters of quality to quantity. Macnaghten and Urry also suggest that opinion polling fails to grasp subjective 'sensing'. They argue more generally that western culture places excessive importance upon the visible and neglects how 'touch, smell and sound are all involved in how we sense nature' (1998: 132). It is not uncommon now, moreover, for polls to report a decline in environmental concern. According to Macnaghten and Urry, research on environmental consciousness must at least be supplemented with qualitative methods or else we will miss what is actually thought and felt in everyday life about the environment of which everyone is a part.

In focus group research in northern England on 'sustainability', Macnaghten and Urry report that '[n]early all groups remarked on the emerging climate of uncertainty and the sense that life was becoming increasingly unpredictable' (1998: 221). A pervasive sense of fear for the future was evident in their research. To quote Macnaghten and Urry:

> the widespread fear of the future and the sense that lived conditions would be harder was also connected to apparently intractable forces of globalisation . . . we might suggest that people were responding to the dark side of modernity. Many people spoke to us in terms of a widespread sense of 'the system' that was geared to serving the interests of business and corporate finance, that was believed to be driving economic

and social life, that was infecting public institutions and the motivations of those employed in them, and that was beginning to structure personal aspects of daily life. Such trends were commonly perceived to be shaped by 'money' and 'self-interest', and to contribute towards an inappropriate 'short-termism' in public policy. Such perspectives were surprisingly shared across age and class variables in the form of pronounced fatalism and even cynicism towards institutions, and to expressed doubts of the willingness or ability of such institutions to contribute towards a better future. This perspective came to light most starkly in discussions about the role of the state and business in contributing towards a better future.

(Macnaghten and Urry 1998: 224)

A general sense of powerlessness meant that 'sustainability' was not in their command: participation did not feel like an option. Further research in the south of England revealed similar attitudes, feelings of loss and powerlessness. Macnaghtan and Urry (1998: 236) note that 'people identify their concerns about the environment in terms of what we have called "glacial" and evolutionary time'. This longer term, popular perspective on the environment is out of sync, then, with the short-term polling and quick-fix culture of government and business.

Although they do not interpret their findings in this way, Macnaghten and Urry's research makes sense in Jurgen Habermas's (1984 [1981]; 1987b [1981]) theoretical framework of the tensions between 'instrumental rationality' and 'communicative rationality' and between 'system' and 'life-world'. Participants in communicatively rational discourse construct their own purposes, whereas most participants in instrumentally rational discourse have the goals of action constructed for them. It may even appear as though nobody is actually responsible for determining the goals and purposes of action. They seem to be just there, dictated by impersonal economic and bureaucratic forces over which ordinary people have no control. These forces are systemic, bound up with complex processes of social reproduction and steered by the media of money and power. By contrast, in the everyday life-world, people may find spaces of communicative freedom that are not dictated by impersonal and systemic forces (see McGuigan 1998b for a fuller discussion of Habermas's conceptual apparatus).

For Habermas, modernity is characterized by the uncoupling of life-world and system. The system is animated by instrumental and strategic rationality which is over and above the comprehension of most people yet with which they have to comply in order, for instance, to earn a living. In comparison, life-world spaces are more open to creativity and self-fulfilment. Habermas has proposed two successive theses on the relationship between life-world and system (Carleheden and Gabriels 1996): the colonization thesis (Habermas 1987b) and the sluicegate model (Habermas 1996 [1992]). The colonization thesis suggests that instrumental rationality is invading the life-world, displacing communicative forms of sense making with the senselessness of instrumentalism. Under these conditions, it is necessary to gather together life-world resources and bring them to bear on systemic processes: hence the importance of social movements as advocates of progressive policy and in putting pressure on formally democratic governments. Feminist, environmental and other movements are thus seen as the necessary antidote to the encroachments of the system on the life-world. In his later work, Habermas supplements the colonization thesis with the sluicegate model whereby social movements force issues onto the political agenda that would not themselves be engendered by the system and the official public sphere:

> The great issues of the last decades give evidence for this. Consider, for example, the spiralling nuclear-arms race; consider the risks involved in the peaceful use of atomic energy or in other large-scale technological projects and scientific experimentation, such as genetic engineering; consider the ecological threats involved in an overstrained natural environment (acid rain, water pollution, species extinction, etc.); consider the dramatically progressing impoverishment of the Third World and problems of the World economic order; or consider such issues as feminism, increasing migration and the associated problems of multiculturalism. Hardly any of these topics were *initially* brought up by exponents of the state apparatus, large organizations or functional systems. Instead, they were broached by intellectuals, concerned citizens, radical professionals, self-proclaimed 'advocates' and the like.
>
> (Habermas 1996: 381)

Habermas's observations here put a politically optimistic gloss on the capacities of the life-world in relation to the system as mediated by progressive social movements. Yet, the mundane sense of hopelessness, with its pessimistic implications, registered by Macnaghten and Urry's research also has to be taken on board. It is not, however, inexplicable. André Gorz refers to

> the reality of Western societies, which stands revealed to those who gain access to it as cruelly bereft of orientation, of perspective, of an openness to goals which it might be meaningful to pursue. Deep down, fear of the future, withdrawal into the private sphere and despair are not products of the hole in the ozone layer or the greenhouse effect, not even of the justified fear of the consequences of – even a local – war. They are caused, rather, by this society's lack of a perspective and a

project, and by the impossibility of continuing much longer with its way of doing things, its way of life – and not merely locally, but on a world scale. And they are caused by the collapse of social cohesion and lived social relations, the crisis of socialization, the fierce competition between job-hunters and, indeed, by all those things that render individuals impotent in the face of autonomized processes and faceless powers, and give rise to impotent protests and hatreds, to abstract glorifications of brute force, to nationalist-racist passions about identity or to finicky religiosities.

(Gorz 1994 [1991]: 4)

Living with uncertainty

Voltaire wrote *Candide*, his satire on knowledge and suffering, in response to the Lisbon earthquake of 1755 in which 50,000 people died. How could Christians make sense of such an event? If God was good, why allow such a terrible disaster to befall his human subjects? The Lisbon earthquake was the topic of considerable theological disputation at the time. One argument in justification of suffering on Earth was the bequest of free will to the human being. God allowed his subjects to choose and, if they chose evil, so be it: they damned themselves. Such reasoning was no use, however, when it came to something like the Lisbon earthquake since nobody had exercised a choice: it was a *natural disaster*. The caricature apologist, Pangloss could argue that there was some ultimate good sense even here, that God had his reasons and, ultimately, it was still the best of all possible worlds. It is hardly surprising, then, that a Voltairean take on the Lisbon earthquake, a ruthless critical questioning of conventional wisdom in the spirit of Enlightenment, should articulate atheistic disbelief.

'Natural disasters' now are no longer just the work of nature and a problem of theology: they are, most significantly, the work of society and a problem for politics. This is the meaning of the risk society thesis, 'the central themes and perspectives' of which 'have to do with *fabricated uncertainty* within our civilization: risk, danger, side-effects, insurability, individualization and globalization' (Beck 1996: 1). Not so long ago, in the era of the Cold War, presaged by the American atom bombs dropped on Japan in 1945 which 'espoused a monstrous uncertainty both of future and morality' (Nuttall 1970 [1968]: 19), the greatest danger seemed to be mutual extermination. This is a danger that has not gone away, however, with the collapse of Soviet communism. The official purpose of the nuclear weapons build-up during the Cold War had been 'deterrence', the safety ensured by a phoney war. In actual fact, military strategists in the west were prepared to calculate the risks of a nuclear exchange, for instance, with the hypothesis, taken seriously in some circles, that it would knock out communism and set capitalism back only to the condition of the 1930s, a risk perhaps worth taking. That particular hypothesis was challenged by the nuclear winter thesis and the estimation that a nuclear war would return its few survivors to a condition somewhat less civilized than the dark ages, including the dissolution of language, which was so powerfully depicted in the BBC docu-drama, *Threads*, in 1984.

We may no longer live so self-consciously under the shadow of the bomb but, apparently, anxiety is a widespread social phenomenon in the richer countries of the world, like the USA and Britain, a feeling that even when and where things seem to be good they are really rather bad. This is, of course, the regular popular fare of certain strands of social and cultural commentary. An example is the book edited by Sarah Dunant and Roy Porter (1997), *The Age of Anxiety*. They remark, 'AIDS, Eboli, asthma from pollution, scientific research, global warming and a freak story of rape from a New York hospital. It doesn't take much to whip up dark-age-type millennial fever' (1997: ix). Again, there are the recurrent themes of a sense of powerlessness and fearfulness for what the future holds in store. Dunant and Porter virtually reduce the problem to psychology: 'As our choices appear to expand and our sense of control appears to diminish, how do we stop ourselves from being frightened of the future?' (1997: xvi). Although the contributors to Dunant and Porter's book consider a number of issues to do with, for instance, the need for community, a realistic attitude to technology rather than a utopian or dystopian one and a generally ironic and reflexive attitude to life, the question posed by the editors seems to call for psychotherapy of one kind or another.

A more sociological understanding is provided by Frank Furedi's (1997) *Culture of Fear*. His view may, at first, be seen as diametrically opposed to that of Ulrich Beck: 'It is striking that despite the many problems that face humanity, we live in a world that is far safer than at any time in history' (1997: 54). While Beck argues that we need not prove the extent of risk in order to argue for safety precautions, Furedi insists that the preoccupation with safety is itself a problem. On second glance, however, the difference between Beck and Furedi is not so great: they are both interested in risk consciousness and its politics. They both question prevailing knowledge strategies and institutionalized remedies. However, Furedi does emphasize the corrosive effects of risk consciousness. He remarks upon how demotic talk of 'risk' has changed from the positive orientation towards risk taking in 'a good risk' to the anxieties concerned with being 'at risk'. More and more people in more and more situations are deemed to be 'at risk'. This is quite apart from the catalogue of global doom and gloom, whereby human beings may destroy themselves and their environment, supplied by writers like John Leslie (1996). There is a common-sense attitude in everyday life which seems to imply that it is probably safest just to stay in bed in the morning provided that you don't smoke, that there are no incestuous members of the family around and the roof is secure. Homes and families, schools, workplaces and leisure venues are now seen as sites of risk, rather like the trenches were in the First World War.

One sign of a risk-conscious everyday life and its professional mediation is the phenomenal rise of counselling. Furedi (1997: 94) observes, 'Uncertainty about issues, an inability to make decisions or the disappointments associated with setbacks in life are now routinely diagnosed as symptoms of some kind of anxiety disorder'. Anti-social behaviour at school, students missing essay deadlines, the stresses of overwork, being made redundant, mid-life crises, bereavement, witnessing all manner of traumatic events and much else besides, are likely to be referred to an expert counsellor. These experts are said to know more about coping with the trials and tribulations of daily existence and the stresses and strains of the life course than the ordinary person for whom it has all become too much. This ubiquitous assumption is allied to a general medicalization of routinely experienced problems, in effect, disabling rather than aiding the person's capacity to cope socially, for people to find solutions for themselves. New syndromes are constantly being discovered to name and medicalize the mundane miseries of humanity and the shock effects of social change. Furedi sees all this as symptomatic of an undermining of subjectivity, resulting in the objectification of the self. The general effect is very conservative, according to Furedi, dissuading people from taking chances, experimenting and innovating, in effect, from being in command of their own lives.

The claims that are made about risk consciousness, particularly the identification of a generalized anxiety in everyday life and pervasive feelings of doubt and uncertainty, might be somewhat exaggerated yet they do, none the less, point up some striking features of the culture of capitalist civilization in the post-Cold War period. This may be linked at least partly to environmental risk but also it must be related to the economic insecurities that now characterize even the wealthiest societies. Furedi's analysis is contradictory in this respect. He asserts that the 'loss of confidence of capitalist society cannot be directly attributed to economics' yet goes on to note:

The stagnation of many leading capitalist economies has had a major impact on the quality of life. It has led to important changes in the structuring of economic life. The decline of manufacturing, the growth of structural unemployment and the shift towards part-time and temporary work are some of the important features of contemporary economic life. However, economic problems do not inexorably lead to a loss of confidence in society. Indeed what is particularly interesting today is that even the beneficiaries of the capitalist system express doubt and anxiety about the future.

(Furedi 1997: 65)

What Furedi fails to address is how the general restructuring of a socio-economic order may create a 'climate of fear' which is mediated for individuals in different ways according to their particular situations. Roughly speaking, it is not the same for everyone. Also, there are other authors, similarly concerned about the complexity of cultural determinations and not just economic determinations, who place greater explanatory emphasis on how changes in capitalist civilization, its organizational principles and ideological justifications, have contributed to the intensification of feelings of anxiety, insecurity and uncertainty that are not exclusively focused upon issues of material well-being. For Larry Elliott and Don Atkinson (1998), the revival of neo-classical economics, the insistence on market mechanisms for the management of everything and the erosion of the welfare state have fostered insecurity both materially and psychologically, for instance, fear of unemployment and proneness to self-doubt, that is, uncertainty about the capacity to fend for oneself alone. They say, if rather too bluffly, 'The "things which really matter" have not changed much over the years. People still want a steady job, decent pay, a healthy environment, personal freedom and somebody to rely on if the going gets a bit tough' (Elliott and Atkinson 1998: 247).

In his history of 'the short twentieth century', from 1914 to 1991, *Age of Extremes* (1994), Eric Hobsbawm attributes the current uncertainty to the eclipse of 'the Golden Age' of western capitalism. This period lasted from the Second World War until the recomposition of hegemony from the 1970s, the switch from state to market solutions, and the crisis of the socialist alternative, including both Soviet communism in the east and social democracy in the west. Over the course of 'the Golden Age', the conditions of ordinary people had been much improved due to full employment, mass consumption, welfare provision and social rights generally, such as grants for higher education. The social revolution had been accompanied by a cultural revolution, which broke with traditional ties and bonds, thus liberating the individual to the existential freedom that is simultaneously exhilarating and terrifying.

The greatest irony of the collapse of communism was not that socialism was now deemed to be in the past rather than in the future but, curiously enough, the malaise that was suddenly revealed at the very heart of triumphant capitalism, casting doubt upon the fundamental assumptions of modernity in its entirety. This had already been simmering for some time among intellectuals, particularly those disappointed by Marxism. There was no longer an available map of the future, either of liberal reform or radical revolution. The future had already arrived and required naming:

> When people face what nothing in their past has prepared them for they grope for words to name the unknown, even when they can neither define nor understand it. Some time in the third quarter of the century we can see the process at work among intellectuals of the West. The keyword was the small preposition 'after', generally used in its latinate form 'post' as a prefix to any of the numerous terms which had, for some generations, been used to mark out the mental territory of twentieth century life. The world, or its relevant aspects, became post-industrial, post-imperial, post-modern, post-structuralist, post-Marxist, post-Gutenberg, or whatever. Like funerals, these prefixes took official recognition of death without implying any consensus or indeed certainty about the nature of life after death. In this way the greatest and most dramatic, rapid and universal social transformation in history entered the consciousness of reflective minds who lived through it.
>
> (Hobsbawm 1994: 287–8)

Not even science was safe, now routinely assailed by sociologists of knowledge and cultural critics as just another myth system upholding a *passé* modernity, the civilization of western capitalism and its offshoot in eastern communism. It was this attack on the greatest sacred cow of the Enlightenment which resulted in *l'affaire Sokal*. In 1996, the American cultural theory journal, *Social Text*, published the physicist Alan Sokal's seminal essay, 'Transgressing the boundaries: toward a transformative hermeneutics of quantum gravity', in which he declared redundant

> the dogma imposed by the long post-Enlightenment hegemony over the Western intellectual outlook, which can be summarized briefly as follows: that there exists an external world, whose properties are independent of any individual human being and indeed of humanity as a whole; that these properties are encoded in 'external' physical laws; and that human beings can obtain reliable, albeit imperfect and tentative, knowledge of these laws by hewing to the 'objective' procedures and epistemological strictures prescribed by the (so-called) scientific method.
>
> (Sokal 1996: 219)

This was a famous hoax. Sokal did not hold to such a view at all. In fact, he believed exactly the opposite: that the real world exists and that objectivity is possible if scientific method is used appropriately. The whole article was a clever parody of a certain kind of cultural studies writing, full of scientific absurdities made credible by deadpan delivery, the full panoply of academic citation and appeal to the authority of 'postmodern' theory. Sokal, a self-declared leftist, perpetrated the hoax because he was fed up with a fashionable cultural studies that had severed emancipatory politics from truth seeking. It is unfortunate that the hoax should have been pulled, however, on Andrew Ross, editor of the special issue of *Social Text* on 'the science wars'. Ross himself had well demonstrated the value of a cultural critique of science, particularly in questioning Richard Dawkins's ideology-laden metaphor for 'the selfish gene' in his 'Chicago gangster theory of life' (Ross 1994) and, also, in generally avoiding the use of science in order to give spurious authority to his own work, which is what Sokal went on to attack in his book with Jean Bricmont, *Intellectual Impostures* (1998 [1997]). There, Bricmont and Sokal identified the casual appropriation of science by a number of French writers who had shaped 'postmodern' thought, including Baudrillard, Kristeva and Lacan. In appropriating bits and pieces of science, not just for analogous and metaphorical purposes but, instead, to beef up their general arguments, these gurus had misunderstood and misrepresented numerous elementary scientific propositions, Sokal and Bricmont demonstrate through close readings. Several specific cases of the misuse of scientific knowledge are thus identified which, by implication, cast doubt upon the work of the doubters themselves. Sokal and Bricmont are clear about their ultimate target:

> Vast sectors of the humanities and the social sciences seem to have adopted a philosophy that we shall call, for want of a better word, 'postmodernism': an intellectual current characterised by the more-or-less explicit rejection of the rationalist tradition of the Enlightenment, by theoretical discourses disconnected from any empirical test, and by a cognitive and cultural relativism that regards science as nothing more than a 'narration', a 'myth' or a social construction among many others.
>
> (Sokal and Bricmont 1998: 1)

In fact, on the question of cultural relativism, Sokal and Bricmont are themselves agnostic; but not so on cognitive or *epistemic* relativism, the assumption that all 'truth', including scientific ones, are particular to the groups and societies that believe them and have no greater universal validity. This might imply, then, that the forces of gravity are socially constructed, a matter of intersubjective agreement, and not 'objective' in any demonstrable sense. Sokal and Bricmont cite an example of this kind of reasoning in a comment by the anthropologist, Yves Winkin, on a dispute that arose between a police officer and a judge over evidence concerning kidnap murders of children in Belgium. The police officer said he had sent a key file to the judge who claimed never to have received it. Winkin commented, 'anthropologically, there are only partial truths, shared by a larger or smaller number of people, a group, a family, a firm. There is no transcendent truth. Therefore, I don't think that judge Doutrewe or officer Lesage are hiding anything: both are telling their truth' (quoted by Sokal and Bricmont 1998: 91). As Sokal and Bricmont observe, the file might have been lost in the post and it is possible that neither the judge nor the police officer were lying. Yet, it is ludicrous to contend, as Winkin does, that the question of truth ends with the incommensurability and subjectivity of participant truths. Evidence of actual loss of the file or the dishonesty of one of the participants (for example, the file discovered in the police officer's or even the judge's bottom drawer) would elicit a different truth: perhaps an objective truth? This is, to be sure, quite a trivial example. Sokal and Bricmont give larger practical examples, for instance, the use of western medicine in, say, a Third World context where local beliefs and practices may have no remedy for a disease that the applied knowledge of modern science can cure.

While Sokal's intervention is dismissed as an illegitimate and mischievous move by postmodern relativists, he has done a service in at least suggesting that the Emperor's new clothes are less in evidence than is generally thought to be the case in the humanities and soft social sciences. He and Bricmont are also right to have drawn attention to the disjunction between a commitment to demystification and truth telling and what frequently passes for radical critique in the academy these days. However, it would be unfortunate if Sokal and Bricmont's intervention was used to discredit the proper questioning of scientific practice, especially concerning the institutional pressures to claim certitude where none exists and routine procedures that are light years away from the Enlightenment's critical reasoning. The sociologist of science, Steve Fuller (1997) has usefully distinguished between Enlightenment and positivist attitudes to science. For the Enlightenment, science was a bold, critical practice that questioned authority; for positivism, it is a professional authority itself. With the institutionalization of science through industrialism, it was inevitable that science would become instrumental and pragmatic in its mainstream orientation; and, often mystifying in practice. Perhaps it is unrealistic now to recall the Enlightenment's critical and emancipatory view of science: however, this is, I believe, what animates Sokal and Bricmont's intervention rather than a conservative defence of institutionalized science. In a

similar vein, Christopher Norris (1998) has made the old story of Enlightenment sound attractive in reflexive times:

> It may be unfashionable, but I think that we must start from the values
> associated with the Enlightenment, such as progress, notions of truth
> and of the concept of ideology and the possibility of criticising ideology.
> Critics of these values, especially 'postmodern' critics, have constructed
> a very crude image of the Enlightenment. It has become a bugbear that
> stands for certain authoritarian ideas of truth and progress – as if the
> Enlightenment were a unitary, monolithic movement. But the En-
> lightenment was nothing if not a movement devoted to criticism and
> debate. Advancing it need not mean imposing some set of narrow, west-
> ern European, post-1750 values onto their cultures. It doesn't tell
> people what to believe; it is about suggesting ways that they might think
> more critically about what they already believe. One standard post-
> modernist objection to the Enlightenment is that this is contradictory.
> Kant says, 'Dare to think for yourself'. The postmodernist might reply:
> 'If you order someone to think for themselves, then you are effectively
> saying: "Don't think for yourself, think like I do and adopt the follow-
> ing prescriptions as to what you should think"'. But what Kant was
> actually saying was: 'Take nothing as gospel. Criticise everything,
> including what I am saying now and my own philosophical ideas and
> beliefs'. That is the core of the Enlightenment: perpetual self-criticism,
> taking nothing on trust.
>
> (Norris 1998: 21)

Conclusion

In this chapter I have sought to show how the kinds of issues raised by a
postmodernist imaginary can be made sense of in the terms of the reflexive
modernization thesis. At its worst postmodernism encourages an ironic
detachment and nihilistic indifference when confronted with the complex
problems of a rapidly changing world. At its best it opens up new terrains of
criticism, for example, concerning the certitudes of science. A sceptical and
questioning attitude in this respect is valuable but there are risks in this as in
everything else. A cavalier challenge to science is in danger of supporting
forms of irrationalism that reject any possibility of addressing the problems
of life and environment in a capitalist civilization that periodically wheels
out of control.

The finer values of the Enlightenment or, if you prefer, the modern project offer a means of remaining sane on what is, admittedly, a crazy scene.

Nothing is certain but rational criticism helps. It has always been difficult to chart a course through life: it is just rather more complicated now when there is so much to think about and decide upon. The questions are not only existential, however: they are also epistemological. An unqualified embrace of uncertainty, in this respect, undercuts the grounds for critique and, consequently, the emancipatory power of social and cultural criticism. The intervention by Sokal and Bricmont, though sobering, does not finally refute epistemic relativism in the humanities and social sciences where it may have greater justification than in the natural sciences but such an intervention should make us think again.

CONCLUSION

To conclude, just one final example of the wit and wisdom of postmodernism:

> At some point in the 1980s, history took a turn in the opposite direction. Once the apogee of time, the summit of the curve of evolution, the solstice of history had been passed, the downward slope of events began and things began to run in reverse. It seems that like cosmic space, historical space-time is also curved. By the same chaotic effect in time as in space, things go quicker and quicker as they approach their term, just as water mysteriously accelerates as it approaches a waterfall.
>
> . . . By this reversion of history to infinity, this hyperbolic curvature, the century itself is escaping its end. By this retroaction of events, we are eluding our own deaths. Metaphorically, then, we shall not even reach the symbolic term of the end, the symbolic turn of the year 2000.
>
> (Baudrillard 1994b [1992]: 10, 11)

Writing in the early 1990s, Jean Baudrillard could thus announce that history had already gone into reverse and the Year 2000 would never be reached; a statement dressed up in quasi-scientific language and meant only as a metaphor, of course, for the implosion of the real in a culture that devours and resignifies everything. I find Baudrillard's quip amusing. It makes me think but not for long. Writing at the end of the 1990s, and anticipating that most of the readings of this book will occur after the Year 2000 happens, I feel that I must look elsewhere for the meaning of the millennium, to Hillel Schwartz (1996 [1990]), for instance, on the history of how centuries have ended and the evidence of what happened at the end of the first Christian millennium (he contests the view that there was a great panic). On why the millennium is arbitrary yet does indeed matter, I might turn to Stephen Jay Gould (1997), who explains how apocalypse turned into calendrics. When the end does not come, time still has to be measured. The apocalypse did not occur when the Year 1000 arrived nor will it (nor did it) with the Year 2000, although some computers may well have gone on the blink. Disputes will no doubt continue over Diminutive Dennis's omission of the Year Zero from the old Julian calendar and, in effect, from what eventually became the Gregorian calendar. Time is a funny business. Human beings impose classificatory schemes on a messy reality and they frequently get it wrong. The timing of a year itself is a tricky problem since it takes 365 days, 5 hours, 48 minutes and 45.96768 seconds for the Earth to go round the Sun, necessitating leap years which are sometimes not leap years. There is no necessary reason for dividing blocks of years into thousands except that it used to mean something to Christians. Now, it means something to everyone since in the modern world time is coordinated to facilitate trade and communication. The meaning of the Year 2000 is instrumental, like any other year, not apocalyptic.

It is conventional to distinguish between instrumental reason and critical reason and, as I have suggested in this book, this is a pertinent distinction if one wants to understand the contradictoriness of modernity, its pragmatic power and its invocation of criticism. To all intents and purposes, Jean-François Lyotard (1984 [1979]) equated postmodern knowledge with instrumental reason in his argument concerning the pragmatics of science after the demise of grand narratives and great promises. For him, critical reason no longer applies to what makes the world go round. Baudrillardian reasoning, on the other hand, is quite different from Lyotard's accommodative attitude, but it is not critical reason. It might usefully be called ironic reason, bordering on unreason. Baudrillard is not prepared to accommodate to the way things really are, to the instrumental reason of an entirely disenchanted modernity. Confronted with an absurd world, Baudrillard displays irony, not criticism since that, for him, is itself absurd. It is this ironic detachment which is the epitome of postmodernism. It is undeniably attractive and not inaccurate, up to a point. The refusal of critical reason is, however, ultimately nihilistic. It is not enough to simply throw your hands up at the absurdity of it all. We live in a world of globalizing capitalism, of environmental risk and great uncertainty. Yet there is considerable hope in the sheer fluidity of culture and identity, of the breaking down of old barriers and the opening up of new networks of possibility. In this kind of context, different modes of reasoning perform different functions. Instrumental reason is useful but blind. Ironic reason is fun but irresponsible. Critical reason is vital.

GLOSSARY

The purpose of this selective glossary is not to provide exact dictionary definitions of words but, rather, to specify how certain key terms in the text of this book are used.

Accentuated modernity: the globalization of modernity's transformative dynamics, characteristic of capitalist civilization, involving the further erosion of tradition; and which gives rise to the anxieties and uncertainties that are inaccurately labelled 'postmodernity', according to Giddens.

Capitalism: an exploitative economic system, driven by the imperative of capital accumulation, the ultimate logic of which is to turn all human products into marketable commodities and to mediate all social relations.

Cognitive mapping: a speculative aesthetic principle, not a particular form, that is supposed to produce a sense of orientation for the human subject in society and space, according to Jameson.

Critical realism: an epistemological perspective which assumes the real world is analytically knowable, though knowledge is infinitely revisable, and that the normative purpose of social and cultural theory is human emancipation.

Cultural racism: the kind of racism that stresses irreconcilable differences between people on grounds of religion, customs and habits, rather than making claims about biological superiority and inferiority. The postmodernist stress on difference, though usually articulated in terms of oppositional and even emancipatory politics, sometimes comes uncomfortably close to cultural racism.

Double-coding: a term originally used by Jencks to refer to the combination of modern techniques and vernacular (local, traditional, popular) styles in architecture, taken up by Eco with reference to the kind of literary text (and, by extension, cultural texts in general, including films) that appeals to both 'intellectual' and 'popular' tastes, such as his own, *The Name of the Rose*.

Enlightenment: an historical phase and persistent strand of modern thought emphasizing critical reason and the questioning of conventional wisdom.

Epistemology: the branch of philosophy concerned with theories of knowledge, how we know and make sense of the world. For Lyotard, postmodernity is an epistemological condition, a state of knowledge in which grand, legitimizing narratives are no longer convincing.

Fordism: a term originally used by the Italian Marxist, Antonio Gramsci, to characterize the kind of social relations and everyday culture that accompany mass production and assembly-line techniques of manufacturing. Whereas Fordism produced standardized products and fostered homogeneous lifestyles, it is said that its successor, post-Fordism, produces an heterogeneity of products customized for increasingly diverse lifestyles and responsive to rapid changes of taste. Some commentators argue, however, that the present situation is better described not as post-Fordist but, instead, as neo-Fordist, a more subtle system of mass production and consumption.

Globalization: processes that work at speed on a world scale, including cultural and political forces but most importantly economic forces. Castells argues that the late-twentieth century global economy is distinguished from the early-twentieth century world economy by the fact that it operates in unitary time so that market information circulates instantaneously, facilitated by computing and telecommunications.

Hyperreality: an artificial yet heightened sense of reality, as in the simulated environments and simulacra of theme parks and cyberspace.

Identity: socially and culturally constructed sense of self that is usually associated with attachment to various collectivities, including nations and ethnic groups, and increasingly takes hybrid rather than pure forms.

Industrialism: use of inanimate sources of energy and the transformation of nature in manufacturing on a widespread and large scale.

Metanarrative: a term used by Lyotard to refer to stories about stories, all-encompassing and totalizing narratives, such as Marxism and various other stories of progress associated with the Enlightenment.

Modernism: the art and culture of avant-garde movements, mainly, but also referring to the representational techniques of modern, mass-reproduced media such as the cinema.

Modernity: the social institutions and principles of capitalist civilization, including the globalization of industrialism, mass surveillance and technological warfare, as theorized by Giddens.

Modes of production: a Marxist term referring to the combination of forces of production (labour power, technology) and relations of production (ultimately class relations, as between capitalists and workers) that characterize different historical periods, such as feudalism and capitalism.

Network society: the advanced form of capitalist civilization, according to Castells, mediated by the informational mode of economic, social and cultural development.

Performativity: the postmodernist version of the old pragmatic assumption that there is no criterion of truth except for that which can be observed working demonstrably in practice. It is usually contrasted with critical knowledge that is not easily tested empirically, if at all.

Post-Fordism: see Fordism.

Postmodernism: the field of a pervasive 'pick'n'mix' and commodified culture in which modern boundaries between forms, media and spheres of social activity are crossed routinely and, in effect, dissolved.

Postmodernity: a cultural and epistemological condition which is said to result in the supersession of modern social institutions, thus bringing about an epochal transition in the direction of a global postmodern society.

Poststructuralism: a set of mainly French theories derived initially from structural linguistics which call into question such notions as referentiality, essentialism, unified subjectivity, methodological objectivity and scientific truth.

Reflexivity: generalized self-awareness and, also, consciousness of the fallibility of knowledge and the unintended consequences of modern social practices.

Relativism: the rejection of universal values, generally agreed aesthetic criteria and the possibility of objective truth.

Risk society: the condition of a reflexive modernity and a pervasive sense of uncertainty, according to Beck, brought about by industrialism's threat to its own existence and that of the planet.

Sign: made up of signifier/signified in semiology/semiotics. The signifier is a word, image or sound referring to a concept, a socially shared idea of something, the signified.

Surveillance: the routine supervision of populations which is greatly enhanced by electronic and information technologies.

Utopia: the notion of an ideal and perfect place either somewhere else or in the future. Utopianism can lead to totalitarianism, as in the cases of Nazism and Stalinism, when ruthlessly sought in politics yet, alternatively, it also functions positively as an idealized contrast to present conditions that are deemed unsatisfactory and may thus facilitate rational critique and result in progressive reform.

REFERENCES

Adam, B. (1998) *Timescapes of Modernity: The Environment and Invisible Hazards*. London and New York: Routledge.

Adorno, T. and Horkheimer, M. (1979 [1944]) *Dialectic of Enlightenment*. London and New York: Verso.

Althusser, L. (1984) *Essays on Ideology*. London: Verso.

Anderson, B. (1991 [1983]) *Imagined Communities*, 2nd edn. London and New York: Verso.

Barthes, R. (1973 [1957]) *Mythologies*. London: Paladin.

Baudelaire, C. (1972) *Selected Writings on Art and Literature*. Harmondsworth: Penguin.

Baudrillard, J. (1975 [1973]) *The Mirror of Production*. St Louis, MO: Telos Press.

Baudrillard, J. (1983 [1981]) *Simulations*. New York: Semiotext(e).

Baudrillard, J. (1988 [1986]) *America*. London and New York: Verso.

Baudrillard, J. (1993 [1973]) *Symbolic Exchange and Death*. London and Thousand Oaks, CA: Sage.

Baudrillard, J. (1994a [1981]) *Simulacra and Simulation*. Ann Arbor, MI: University of Michigan Press.

Baudrillard, J. (1994b [1992]) *The Illusion of the End*. Cambridge: Polity Press.

Baudrillard, J. (1995) *The Gulf War Did Not Take Place*. Sydney: Power Publications.

Baudrillard, J. (1996 [1968]) *The System of Objects*. London and New York: Verso.

Bauman, Z. (1989) *Modernity and the Holocaust*. Cambridge: Polity Press.

Bauman, Z. (1991) *Modernity and Ambivalence*. Cambridge: Polity Press.

Bauman, Z. (1992) *Intimations of Postmodernity*. London and New York: Routledge.

Beck, U. (1992a [1986]) *Risk Society: Towards a New Modernity*. London and Newbury Park, CA: Sage.

Beck, U. (1992b) From industrial society to the risk society: questions of survival, social structure and ecological enlightenment, *Theory, Culture and Society*, 9: 97–123.

Beck, U. (1995a [1991]) *Ecological Enlightenment: Essays on the Politics of the Risk Society*. Atlantic Highlands, NJ: Humanities Press International.

Beck, U. (1995b [1988]) *Ecological Politics in an Age of Risk*. Cambridge: Polity Press.

Beck, U. (1996) World risk society as cosmopolitan society? Ecological questions in a framework of manufactured uncertainties, *Theory, Culture and Society*, 13(4): 1–32.

Beck, U. (1997 [1996]) *The Reinvention of Politics: Rethinking Modernity in the Global Social Order*. Cambridge: Polity Press.

Beck, U. and Beck-Gernsheim, E. (1995 [1990]) *The Normal Chaos of Love*. Cambridge: Polity Press.

Beck, U., Giddens, A. and Lash, S. (1994) *Reflexive Modernization: Politics, Tradition and Aesthetics in the Modern Social Order*. Cambridge: Polity Press.

Benjamin, W. (1973a [1969]) *Charles Baudelaire: A Lyric Poet in the Era of High Capitalism*. London: New Left Books.

Benjamin, W. (1973b [1936]) The work of art in the age of mechanical reproduction, in *Illuminations*. London: Fontana.

Berger, J. (1972 [1969]) The moment of Cubism, in *Selected Essays and Articles: The Look of Things*. Harmondsworth: Penguin.

Berman, M. (1983) *All That is Solid Melts into Air: The Experience of Modernity*. London: Verso.

Bhaskar, R. (1989) *Reclaiming Reality: A Critical Introduction to Contemporary Philosophy*. London and New York: Verso.

Bloch, E., Lukács, G., Brecht, B., Benjamin, W. and Adorno, T. (1980) *Aesthetics and Politics*. London: Verso.

Bryman, A. (1995) *Disney and his Worlds*. London and New York: Routledge.

Butler, J. (1990) *Gender Trouble: Feminism and the Subversion of Identity*. London and New York: Routledge.

Butler, J. (1993) *Bodies that Matter: On the Discursive Limits of 'Sex'*. London and New York: Routledge.

Callinicos, A. (1989) *Against Postmodernism: A Marxist Critique*. Cambridge: Polity Press.

Carleheden, M. and Gabriels, R. (1996) An interview with Jurgen Habermas, *Theory, Culture and Society*, 13(3): 1–17.

Castells, M. (1996) *The Rise of the Network Society*. Malden, MA and Oxford: Basil Blackwell.

Castells, M. (1997a) *The Power of Identity*. Malden, MA and Oxford: Basil Blackwell.

Castells, M. (1997b) An introduction to the Information Age, *City*, 7: 6–16.

Castells, M. (1998) *End of Millennium*. Malden, MA and Oxford: Basil Blackwell.

Chomsky, N. (1992) The media and the war – what war?, in H. Mowlana, G.

Gerbner and H. Schiller (eds) *Triumph of the Image: The Media's War in the Persian Gulf – A Global Perspective*. Boulder, CO: Westview Press.

Cohen, S. (1996) Witnessing the Truth, *Index on Censorship*, 1: 36–45.

Cottle, S. (1998) Ulrich Beck, 'Risk Society' and the media – a catastrophic view?, *European Journal of Communication*, 13(1): 5–32.

Crook, S., Pakulski, J. and Waters, M. (1992) *Postmodernization: Change in Advanced Society*. London and Newbury Park, CA: Sage.

Culler, J. (1976) *Saussure*. London: Fontana.

D'Alembert, J. Le R. (1963 [1751]) *Preliminary Discourse to the Encyclopedia of Diderot*. New York: Bobbs-Merrill.

Davis, S. (1996) The theme park – global industry and cultural form, *Media, Culture and Society*, 18: 399–422.

Debord, G. (1995 [1967]) *The Society of the Spectacle*. New York: Zone Books.

Deleuze, G. and Guattari, F. (1984 [1972]) *Anti-Oedipus: Capitalism and Schizophrenia*. London: Athlone Press.

Denzin, N. (1991) *Images of Postmodern Society: Social Theory and Contemporary Cinema*. London and Newbury Park, CA: Sage.

Derrida, J. (1976 [1967]) *Of Grammatology*. Baltimore, MD: Johns Hopkins University Press.

Dunant, S. and Porter, R. (eds) (1997) *The Age of Anxiety*. London: Virago.

Eagleton, T. (1996) *The Illusions of Postmodernism*. Oxford and Cambridge, MA: Basil Blackwell.

Eco, U. (1987) *Travels in Hyperreality*. London: Picador.

Eliot, M. (1994) *Walt Disney: Hollywood's Dark Prince*. London: André Deutsch.

Ellin, N. (1996) *Postmodern Urbanism*. Cambridge, MA and Oxford: Basil Blackwell.

Elliott, L. and Atkinson, D. (eds) (1998) *The Age of Insecurity*. London and New York: Verso.

Ferguson, M. (1991) Marshall McLuhan revisited – 1960s Zeitgeist victim or pioneer postmodernist? *Media, Culture and Society*, 13(1): 71–90.

Flax, J. (1992) Is enlightenment emancipatory? A feminist reading of 'what is enlightenment?', in F. Barker, P. Hulme and M. Iverson (eds) *Postmodernism and the Re-Reading of Modernity*. Manchester and New York: Manchester University Press.

Foucault, M. (1967 [1961]) *Madness and Civilization: A History of Insanity in the Age of Reason*. London: Tavistock.

Foucault, M. (1970 [1966]) *The Order of Things: An Archaeology of the Human Sciences*. London: Tavistock.

Foucault, M. (1977 [1975]) *Discipline and Punish: The Birth of the Prison*. London: Allen Lane.

Foucault, M. (1981 [1976]) *The History of Sexuality, Volume 1: An Introduction*. Harmondsworth: Penguin.

Foucault, M. (1986 [1984]) What is Enlightenment?, in P. Rabinow (ed.) *The Foucault Reader*. Harmondsworth: Penguin.

Fukuyama, F. (1989) The end of history? *National Interest*, 16 (summer): 3–18.

Fukuyama, F. (1992) *The End of History and the Last Man*. Harmondsworth: Penguin.

Fuller, S. (1997) *Science*. Buckingham: Open University Press.

Furedi, F. (1997) *Culture of Fear: Risk-Taking and the Morality of Low Expectation*. London and Washington, DC: Cassell.

Gane, M. (1991) *Baudrillard's Bestiary: Baudrillard and Culture*. London and New York: Routledge.

Gane, M. (ed.) (1993) *Baudrillard Live: Selected Interviews*. London and New York: Routledge.

Gay, P. (1977a [1966]) *The Enlightenment: The Rise of Modern Paganism*. New York: W.W. Norton.

Gay, P. (1977b [1969]) *The Enlightenment: The Science of Freedom*. New York: W.W. Norton.

Gerth, H. and Wright Mills, C. (1970 [1948]) *From Max Weber: Essays in Sociology*. London: Routledge & Kegan Paul.

Gibson, W. (1984) *Neuromancer*. London: Victor Gollancz.

Giddens, A. (1990) *The Consequences of Modernity*. Cambridge: Polity Press.

Giddens, A. (1991) *Modernity and Self-Identity: Self and Society in the Late Modern Age*. Cambridge: Polity Press.

Giddens, A. (1992) *The Transformation of Intimacy: Sexuality, Love and Eroticism in Modern Societies*. Cambridge: Polity Press.

Giddens, A. (1996) Out of place, *The Higher*, 13 December.

Gitlin, T. (1989) Postmodernism – roots and politics, in I. Angus and S. Jhally (eds) *Cultural Politics in Contemporary America*. London and New York: Routledge.

Goldberg, D. (ed.) (1994) *Multiculturalism: A Critical Reader*. Cambridge, MA and Oxford: Basil Blackwell.

Gomery, D. (1994) Disney's business history: a reinterpretation, in E. Smoodin (ed.) *Disney Discourse: Producing the Magic Kingdom*. London and New York: Routledge.

Gorz, A. (1994 [1991]) *Capitalism, Socialism, Ecology*. London and New York: Verso.

Gould, S.J. (1988 [1987]) *Time's Arrow, Time's Cycle: Myth and Metaphor in the Discovery of Geological Time*. Harmondsworth and New York: Penguin.

Gould, S.J. (1997) *Questioning the Millennium*. London: Jonathan Cape.

Grove-White, R. (1996) Environmental knowledge and public policy needs – on humanising the research agenda, in S. Lash, B. Szerszynski and B. Wynne (eds) *Risk, Environment and Modernity: Towards a New Ecology*. London and Thousand Oaks, CA: Sage.

Habermas, J. (1979 [1976]) *Communication and the Evolution of Society*. London: Heinemann.

Habermas, J. (1984 [1981]) *The Theory of Communicative Action, Volume 1: Reason and the Rationalization of Society*. Cambridge: Polity Press.

Habermas, J. (1985 [1981]) Modernity – an incomplete project, in H. Foster (ed.) *Postmodern Culture*. London: Pluto.

Habermas, J. (1987a [1985]) *The Philosophical Discourse of Modernity*. Cambridge: Polity Press.

Habermas, J. (1987b [1981]) *The Theory of Communicative Action, Volume 2: The Critique of Functionalist Reason*. Cambridge: Polity Press.

Habermas, J. (1988 [1967]) *On the Logic of the Social Sciences*. Cambridge: Polity Press.

Habermas, J. (1989 [1962]) *The Structural Transformation of the Public Sphere: An Inquiry into a Category of Bourgeois Society*. Cambridge: Polity Press.

Habermas, J. (1992a [1988]) *Postmetaphysical Thinking*. Cambridge: Polity Press.

Habermas, J. (1992b) *Autonomy and Solidarity: Interviews with Jurgen Habermas*, P. Dews (ed.), London and New York: Verso.

Habermas, J. (1994) Taking aim at the heart of the present – on Foucault's lecture on Kant's 'What is Enlightenment?', in M. Kelly (ed.) *Critique and Power: Recasting the Foucault/Habermas Debate*. Cambridge, MA and London: Massachusetts Institute of Technology Press.

Habermas, J. (1996 [1992]) *Between Facts and Norms: Contribution to a Discourse Theory of Law and Democracy*. Cambridge: Polity Press.

Hall, S. (1992) The west and the rest – discourse and power, in S. Hall and B. Gieben (eds) *Formations of Modernity*. Cambridge: Polity Press.

Hall, S. (1996) Who needs 'identity'?, in S. Hall and P. du Gay (eds) *Questions of Cultural Identity*. London and Thousand Oaks, CA: Sage.

Hamilton, P. (1992) The Enlightenment and the birth of social science, in S. Hall and B. Gieben (eds) *Formations of Modernity*. Cambridge: Polity Press.

Haraway, D. (1991) *Simians, Cyborgs, and Women: The Reinvention of Nature*. London: Free Association Books.

Harvey, D. (1989) *The Condition of Postmodernity*. Oxford and Cambridge, MA: Basil Blackwell.

Hayward, P. (1993) Situating cyberspace – the popularisation of virtual reality, in P. Hayward and T. Wollen (eds) *Future Visions: New Technologies of the Screen*. London: British Film Institute.

Hayward, P. and Wollen, T. (eds) (1993) *Future Visions: New Technologies of the Screen*. London: British Film Institute.

Heath, S. (ed.) (1977) *Roland Barthes: Image-Music-Text*. London: Fontana.

Heelas, P., Lash, S. and Morris, P. (eds) (1996) *Detraditionalization*. Oxford and Cambridge, MA: Basil Blackwell.

Herman, E. and McChesney, R. (1997) *The Global Media: The New Missonaries of Global Capitalism*. London and Washington, DC: Cassell.

Hirst, P. and Thompson, G. (1996) *Globalization in Question*. Cambridge: Polity Press.

Hitchcock, H.-R. and Johnson, P. (1966 [1932]) *The International Style*. New York: W.W. Norton.

Hobsbawm, E. (1994) *Age of Extremes: The Short Twentieth Century 1914–1991*. London: Michael Joseph.

Hobsbawm, E. (1996) Identity politics and the Left, *New Left Review*, 217 (May/June): 38–47.

Homer, S. (1998) *Fredric Jameson: Marxism, Hermeneutics, Postmodernism*. Cambridge: Polity Press.

Hughes, R. (1991 [1980]) *The Shock of the New: Art and the Century of Change*, 2nd edn. London: Thames & Hudson.

Huntington, S. (1993) The clash of civilizations? *Foreign Affairs*, 72.3 (July/August): 22–49.

Huntington, S. (1996) *The Clash of Civilizations and the Remaking of World Order*. New York: Simon & Schuster.

Huntington, S. (1997) The west and the rest, *Prospect*, February: 34–9.

Huyssen, A. (1992) Mapping the postmodern, in C. Jencks (ed.) *The Post-Modern Reader*. London: Academy Editions.

James, C.L.R. (1980 [1938]) *The Black Jacobins: Toussaint L'Ouverture and the San Domingo Revolution*. London: Allison & Busby.

Jameson, F. (1981) *The Political Unconscious: Narrative as Socially Symbolic Act*. London: Methuen.

Jameson, F. (1984) Postmodernism, or the cultural logic of late capitalism, *New Left Review*, 146: 53–92.

Jameson, F. (1988) Cognitive mapping, in C. Nelson and L. Grossberg (eds) *Marxism and the Interpretation of Culture*. London: Macmillan.

Jameson, F. (1991) *Postmodernism, or, The Cultural Logic of Late Capitalism*. London and New York: Verso.

Jameson, F. (1992) *The Geopolitical Aesthetic: Cinema and Space in the World System*. London: British Film Institute.

Jameson, F. (1994) *The Seeds of Time*. New York: Columbia University Press.

Jay, M. (1986) In the empire of the gaze, in L. Apignanesi (ed.) *ICA Documents 4/5 – Postmodernism*. London: Institute of Contemporary Arts.

Jay, M. (1992) Scopic regimes of modernity, in S. Lash and P. Friedman (eds) *Modernity and Identity*. Oxford and Cambridge, MA: Basil Blackwell.

Jencks, C. (1984 [1977]) *The Language of Post-Modern Architecture*, 4th edn. London: Academy Editions.

Jencks, C. (1986) *What is Post-Modernism?* London: Academy Editions.

Jencks, C. (1997 [1995]) *The Architecture of the Jumping Universe*, revised edn. London: Academy Editions.

Jenks, C. (ed.) (1995) *Visual Culture*. London and New York: Routledge.

Kaufmann, W. (1968 [1950]) *Nietzsche: Philosopher, Psychologist, Antichrist*, 3rd edn. New York: Vintage Books.

Kellner, D. (1989a) *Jean Baudrillard: From Marxism to Postmodernism and Beyond*. Cambridge: Polity Press.

Kellner, D. (ed.) (1989b) *Postmodernism, Jameson, Critique*. Washington, DC: Maissoneuve Press.

Kellner, D. (1992) *The Persian Gulf TV War*. Boulder, CO: Westview Press.

Kellner, D. (ed.) (1994) *Baudrillard: A Critical Reader*. Oxford and Cambridge, MA.: Basil Blackwell.

Kellner, D. (1995) *Media Culture: Cultural Studies, Identity and Politics between the Modern and the Postmodern*. London and New York: Routledge.

Kelly, M. (ed.) (1994) *Critique and Power: Recasting the Foucault/Habermas Debate*. Cambridge, MA and London: Massachusetts Institute of Technology Press.

Kramnick, I. (ed.) (1995) *The Portable Enlightenment Reader*. Harmondsworth: Penguin.

Kumar, K. (1987) *Utopia and Anti-Utopia in Modern Times*. Oxford and Cambridge, MA: Basil Blackwell.

Kumar, K. (1995) *From Post-Industrial to Post-Modern Society: New Theories of the Contemporary World*. Oxford and Cambridge, MA: Basil Blackwell.

Laing, R.D. (1965 [1960]) *The Divided Self: An Existential Study in Sanity and Madness*. Harmondsworth: Penguin.

Lash, S. (1990) *Sociology of Postmodernism*. London and New York: Routledge.

Lash, S. and Urry, J. (1994) *Economies of Signs and Space*. London and Thousand Oaks, CA: Sage.

Lash, S., Szerszynski, B. and Wynne, B. (eds) (1996) *Risk, Environment and Modernity: Towards a New Ecology*. London and Thousand Oaks, CA: Sage.

Lechte, J. (1994) *Fifty Key Contemporary Thinkers: From Structuralism to Postmodernity*. London and New York: Routledge.

Leslie, J. (1996) *The End of the World: The Science and Ethics of Human Extinction*. London and New York: Routledge.

Lukes, S. (1995) *The Curious Enlightenment of Professor Caritat*. London and New York: Verso.

Lynch, K. (1960) *The Image of the City*. Cambridge, MA: Massachusetts Institute of Technology.

Lyotard, J.-F. (1984 [1979]) *The Postmodern Condition: A Report on Knowledge*. Manchester: Manchester University Press.

McGuigan, J. (1992) *Cultural Populism*. London and New York: Routledge.

McGuigan, J. (1996) *Culture and the Public Sphere*. London and New York: Routledge.

McGuigan, J. (1997) Cultural populism revisited, in M. Ferguson and P. Golding (eds) *Cultural Studies in Question*. London and Thousand Oaks, CA: Sage.

McGuigan, J. (1998a) National government and the cultural public sphere, *Media International Australia incorporating Culture and Policy*, 87 (May): 68–83.

McGuigan, J. (1998b) What price the public sphere?, in D. Thussu (ed.) *Electronic Empires: Global Media and Local Resistance*. London and New York: Arnold.

McLennan, G. (1992) The Enlightenment Project revisited, in S. Hall, D. Held and T. McGrew (eds) *Modernity and its Futures*. Cambridge: Polity Press.

McLuhan, M. (1964) *Understanding Media*. London: Routledge & Kegan Paul.

Macnaghtan, P. and Urry, J. (1998) *Contested Natures*. London and Thousand Oaks, CA: Sage.

Mandel, E. (1975) *Late Capitalism*. London: New Left Books.

Marx, K. and Engels, F. (1967 [1848]) *The Communist Manifesto*. Harmondsworth: Penguin.

Marx, K. and Engels, F. (1970) *The German Ideology*. London: Lawrence & Wishart.

Massey, D. (1997 [1991]) A global sense of place, in A. Gray and J. McGuigan (eds) *Studying Culture*, 2nd edn. London and New York: Arnold.

Mercer, K. (1994) *Welcome to the Jungle: New Positions in Black Cultural Studies*. London and New York: Routledge.

Mestrovic, S. (1998) *Anthony Giddens: The Last Modernist*. London and New York: Routledge.

Mowlana, H., Gerbner, G. and Schiller, H. (eds) (1992) *Triumph of the Image: The Media's War in the Persian Gulf – A Global Perspective*. Boulder, CO: Westview Press.

Murdock, G. (1993) Communications and the constitution of modernity, *Media, Culture and Society*, 15: 521–39.

Negroponte, N. (1995) *Being Digital*. London: Hodder and Stoughton.

Norris, C. (1987) *Derrida*. London: Fontana.

Norris, C. (1990) *What's Wrong with Postmodernism: Critical Theory and the Ends of Philosophy*. Hemel Hempstead: Harvester Wheatsheaf.

Norris, C. (1992) *Uncritical Theory: Postmodernism, Intellectuals and the Gulf War*. London: Lawrence & Wishart.

Norris, C. (1993) *The Truth about Postmodernism*. Oxford and Cambridge, MA: Basil Blackwell.

Norris, C. (1998) Reason reawakens, *Red Pepper*, 45 (February): 21–4.

Nuttall, J. (1970 [1968]) *Bomb Culture*. London: Paladin.

O'Neill, J. (1995) *The Poverty of Postmodernism*. London and New York: Routledge.

Osborne, P. and Segal, L. (1994) Gender as performance – an Interview with Judith Butler, *Radical Philosophy*, 67 (summer): 32–5.

Patton, P. (1995) Introduction, to J. Baudrillard, *The Gulf War Did Not Take Place*. Sydney: Power Publications.

Peters, T. (1994a) *The Pursuit of Wow! Every Person's Guide to Topsy-Turvy Times*. New York: Vintage.

Peters, T. (1994b) *The Tom Peters Seminar: Crazy Times Call for Crazy Organizations*. New York: Vintage.

Pickering, M. (1997) *History, Experience and Cultural Studies*. London: Macmillan.

Plant, S. (1996) On the matrix – cyberfeminist simulations, in R. Shields (ed.) *Cultures of Internet: Virtual Spaces, Real Histories, Living Bodies*. London and Thousand Oaks, CA: Sage.

Plant, S. (1997) *Zeros and Ones: Digital Women and the New Technoculture*. London: Fourth Estate.

Plummer, K. (1995) *Telling Sexual Stories: Power, Change and Social Worlds*. London and New York: Routledge.

Poster, M. (ed.) (1988) *Jean Baudrillard: Selected Writings*. Cambridge: Polity Press.

Ritzer, G. (1993) *The McDonaldization of Society*. Thousand Oaks, CA and London: Sage.

Ritzer, G. (1998) *The McDonaldization Thesis*. Thousand Oaks, CA and London: Sage.

Robins, K. (1996) *Into the Image: Culture and Politics in the Field of Vision*. London and New York: Routledge.

Rorty, R. (1985) Habermas and Lyotard on postmodernity, in R. Bernstein (ed.) *Habermas and Modernity*. Cambridge: Polity Press.

Ross, A. (1994) *The Chicago Gangster Theory of Life: Nature's Debt to Society*. London and New York: Verso.

Rowbotham, S. (1974) *Women, Resistance and Revolution*. Harmondsworth: Penguin.

Rustin, M. (1994) Incomplete modernity – Ulrich Beck's *Risk Society*, *Radical Philosophy*, 67 (summer): 3–12.

Ryan, A. (1996) Propagate a new ivy variety, *The Times Higher*, 29 November.

Said, E. (1985 [1978]) *Orientalism*. Harmondsworth: Penguin.

Said, E. (1993) Orientalism and after, *Radical Philosophy*, 63 (spring): 22–32.

Sardar, Z. (1998) *Postmodernism and the Other: The New Imperialism of Western Culture*. London: Pluto.

Sarup, M. (1993 [1988]) *An Introductory Guide to Poststructuralism and Postmodernism*, 2nd edn. Hemel Hempstead: Harvester Wheatsheaf.

Sarup, M. (1996) *Identity, Culture and the Postmodern World*. Edinburgh: Edinburgh University Press.

Schwartz, H. (1996 [1990]) *Centuries End: An Orientation Manual Toward the Year 2000*, 2nd edn. New York: Doubleday.

Segal, L. (1997) Sexualities, in K. Woodward (ed.) *Identity and Difference*. London and Thousand Oaks, CA: Sage.

Shilling, C. (1993) *The Body and Social Theory*. London and Thousand Oaks, CA: Sage.

Shilling, C. (1997) The body and difference, in K. Woodward (ed.) *Identity and Difference*. London and Thousand Oaks, CA: Sage.

Smith, A. and Webster, F. (eds) (1997) *The Postmodern University? Contested Visions of Higher Education in Society*. Buckingham: Society for Research in Higher Education and Open University Press.

Soja, E. (1989) *Postmodern Geographies: The Reassertion of Space in Critical Social Theory*. London and New York: Verso.

Soja, E. (1996) *Thirdspace: Journeys to Los Angeles and Other Real-and-Imagined Places*. Cambridge, MA and Oxford: Basil Blackwell.

Sokal, A. (1996) Transgressing the boundaries: toward a transformative hermeneutics of quantum gravity, *Social Text*, 46–7: 217–52.

Sokal, A. and Bricmont, J. (1998 [1997]) *Intellectual Impostures*. London: Profile Books.

Sontag, S. (1979) *On Photography*. Harmondsworth: Penguin.

Strinati, D. (1992) Postmodernism and popular culture, *Sociology Review*, April: 2–7.

Taylor, M. and Saarinen, E. (1994) *Imagologies: Media Philosophy*. London and New York: Routledge.

Tester, K. (ed.) (1994) *The Flaneur*. London and New York: Routledge.

Thompson, E.P. (1976) Romanticism, Utopianism and moralism – the case of William Morris, *New Left Review*, 99: 83–111.

Thompson, E.P. (1993 [1967]) Time, work-discipline and industrial capitalism, in *Customs in Common*. Harmondsworth: Penguin.

Thompson, J.B. (1995) *The Media and Modernity: A Social Theory of the Media.* Cambridge: Polity Press.

Tomlinson, J. (1997) Cultural globalization and cultural imperialism, in A. Mohammadi (ed.) *International Communication and Globalization.* London and Thousand Oaks, CA: Sage.

Turkle, S. (1997) *Life on the Screen: Identity in the Age of the Internet.* London: Phoenix.

Venturi, R. (1977 [1966]) *Complexity and Contradiction in Architecture*, 2nd edn. New York: Museum of Modern Art.

Venturi, R., Scott Brown, D. and Izenour, S. (1977 [1972]) *Learning from Las Vegas*, revised edn. Cambridge, MA: Massachusetts Institute of Technology.

Virilio, P. (1994 [1988]) *The Vision Machine.* London: British Film Institute.

Voltaire, F.M.A. de (1947 [1758]) *Candide.* Harmondsworth: Penguin.

Voltaire, F.M.A. de (1961 [1732]) *Philosophical Letters.* New York: Bobbs-Merrill.

Wasko, J. (1994) *Hollywood in the Information Age.* Cambridge: Polity Press.

Wasko, J. (1996) Understanding the Disney Universe, in J. Curran and M. Gurevitch (eds) *Mass Media and Society*, 2nd edn. London and New York: Arnold.

Weber, M. (1964 [1947]) *The Theory of Social and Economic Organization*, T. Parsons (ed.). New York: Free Press.

Williams, R. (1974) *Television: Technology and Cultural Form.* London: Fontana.

Williams, R. (1977) *Marxism and Literature.* Oxford: Oxford University Press.

Williams, R. (1980) Utopia and science fiction, in *Problems in Materialism and Culture.* London: Verso.

Williams, R. (1985 [1983]) *Towards 2000.* Harmondsworth: Penguin.

Winston, B. (1996) *Technologies of Seeing: Photography, Cinematography and Television.* London: British Film Institute.

Wittgenstein, L. (1958 [1953]) *Philosophical Investigations*, 2nd edn. Oxford: Basil Blackwell.

Wolfe, T. (1983) *From Bauhaus to Our House.* London: Abacus.

Wolff, J. (1990) *Feminine Sentences: Essays on Women and Culture.* Cambridge: Polity Press.

Wynne, B. (1996) May the sheep safely graze? A reflexive view of the expert–lay knowledge divide, in S. Lash, B. Szerszynski and B. Wynne (eds) *Risk, Environment and Modernity: Towards a New Ecology.* London and Thousand Oaks, CA: Sage.

Zeldin, T. (1995) *An Intimate History of Humanity.* London: Minerva.

Zukin, S. (1991) *Landscapes of Power: From Detroit to Disney World.* Berkeley, CA: University of California Press.

Zukin, S. (1992) Postmodern urban landscapes – mapping culture and power, in S. Lash and J. Freedman (eds) *Modernity and Identity.* Oxford and Cambridge, MA: Basil Blackwell.

Zurbrugg, N. (1993) *The Parameters of Postmodernism.* London and New York: Routledge.

INDEX